# EASTERN CANADA

## TRAVEL✦SMART™ TRIP PLANNER

Felicity Munn

John Muir Publications
Santa Fe, New Mexico

John Muir Publications, P.O. Box 613, Santa Fe, New Mexico 87504
© 1996 Felicity Munn
Cover and maps © 1996 by John Muir Publications
All rights reserved.

Printed in the United States of America.
Second printing November 1996.

Parts of this book were originally published in *2 to 22 Days in Eastern Canada* © 1994, 1995

ISSN 1086-8119
ISBN 1-56261-254-9

Cover photo: Toronto's Casa Loma, Bob Krist/Leo de Wys Inc.
Back cover photos: Derek Trask/Leo de Wys Inc.
Map Design: American Custom Maps—Albuquerque, NM USA
Graphics Manager: Sarah Horowitz
Editors: Dianna Delling, Peggy Schaefer
Design: Janine Lehmann, Linda Braun
Typesetting: Suzanne Rush
Production: Nikki Rooker, Janine Lehmann
Printing: Publishers Press

Distributed to the book trade by
Publishers Group West
Emeryville, California

# HOW TO USE THIS BOOK

The *Eastern Canada Travel♦Smart™ Trip Planner* is organized in 18 destination chapters, each covering the best sights and activities, restaurants, and lodging available in a specific destination. The author has thoroughly researched the numerous choices in each destination to bring you only the best options, saving you time and money in your travels. The chapters are in geographic sequence so you can follow an easy route from one to the next. If you were to visit each destination in chapter order, you'd enjoy a complete tour of the best of Eastern Canada.

**Each chapter contains:**

• User-friendly maps of the area, showing all recommended sights, restaurants, and accommodations.

• "A Perfect Day" description—how the author would spend her time if she had just one day in that destination.

• Sightseeing highlights, each rated by degree of importance: ★★★ Don't miss; ★★ Try hard to see; ★ See if you have time; and No stars—Worth knowing about.

• Selected restaurant, lodging, and camping recommendations to suit a variety of budgets.

• Helpful hints, fitness and recreation ideas, insights, and random tidbits of information to enhance your trip.

**The Importance of Planning.** A trip itinerary is the best way to get the most satisfaction from your travels, and this guidebook makes it easy. First, read through the book and choose the places you'd most like to visit. Then, study the color map on the inside cover flap and the mileage chart (page 12) to determine which you can realistically see in the time you have available and at the travel pace you prefer. Using the Planning Map (pages 10–11), map out your route. Finally, use the lodging recommendations to determine your accommodations.

**Some Suggested Itineraries.** To get you started, six itineraries of varying lengths and based on specific interests follow. Mix and match according to your interests and time constraints, or follow a given itinerary from start to finish. The possibilities are endless. *Happy travels!*

# SUGGESTED ITINERARIES

With the *Eastern Canada Travel•Smart*™ Trip Planner you can plan a trip of any length—a 1-day excursion, a getaway weekend, or a 3-week vacation—around any special interest. To get you started, the following pages contain six suggested itineraries geared toward a variety of interests. For more information, refer to the chapters listed—chapter names are bolded and chapter numbers appear inside black bullets. You can follow a suggested itinerary in its entirety, or shorten, lengthen, or combine parts of each, depending on your starting and ending points.

Discuss alternative routes and schedules with your travel companions—it's a great way to have fun, even before you leave home. And remember: don't hesitate to change your itinerary once you're on the road. Careful study and planning ahead of time will help you make informed decisions as you go, but spontaneity is the extra ingredient that will make your trip memorable.

# Eastern Canada in One to Three Weeks

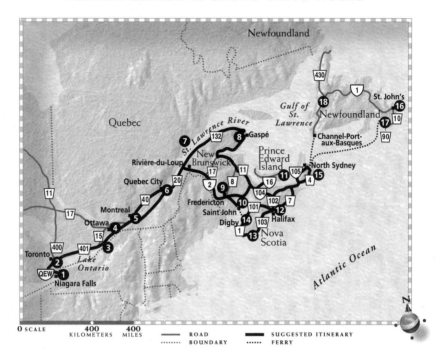

If you have one week to visit, see:
1 **Niagara Falls**
2 **Toronto**
3 **The Thousand Islands**
4 **Ottawa**
5 **Montreal**

If you have two weeks to visit, add:
6 **Quebec City**
7 **Charlevoix and Tadoussac**
8 **The Gaspè Peninsula**
9 **Fredericton**
10 **The Fundy Shore**
11 **Prince Edward Island**

If you have three weeks, add:
12 **Halifax**
13 **The Lighthouse Route**
14 **Evangeline Trail**
15 **Cape Breton Island**
16 **St. John's**
17 **The Avalon Peninsula**
18 **Western Newfoundland**

Time needed for this tour: 1 to 3 weeks

# Eastern Canada: The Nature-Lover's Tour

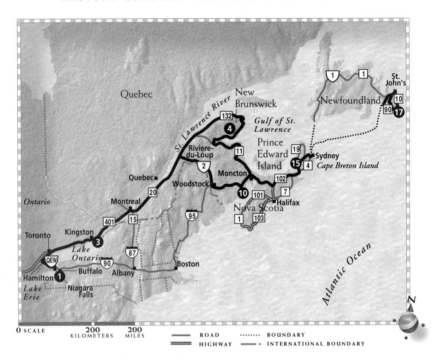

Canada is famous for its wide-open spaces and pristine natural beauty. On the Nature Lover's Tour, you'll see some of the best it has to offer, from the raging torrent of Niagara Falls to the eerie beauty of Newfoundland's rocky coast. You can cruise in the Thousand Islands, whale-watch on the Saguenay and hike in the Park de la Gaspésie. Off Newfoundland, you may even spot monster icebergs floating regally southwards.

- ❶ Niagara Falls
- ❸ The Thousand Islands
- ❹ The Gaspè Peninsula
- ❿ The Fundy Shore
- ⓖ Cape Breton Island
- ⓗ The Avalon Peninsula

Time needed for this tour: 2 weeks

# Eastern Canada: The Art- and Culture-Lover's Tour

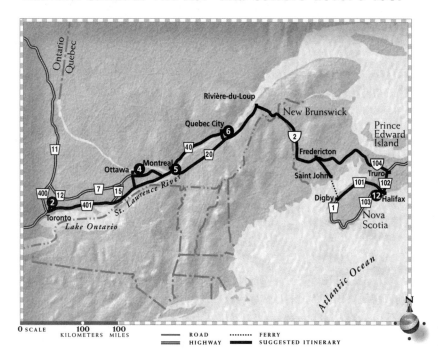

With its hyperactive theater scene—Canada's answer to Broadway, only with more reasonable ticket prices—and plentiful art galleries and museums, Toronto is a must for any culture-lover. As the national capital, Ottawa is home to numerous museums as well as the National Arts Center. Montreal comes alive in the summer with wall-to-wall cultural festivals, from the famous jazz fest in late June through the World Film Festival in late August. History is everywhere in the old part of Quebec City, while Halifax has the Neptune Theater, the fascinating Maritime Museum of the Atlantic and, for budget-conscious lovers of literature, an enticing array of second-hand bookstores.

- ❷  Toronto
- ❹  Ottawa
- ❺  Montreal
- ❻  Quebec City
- ⓬  Halifax

Time needed for this tour: 2 weeks

# Eastern Canada: The Family Fun Tour

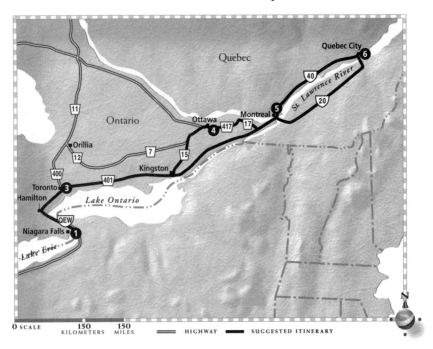

Everyone, no matter how old, is amazed by Niagara Falls, which also offers nearby Marineland, a popular theme park. Toronto has a world-class zoo and a terrific hands-on science and technology museum, while Ottawa is home to kid-friendly museums devoted to everything from airplanes to caricatures. Montreal has La Ronde, an amusement park built for Expo '67, while Prince Edward Island was the setting of that perennial favorite of children's literature, *Anne of Green Gables*.

❶   **Niagara Falls**
❸   **Toronto**
❹   **Ottawa**
❺   **Montreal**
❻   **Quebec City**

Time needed for this tour:  2 weeks

# Eastern Canada: The Literary Tour

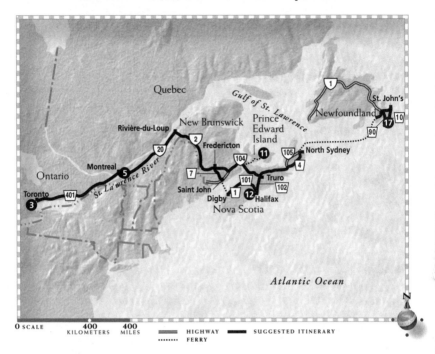

There's more to Canadian literature than *Anne of Green Gables*, the famous book set on Prince Edward Island. Toronto has been the setting for novels by Margaret Atwood and Robertson Davies, among others. Mordecai Richler, whose *The Apprenticeship of Duddy Kravitz* was made into a movie, sets most of his books in his hometown of Montreal. Poet, novelist, singer, and songwriter Leonard Cohen, another Montrealer, sometimes uses the city as a backdrop in his work. Hugh MacLennan, a boy in Halifax at the time of the Halifax Explosion, later wrote a novel about that tragedy, *Barometer Rising*. Farley Mowat set *The Boat Who Wouldn't Float* on Newfoundland's Avalon Peninsula, and National Book Award winner E. Annie Proulx chose Newfoundland as a backdrop for *The Shipping News*.

**❸ Toronto**
**❺ Montreal**
**⓫ Prince Edward Island**
**⓬ Halifax**
**⓱ Avalon Peninsula**

Time needed for this tour: 1 to 2 weeks

# Eastern Canada: The Historical Tour

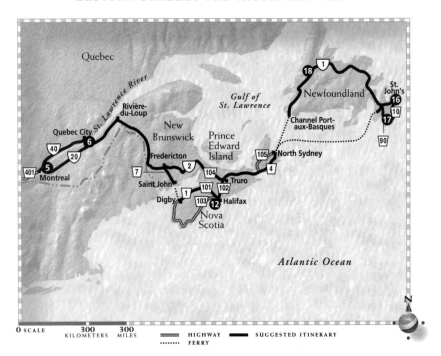

History buffs won't want to miss Montreal and Quebec City—the old sections of these towns, with their cobblestoned streets, offer the ambiance of bygone centuries. Next, visit the historic and picturesque waterfront of Halifax, sight of the Halifax Explosion of 1917. Make an effort to visit the Fortress of Louisbourg, a living museum many visitors describe as the best historic re-creation in Canada. Finish your tour by exploring Newfoundland, the reputed site of explorer John Cabot's landing in North America (although some historians believe he made landfall at the eastern tip of Nova Scotia). L'Anse aux Meadows, at the tip of the Great Northern Peninsula, was the site of a Viking settlement some 1,000 years ago.

If you have one to two weeks, see:
- ❺   Montreal
- ❻   Quebec City
- ⓬   Halifax
- ⓰   St. John's
- ⓱   Avalon Peninsula
- ⓲   Western Newfoundland

Time needed for this tour: 1 to 2 weeks

# USING THE PLANNING MAP

A major aspect of itinerary planning is determining the mode of transportation and the route you will follow as you travel from destination to destination. The Planning Map on the following pages will allow you to do just that.

First, read through the destination chapters carefully and note the sights that intrigue you. Then, photocopy the Planning Map so you can try out several different routes that will take you to these destinations. (The mileage chart that follows will allow you to calculate your travel times and distances.) Decide where you will be starting your tour of Eastern Canada. Will you fly into Toronto, Montreal, or Halifax, or will you start from somewhere in between? Will you be driving from place to place or flying into major transportation hubs and renting a car for daytrips? The answers to these questions will form the basis for your travel route design.

Once you have a firm idea of where your travels will take you, copy your route onto the additional Planning Map in the Appendix. You won't have to worry about where your map is, and the information you need on each destination will always be close at hand.

Leo de Wys Inc./Fridmar Damm

# Planning Map: Eastern Canada

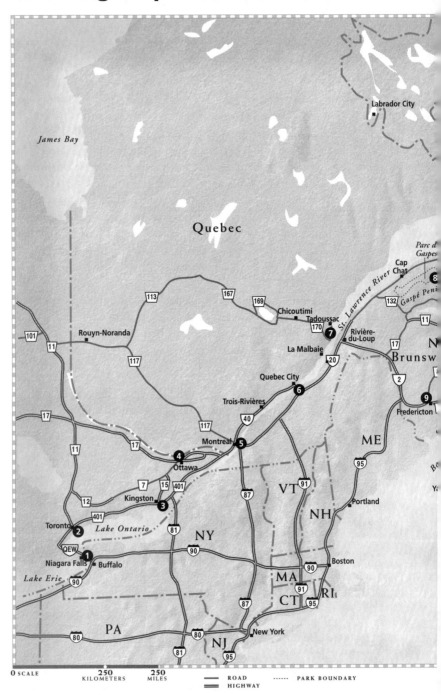

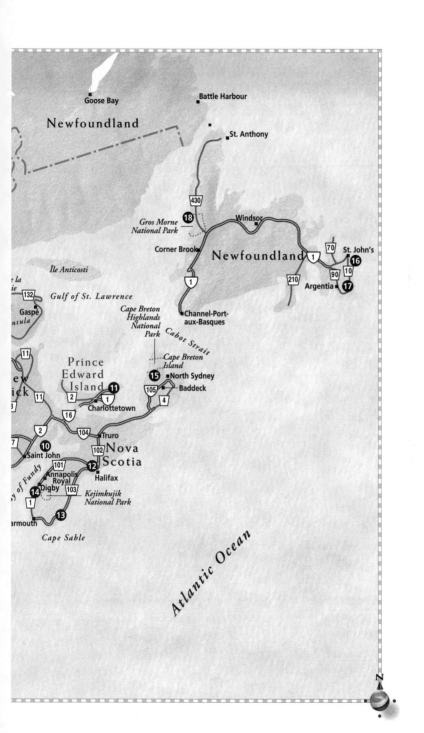

Goose Bay

Battle Harbour

**Newfoundland**

St. Anthony

[430]

*Gros Morne National Park* 🅳

Windsor

Corner Brook

**Newfoundland** [1]

[70] St. John's

🅯

[90] [10]

[210] Argentia 🅱

*Île Anticosti*

*Gulf of St. Lawrence* [132]

Gaspé
*Peninsula* [132]

*la*
*e*
*sula*

*Cape Breton Highlands National Park*

Channel-Port-aux-Basques

*Cabot Strait*

**Prince Edward Island** [11]

*Cape Breton Island*

🅭 North Sydney
[105] Baddeck
[4]

[2] [1]
Charlottetown

*ew*
*ick* [11]

[16]

[2]

[104] Truro
[102]

🅰

Saint John

**Nova Scotia**

[101] 🅲
Annapolis Royal    Halifax
[7]

🅽 Digby [103]  *Kejimkujik National Park*

*y of Fundy*

[1]

*armouth*
🅼

*Cape Sable*

*Atlantic Ocean*

N

# EASTERN CANADA MILEAGE CHART (km/miles)

| | Niagara Falls | Toronto | Kingston | Ottawa | Montreal | Quebec City | Tadoussac | Gaspé | Fredericton | St. John | Charlottetown | Halifax | Lunenberg | Annapolis Royal | Baddeck | St. John's | Placentia |
|---|---|---|---|---|---|---|---|---|---|---|---|---|---|---|---|---|---|
| Toronto | 180/112 | | | | | | | | | | | | | | | | |
| Kingston | 462/287 | 206/128 | | | | | | | | | | | | | | | |
| Ottawa | 576/358 | 398/247 | 192/119 | | | | | | | | | | | | | | |
| Montreal | 704/437 | 589/366 | 383/238 | 203/126 | | | | | | | | | | | | | |
| Quebec City | 962/597 | 837/520 | 646/401 | 481/299 | 262/163 | | | | | | | | | | | | |
| Tadoussac | 1188/738 | 1064/661 | 873/542 | 708/440 | 489/304 | 227/141 | | | | | | | | | | | |
| Gaspé | 1748/1086 | 2079/1291 | 1887/1172 | 1723/1070 | 1504/934 | 1241/771 | 1014/630 | | | | | | | | | | |
| Fredericton | 1596/991 | 1380/857 | 1187/737 | 997/619 | 805/499 | 578/359 | 805/500 | 742/461 | | | | | | | | | |
| St. John | 1699/1055 | 1423/921 | 1290/801 | 1100/683 | 906/563 | 681/423 | 908/564 | 845/525 | 103/64 | | | | | | | | |
| Charlottetown | 1963/1219 | 1771/1100 | 1501/932 | 1362/846 | 1117/694 | 947/588 | 1174/729 | 1111/690 | 369/229 | 317/197 | | | | | | | |
| Halifax | 2065/1283 | 1850/1149 | 1663/1033 | 1465/910 | 1280/795 | 1045/649 | 1272/790 | 1212/753 | 470/292 | 422/262 | 224/139 | | | | | | |
| Lunenberg | 2169/1347 | 1953/1213 | 1766/1097 | 1568/974 | 1383/859 | 1148/713 | 1375/854 | 1319/819 | 576/358 | 526/327 | 327/203 | 103/64 | | | | | |
| Annapolis Royal | 2204/1369 | 2050/1273 | 1832/1138 | 1652/1026 | 1449/900 | 1187/737 | 1414/878 | 1351/839 | 609/378 | 559/347 | 380/236 | 206/128 | 129/80 | | | | |
| Baddeck | 2222/1380 | 2067/1284 | 1850/1149 | 1670/1037 | 1467/911 | 1204/748 | 1431/889 | 1369/850 | 626/389 | 576/358 | 290/180 | 364/226 | 467/290 | 535/332 | | | |
| St. John's | 3181/1976 | 3027/1880 | 2809/1745 | 2629/1633 | 2426/1507 | 2164/1344 | 2390/1485 | 2328/1446 | 1586/985 | 1536/954 | 1249/776 | 1323/822 | 1428/887 | 1496/929 | 960/596 | | |
| Placentia | 3091/1920 | 2937/1824 | 2719/1689 | 2539/1577 | 2336/1451 | 2074/1288 | 2301/1429 | 2238/1390 | 1496/929 | 1446/898 | 1159/720 | 1233/766 | 1336/830 | 1404/872 | 869/540 | 116/72 | |
| Port au Choix | 2764/1717 | 2610/1621 | 2392/1486 | 2212/1374 | 2009/1248 | 1747/1085 | 1974/1226 | 1911/1187 | 1169/726 | 1119/695 | 838/517 | 906/563 | 1009/627 | 1078/670 | 543/337 | 847/543 | 808/502 |

# WHY VISIT EASTERN CANADA?

From the heady rush of Niagara Falls to the craggy charm of tiny fishing outposts along the rocky Newfoundland coast, from the bustle of big cities to the soothing serenity of oceanside vistas, Eastern Canada holds the promise of infinite discoveries.

Nature lovers, history buffs, big-city aficionados—there's something here for everyone. You can tour the wineries of the Niagara Peninsula or meander along New Brunswick's Fundy Shore, where the tides are the highest in the world. You can savor the lively French-flavored nightlife in Montreal or explore Prince Edward Island's gently rolling hills and sweeping beaches. You can cruise the Thousand Islands, where some islets are so small they scarcely have enough room for a house, a dock, and a single tree. You can step back in time at the Fortress of Louisbourg or stroll the Plains of Abraham in Quebec City, setting of a long-ago battle whose ramifications are still felt from one end of the country to the other.

The great outdoors usually springs to mind when you think of Canada, but Canadian cities are cultured and cosmopolitan enough to suit the most sophisticated tastes. Toronto, for instance, likes to think of itself as New York City, only without the crime and grime (that's why some wags call it The Big Lemon). Ottawa, the nation's capital, comes gloriously alive every spring, when hundreds of thousands of tulips burst into bloom all over the city. Montreal, the so-called Paris of North America, offers wall-to-wall summer festivals, a dizzying range of restaurants, and several unique museums, including a humor museum. Up the road a piece, Quebec City's remarkable clifftop setting is dominated by the stately Château Frontenac, one of the most photographed hotels in Canada.

Atlantic Canada, made up of New Brunswick, Nova Scotia, Prince Edward Island, and Newfoundland, has some of the best scenery in the country. It also has one of Canada's most-visited natural attractions, Magnetic Hill in New Brunswick, where your vehicle gets pulled backwards up a hill by a mysterious force. The Cabot Trail on Nova Scotia's Cape Breton Island provides so many wondrous vistas of cliffs and ocean that there's a danger of scenic overdose. In Newfoundland, known affectionately as The Rock, the people are the most unaffected, hardy, and humorous anywhere. Offshore, huge, luminous icebergs float serenely past, even in the heat of summer.

# HISTORY

Indians and Inuit (Eskimo) peoples lived in Canada for many thousands of years before the arrival of the first Europeans—namely, the Vikings, who set up a community in Newfoundland 1,000 years ago. That settlement was abandoned fairly quickly, thanks to a climate even the Norse found harsh. But in the 1400s another wave of Europeans began to arrive. John Cabot, a Venetian commissioned by the English, lit in either Newfoundland or Nova Scotia in 1497. Several decades later, the French explorer Jacques Cartier sailed up the St. Lawrence River, claiming the land for France.

The British-French rivalry continued off and on until Quebec fell to the British at the Battle of the Plains of Abraham in 1759 and Montreal surrendered to the British fleet a year later. As a result, under the Treaty of Paris (1763), New France came under British rule. Chiefly because it enabled them to govern more effectively, the British guaranteed that the French could keep their traditional language, civil law, and Roman Catholic religion. In the War of 1812, the U.S. decided to invade British North America, specifically Upper Canada (now Ontario). But the Upper Canadians forged an alliance with the chief of the Native American nations, which were already fighting the Americans on their own turf, and ultimately repelled the invaders.

In 1867, with confederation, Canada achieved self-government without leaving the British empire. The new nation was a federation of Nova Scotia, New Brunswick, Quebec (Lower Canada), and Ontario (Upper Canada). Later, Prince Edward Island, Newfoundland, and the western provinces (British Columbia, Alberta, Manitoba, and Saskatchewan) joined.

More recently, the issue of French-Canadian separatism has ebbed and flowed, sometimes languishing but always eventually bursting into bloom again. Things reached something of a boiling point in the 1960s, when extremist separatists set off bombs in Montreal. In the autumn of 1970, in what came to be known as the October Crisis, some of the extremists kidnapped the British trade commissioner of the day. He was later released. Meanwhile, however, another cell of the group kidnapped and murdered a provincial cabinet minister.

Things have quieted down a lot since then, but the Quebec-Canada wrangling continues endlessly. In 1980 there was a referendum in Quebec to decide whether the province should separate from the rest of the country; the vote was against separation, by a 60-40 margin. In the autumn of 1995, with the pro-separation Parti Quebecois in power again in the province, there was another referendum (or "neverendum," as some called it) on the same issue. The vote, once again, was for Quebec to remain a part of Canada—but only by a razor-thin margin of less than two percentage points. Another referendum seems inevitable within a couple of years.

## CULTURES

We Canadians are a mishmash, but the largest share of the population is made up of people of British descent (about 35 percent) and French descent (about 25 percent). The vast majority of French-Canadians live in the province of Quebec, but sizable numbers also live in New Brunswick and Ontario. New Brunswick is the only officially bilingual province in Canada. French is the official language in Quebec and English is the official language in the rest of the country. The federal government, however, has long had a bilingualism policy, meaning that all federal government services are supposed to be available in your choice of English or French.

The remainder of the population is composed of people of various ethnic origins, ranging from Greek and Italian to Chinese and Vietnamese. Native peoples and Inuit collectively account for less than 2 percent of the population. Blacks, who make up less than one per cent of the population, are descendants of early immigrants from the United States—mainly runaway slaves. Canada abolished slavery early on, and many slaves came here via the Underground Railroad.

Canada's total population, according to the 1991 census, is a little over 27 million. About three-quarters of the population live in a fairly narrow band along the U.S. border. The overall population density is somewhere around three people per square kilometer (or 7.8 people per square mile).

## THE ARTS

Toronto is now the third-largest English-language theater city in the world, after London and New York City. Toronto loves to boast about its culture, but major theater, opera, and dance groups are found in other big cities too. The National Ballet of Canada and Les Grand Ballets Canadiens, based in Montreal, are the major ballet companies, while the best-known orchestras are the Montreal Symphony and the Toronto Symphony.

If you still think Canada's a cultural backwater, drop in on one of the country's numerous festivals. Montreal and Toronto both host world-class film festivals late every summer. In Montreal, the Just for Laughs Comedy Festival attracts comedians from around the globe. The city's jazz festival, much of it held outdoors with free admission, is hugely popular. Ottawa and Toronto also host big jazz festivals every year. Also not to be missed are the Stratford Festival in Stratford, Ontario, devoted to the works of Shakespeare, and the Shaw Festival in Niagara-on-the-Lake, Ontario, showcasing the works of George Bernard Shaw and his contemporaries. Another Canadian claim to cultural fame is the Cirque du Soleil, the magical and original circus that was started by a bunch of street performers in Baie-St-Paul, Quebec, and gradually evolved into an international sensation.

And for the record, it sometimes seems that half of Hollywood is made up of Canadian expatriates, among them Jim Carrey; Keanu Reeves; Leslie Nielsen (whose brother was for years a senior cabinet minister with the federal government); Dan Aykroyd; Keifer Sutherland and his father Donald; Pamela Sue Anderson; and the late John Candy.

## CUISINE

C anada's cultural diversity is reflected in its eclectic cuisine. And a good thing, too, because aside from a few things like maple syrup, rainbow trout, and the fresh seafood in Atlantic Canada, indigenous dishes aren't much to write home about.

Especially in the big cities, you'll find something for virtually any taste, from hot dogs sold by street vendors to the finest, and priciest, French foods. Popular ethnic cuisines run the usual gamut, from Mexican and Chinese to Italian and Greek. In recent years, Thai and Cajun restaurants have also been gaining in popularity. In Toronto, which has a large Caribbean population, the selection of Bahamian and other Caribbean-themed restaurants is probably larger than elsewhere. Don't forget to try the local wines when you're in Ontario. Montreal has a good number of Vietnamese restaurants operated by immigrants from that country who chose Quebec because of the language. And as noted, in Atlantic Canada fresh seafood is the way to go, especially lobster. As to indigenous dishes, the most notorious is probably *poutine*, sold in many Quebec greasy spoons. It consists of French fries and cheese curds smothered in gravy.

## FLORA AND FAUNA

Forests—endless acres of everything from spruce, balsam fir, and jack pine to maple, beech, walnut, oak, elm, poplar, aspen, and birch—blanket much of the part of Canada covered in this book. Flowering plant species include the aster, buttercup, goldenrod, trillium, and violet; Nova Scotia in particular is known for its wildflowers. The forests are populated with wolf, black bear, caribou, deer, and moose, among other species. Red fox, marten, muskrat, otter, mink, squirrel, and rabbit are also numerous. So are beavers, but you're more likely to see a beaver dam than you are an actual beaver, since they are rather shy. In cities, it's not all that unusual to spot raccoons. In Toronto, in fact, they're a real problem because they can cause damage to houses. Hunters are attracted by game birds like duck, goose, ruffled grouse, and partridge. Other bird species include heron, woodpecker, warbler, finch, and loon—another creature you may never see but whose haunting call you will always remember, should you be lucky enough to hear it on a quiet woodland lake.

In the four provinces of Atlantic Canada, shorebirds include the gull, tern, gannet, kittiwake, cormorant, and puffin. Coastal waters are inhabited by lobster, oysters, scallops, and salmon; inland, freshwater fish like trout, pickerel, pike, and bass lure fishermen. There are practically no snakes in Canada, and those that are present tend to be the harmless garter variety.

## THE LAY OF THE LAND

With a total land area of 9,922,330 square kilometers (3,831,033 square miles), Canada is the second-largest country in the world, behind only Russia. It also contains more lakes and inland waters than any other country—a legacy of a massive glacier that at one time covered nearly the whole country and left in its wake thousands upon thousands of lakes. In eastern Canada, the great rivers include the Saint Lawrence, which runs from the Great Lakes to the Gulf of Saint Lawrence; the Saguenay, which drains into the Saint Lawrence; and the Saint John, which empties into the Bay of Fundy between Nova Scotia and New Brunswick.

All of Labrador and much of Quebec is made up of the so-called Canadian Shield, a region of ancient granite rock sparsely covered with soil. Newfoundland, Nova Scotia, New Brunswick, and Prince Edward Island, as well as Quebec's Gaspé Peninsula, are all part of the

Appalachian-Acadian region, running into the Appalachian mountain system that also includes the Green Mountains in Vermont and the White Mountains in New Hampshire. The St. Lawrence and Lower Lakes region, covering much of southern Quebec and Ontario, is a level plain with a large expanse of arable land.

## OUTDOOR ACTIVITIES

Someone once told me that people in New Zealand look disgustingly fit and healthy because they're all very outdoorsy. It's not quite that way in Canada— some of us are still pasty-faced and indolent—but anyone who's into the whole biking and hiking thing will no doubt find Canada something of a paradise. Outdoor activities in summer run the gamut. Even in big cities, there are invariably bicycle paths, and increasingly you'll find them in the countryside, too, as unused rail beds are converted into recreation trails. (It's expected that eventually a recreation path will run right across the entire country, but that's still a few years off.) If you're on a bicycle, you'll have to dodge in-line skaters—and vice versa—on many bicycle paths.

Canada's relatively short summers, combined with the fact that it has a gazillion lakes, make boating and water sports extremely popular. Much the same goes for fishing; you haven't lived until you've had fresh rainbow trout, out of the lake and into the frying pan. The hiking possibilities are endless; all you have to do is head for the nearest national or provincial park. And if you're fool enough to come in winter, you can do some ice-skating. In some places, you can go dog-sledding—a fascinating experience on account of the dogs, who behave as if all they want to do in life is tear at top speed across the frozen landscape. Or you might consider snowshoeing. Seemingly the easiest outdoor activity of all, it can take you deep into winter wonderlands and it's environmentally correct, unlike ski-dooing.

# PRACTICAL TIPS

## HOW MUCH WILL IT COST?

The Canadian dollar varies in value against the U.S. currency but lately U.S.$1 has been worth from $1.30 to $1.40 Cdn. So American visitors get a lot more bang for their buck in Canada.

All prices in the book are in Canadian dollars. Canadian money comes in a couple of denominations that may seem strange to Americans—the $1 coin, which has a loon on it and so is known as a "loony," and the $2 bill (which is being phased out in favor of a $2 coin). There are also $5, $10, $20, $50, and larger bills. Each denomination is a different color.

Be forewarned that prices for just about everything in Canada tend to be higher than in the United States. If you're a budget traveler, expect to spend about $50 a night for a motel room or $75 a night for a hotel room for two people. In the moderate range, figure on about $100 a night. Upscale hotel rooms cost anywhere from $100 to $200. Bed and breakfasts run around $50 and up a night. Camping rates generally range from about $10 to $20, as do youth-hostel rates.

To calculate food costs, figure inexpensive restaurant meals at under $20 per person for dinner, moderate establishments at $20 to $40, and pricey places at $40 and up. Budget about $10 per person for breakfast and lunch.

Admission prices to parks, museums, and attractions vary widely. To be on the safe side, figure an average $5 to $8 per person.

If you're driving and plan to visit every destination in this book, base gas estimates on approximately 2,500 miles. If you are flying or taking the train to Canada, expect to pay about $300 per week for a small rental car.

On top of the prices, there is also a little something in Canada called the GST, the federal goods-and-services tax. Canadians loathe the GST and grit their teeth whenever they have to pay it—as they do on virtually everything, be it a haircut, a hotel room, or a toothbrush. Visitors have to pay it too, but at least they can get a rebate for GST paid on goods purchased and transported out of the country within 60 days of purchase. Tax charged on hotel and motel accommodations is also eligible for refund.

You can apply for a rebate as long as the GST paid is $7 or more; in other words, you need only buy $100 worth of goods to be eligible for the rebate. Remember to keep all original receipts, which must clearly show that the GST was paid. You have one year from the date of purchase to claim the rebate. GST rebate application forms are available at participating Canadian duty-free shops, tourist information centers, and, in other countries, Canadian embassies and consulates. The easiest way to get a rebate is to hand in the form at a participating duty-free shop, in which case you'll get a cash rebate on the spot. Or you can mail the form, with receipts, to Revenue Canada, Customs and Excise, Visitor Rebate Program, Ottawa, Ont., Canada K1A 1J5. Proof that you are not a Canadian resident and a sample signature are required.

For more information, call (800) 66-VISIT toll-free from within Canada or (613) 991-3346 from outside Canada, or write to Revenue Canada at the above address.

Each of the provinces has its own sales tax as well; at 12 percent, Newfoundland's is the highest. But again, rebates are available for visitors from other countries. Call provincial tourism departments for more information. The phone numbers are listed under Resources at the end of this chapter.

## WHEN TO GO

Given the Canadian climate, June, July, and August are the best months to visit. But in southern Ontario, for example, April and May aren't bad. September and October, when the autumn colors kick in, are generally a safe bet—except maybe in Newfoundland, which can have pretty variable and unpleasant weather.

Visually, the most stunning period is late September and early October, when the changing leaves paint a sublime tableau of scarlet, yellow, and orange as far as the eye can see. It's been called the greatest natural show on earth, and it's worth seeing. The height of the colors varies depending on several factors, but Canadian Thanksgiving, the first weekend of October, is often when they peak. On the plus side, the peak summer travel season is over at this time, so tourist facilities are less crowded and prices may even be lower.

Winter is characterized by sub-zero temperatures and bone-numbing cold. However, there are always winter sports, from skiing and snowshoeing to skating and ski-dooing. Most cities also host winter festivals of one sort or another. Among the best are Ottawa's Winterlude and Quebec City's Carnaval. Winterlude is centered on the frozen Rideau Canal, billed as the longest skating rink in the world. Carnaval centers on a massive ice palace and features hoards of merry-makers warding off the cold with copious amounts of an alcoholic concoction called Caribou.

Canadian temperatures are measured in Celsius, not Fahrenheit. Officially, to convert Celsius to Fahrenheit, you multiply the Celsius figure by 9, divide the result by 5 and add 32 (don't forget your pocket calculator, eh?). Or, to figure out the approximate temperature in Fahrenheit, double the Celsius temperature and add 30; 20 degrees C, for example, becomes roughly 70 degrees F.

## TRANSPORTATION

To get the most from your trip, travel by car is the best bet; that way, you can noodle along at your own pace, exploring and lingering as you please. Driving in Canada shouldn't hold any surprises, but there are a few things to keep in mind. Distance is measured in kilometers, so a speed limit of 100 khp does not give you license to floor it. The 100-kilometer highway speed limit is roughly 60 miles an hour. In town, the 50-kilometer speed limit is roughly 30 miles an hour.

Roads in Ontario, Prince Edward Island, and Nova Scotia tend to be better maintained than in the other three provinces. In the Newfoundland countryside, you also have to beware of wandering animals.

If traveling by car isn't feasible, virtually all the cities and towns en route are accessible by public transportation.

Air Canada and Canadian Airlines International are the major air carriers. Each is affiliated with half-a-dozen regional airlines serving smaller centers. In summer, several charter airlines such as Canada 3000 and Air Transat also offer discount flights on domestic routes; to book such a trip, see a travel agent.

If you love train travel, look to Via Rail, the national passenger railway service. Trains runs frequently between Toronto, Ottawa, Montreal, and Quebec City, which collectively form the busiest railway corridor in the country. The express train between Toronto and Montreal makes the trip in 4 hours flat, while the Montreal–Quebec City express service takes less than 3 hours. From Montreal, Via also runs trains to the scenic Gaspé Peninsula and to Halifax.

Via offers both coach-class and first-class travel. Coach passengers who book at least five days ahead get a 40 percent discount for travel on off-peak days, meaning any day except Friday, Sunday, and public holidays. Between Toronto and Montreal, for example, an adult one-way first-class ticket costs $123, while full economy fare is $83 and the off-peak discount fare $50. Via also offers discounted rates for seniors 60 and up, youths 12 to 24, and kids under 12. Via trains are wheelchair accessible, at least in the so-called corridor.

For extensive train travel, consider the Canrailpass, valid for any 12 days of travel in a 30-day period throughout Via's network. The 1995 peak-season rates were $535 for adults and $480 for youths and seniors for travel between June 1 and September 30, while low-season rates were $365 for adults and $329 for youths and seniors. Via has ticket offices in all the major cities on this itinerary. Otherwise, see a travel agent for information.

Towns served by neither Via nor any airlines are usually on the network of intercity bus routes. Buses are operated by different companies depending on the area. In Ontario, the major bus lines are Greyhound Canada (800-661-8747 from Canada) and Voyageur Colonial (800-668-4438 from Canada); in Quebec, Voyageur Colonial; in Nova Scotia, Acadian Lines, at (902) 454-9321; in Newfoundland, Road Cruisers, at (709) 737-5915; and in New Brunswick and Prince Edward Island, S.M.T. (800-567-5151 toll-free from within New Brunswick or 506-859-5060 from elsewhere).

## EASTERN CANADA'S CLIMATE

This chart shows average high and low temperatures for selected cities. Temperatures are given in Celsius, rounded to the nearest degree; Fahrenheit conversions are shown inside the parentheses.

|        | Toronto   | Montreal  | Halifax   | St. John's |
|--------|-----------|-----------|-----------|------------|
| Jan.   | -3 (27)   | -6 (21)   | -2 (28)   | -1 (30)    |
|        | -11 (12)  | -15 (5)   | -10 (14)  | -7 (19)    |
| March  | 3 (38)    | -2 (28)   | 3 (37)    | 1 (34)     |
|        | -5 (23)   | -6 (21)   | -6 (21)   | -6 (21)    |
| May    | 18 (64)   | 18 (64)   | 15 (59)   | 10 (50)    |
|        | 6 (43)    | 7 (45)    | 4 (39)    | 1 (34)     |
| July   | 27 (81)   | 26 (79)   | 23 (73)   | 20 (68)    |
|        | 14 (57)   | 16 (61)   | 13 (55)   | 10 (50)    |
| Sept.  | 21 (70)   | 20 (68)   | 18 (64)   | 16 (61)    |
|        | 10 (50)   | 10 (50)   | 9 (48)    | 8 (46)     |
| Nov.   | 7 (45)    | 5 (41)    | 7 (45)    | 7 (45)     |
|        | -1 (30)   | -2 (28)   | -1 (30)   | 0 (32)     |

## FOOD AND LODGING

I've included a wide cross-section of eateries in an attempt to appeal to divergent budgets and tastes. But don't let what's in the book limit you, especially since new restaurants are opening—and others folding, alas—all the time. Ask local residents for recommendations and check the restaurant-review sections of local newspapers.

In terms of accommodation, the selection is pretty much similar to what you get in the United States. For the budget-minded, there are campgrounds, youth hostels and no-frills motels. From there, the options rise to the ritziest downtown hotels.

If you're planning to visit in summer, make hotel reservations ahead of time. Always ask about special or weekend rates, which can be much cheaper than the so-called "rack" rate, the official published rate.

As a general rule, the high-end hotels are accessible to people in wheelchairs. Among moderate and budget hotels, the accessibility situation varies widely. The good news is that the Hotel Association of Canada has been encouraging all 10,000 or so hotels, motels, and resorts across the country to join a program called Access Canada. It's based on a series of accessibility standards and criteria for hotels that the Alberta Hotel Association came up with a couple of years back. The standards cover everything from the height of the grab bars in bathrooms to the decibel level at which a telephone bell must ring in order to get the attention of the hard-of-hearing. Many Alberta hotels have since been graded from level-one accessibility (basic) to level-four accessibility (advanced). Now the national hotel association is extending the concept across the country.

Hotel operators can use the standards to grade their properties and, if they decide to renovate, they now know precisely what's needed to meet the requirements for each level. Hotels won't receive Access Canada gradings until the general manager has signed a lengthy checklist and at least one staff member has had a half-day of training. Participation in the program is entirely voluntary, but the hotel association has been reminding hoteliers that people with disabilities are an important untapped market—one that will likely grow as the population ages. By early 1996, travelers were expected to be able to phone hotels and find out their Access Canada level.

Bed and breakfasts are an option worth considering. Fifteen years ago they were a novel concept in Canada, but now they're found almost everywhere. B&Bs are usually reasonably priced, especially considering the ample breakfasts served, and offer comfortable, homey surroundings. Best of all for travelers, they provide a ready-made opportunity to meet locals. But remember to book at least 24 hours ahead. Would-be guests rolling up at 8:00 p.m. with no advance notice make life difficult for the people who operate B&Bs. There are a variety of B&B reservations services in the larger cities on the itinerary; contact numbers are included in those sections. For guidebooks to B&Bs in Canada, see the Recommended Reading section, below.

It's a good idea to book campgrounds in advance too, whether they're in national or provincial parks or privately operated.

## CUSTOMS

Adult visitors from the U.S. entering Canada may bring in 50 cigars, 200 cigarettes, or 2 pounds of tobacco duty-free, plus 1.1 liters (40 ounces) of liquor or wine. After a minimum of 48 hours in Canada, returning United States residents can take back, duty-free, $400 worth of articles for personal use, including up to 100 cigars (as long as they're non-Cuban), 1 liter (33.8 ounces) of alcoholic beverages (if the bearer is at least 21), and 200 cigarettes. If the stay is less than 48 hours, the allowance shrinks to $25 worth of goods, which can include 50 cigarettes and 10 (non-Cuban) cigars.

A trip to Canada, by the way, provides cigar smokers with a rare chance to find out whether the mystique surrounding Cuban cigars is really justified. Specialty smoke shops sell them individually or in boxes; prices begin at $4 per cigar.

## LANGUAGE

It may cause much bickering within Canada, but for English-speaking visitors language shouldn't be a problem. Oddly enough, New Brunswick is the only one of the 10 provinces that's officially bilingual (French and English). The federal government is also officially bilingual. Quebec is officially French and it's the one place visitors may have language problems. Most traffic and commercial signs are in French only. Some merchants around Montreal post "F/E" stickers in their shop windows, indicating that they will serve you in French or English, whichever you prefer. When driving, try to remember that *est* means east, *ouest* means west, *sud* means south, and *nord* means north.

Generally, Quebecers seem more willing these days to speak English if necessary; recent figures from Statistics Canada show that 83 percent of Quebecers speak French at home but fully 35 percent are bilingual. In any situation, there ought to be someone around who can translate. Quebec City is such a tourist mecca that people working in the tourism industry routinely speak English to visitors from elsewhere in Canada and the United States.

## NATIONAL HOLIDAYS

New Year's Day, January 1, is a holiday across Canada. In Quebec only, where New Year's is a big family holiday, businesses also remain closed January 2. At Easter, some businesses take Good Friday, some Easter Monday, and others both days. The Monday closest to May 24 is a holiday known as Dollard Day in Quebec and Victoria Day in the other provinces. Quebec alone celebrates St. Jean-Baptiste Day on June 24, while the whole country marks Canada Day a week later, on July 1. The first Monday in August is a civic holiday in all the provinces except Quebec. The first Monday of September is Labor Day and the second Monday in October is Canadian Thanksgiving. November 11, Remembrance Day, is a semi-holiday in that some businesses close and some don't. And December 25 and 26, Christmas and Boxing Day, are holidays for everyone.

## RECOMMENDED READING

A *Short History of Canada* (Toronto: McClelland and Stewart) is written by a professional historian, but don't let that put you off—it's both entertaining and informative. Author Desmond Morris covers a lot of ground in what is, indeed, a fairly short book. And the history lesson is easily digestible thanks to his storytelling talents. It was first published in 1983 but has been updated a couple of times since then; the latest edition takes us into the 1990s.

*The Story of Canada* (Toronto: Lester Publishing/Key Porter Books) may be meant for kids 10 and up, but it also provides adults with a delightfully readable overview of Canadian history and culture. The bright, anecdote-filled text by Janet Lunn and Christopher Moore is complemented perfectly by Alan Daniel's lavish illustrations. The book chronicles everything from the first people to cross the Bering land bridge thousands of years ago to Roberta Bondar's 1992 flight into history as the first Canadian female astronaut.

Travel writer Jan Morris casts her discerning eye on 10 Canadian cities, including Toronto, Montreal, Ottawa, St. Andrews, and St.

John's, in *City to City* (Toronto: Macfarlane Walter and Ross; published in the U.S. by HarperCollins under the title *O Canada: Travels in an Unknown Country*).

As an apt counterpoint, check out *Welcome Home—Travels in Smalltown Canada*, by Stuart McLean (Toronto: Viking). McLean spent 2 years traveling across Canada and in the end wrote about seven small communities, including Dresden, Ontario; St-Jean-de-Matha, Quebec; Sackville, New Brunswick; and Ferryland, Newfoundland. McLean says he's always most interested in people stories, and this book reflects that.

*Local Colour* (Toronto: Douglas and McIntyre), an anthology devoted to contemporary travel in Canada, covers most of the country via articles and book excerpts by Canadian writers. For example, Wendy Penfield tours along the St. Lawrence River from Montreal to the Saguenay River, while Margaret Laurence visits small towns in southern Ontario, Eugene Cloutier explores New Brunswick, and Clare Mowat voyages along the Newfoundland coast with her husband, author Farley Mowat.

*Oh Canada! Oh Quebec!* (Toronto: Penguin Books) is Mordecai Richler's take on why Canada seems on the verge of fracturing. Richler's sharp eye and acerbic wit have won him international critical acclaim, and this book paints an often devastating portrait of pettiness, paranoia, and anti-Semitism in Canada, particularly Quebec. Subtitled "Requiem for a Divided Country," the book created a big brouhaha when it was published, to which Richler replied: "There is nothing like pointing at childish behavior to make people even more petulant."

*Niagara—A History of the Falls* (Toronto: McClelland and Stewart) is by Pierre Berton, a prolific writer and well-known Canadian personality. Berton's use of memorable characters—stunt men and women, explorers, artists, and suicides among them—make for a lively social history of the Falls.

If you're heading for Newfoundland, consider first reading *The Shipping News* (New York: Charles Scribner's Sons), the Pulitzer-prize-winning novel by E. Annie Proulx that's set largely in Newfoundland.

*The Canadian Book of the Road* (Montreal: Reader's Digest) is a marvelous companion for road trips, replete with brightly written nuggets of information, illustrations, and photographs detailing the history, culture, and sights along Canada's highways and byways. Another very helpful Reader's Digest book is *Backroads and Getaway Places of Canada*, published in a similar format to *Book of the Road* but concentrating on areas outside major urban centers. It features suggested drives, national park closeups, places to see, regional maps, and so on. Together, the two books cover just about every part of Canada that can be reached by car.

*The Canadian Bed and Breakfast Guide*, by Gerda Pantel (Toronto: Penguin Books) is billed as the most comprehensive guide available to the rapidly growing B&B scene in Canada. Regional B&B guides include *The Best Places to Bed & Breakfast in Ontario*, by Janette Higgens (Port Hope, Ont.: Juno Press), and *Affordable Bed & Breakfasts in Quebec* (Montreal: Ulysses Travel Publications).

For current suggestions on restaurants, shows, and galleries, check local dailies such as the Toronto *Star* or the *Globe and Mail*, the Kingston *Whig-Standard*, the Ottawa *Citizen*, the Montreal *Gazette*, the Halifax *Chronicle-Herald*, or the St. John's *Evening Telegram*.

# RESOURCES

**Ontario Travel:** (800) 668-2746.
**Toronto Convention and Visitors Association:** (800) 363-1990.
**Ottawa Tourism and Convention Authority:** (800) 465-1867.
**Tourisme Quebec:** (800) 363-7777.
**Montreal Convention & Tourism Bureau:** (800) 363-7777.
**Greater Quebec Tourism & Convention Bureau:** (800) 363-7777.
**New Brunswick Tourism:** (800) 561-0123.
**Fredericton Tourism:** (506) 452-9500.
**Saint John Visitor and Convention Bureau:** (506) 658-2990.
**Prince Edward Island Visitor Services:** (800) 463-4734.
**City of Charlottetown:** (902) 566-5548.
**Nova Scotia Tourism:** (800) 565-0000.
**Tourism Halifax:** (800) 565-0000.
**Newfoundland and Labrador:** (800) 563-6353.
**St. John's Economic Development and Tourism:** (709) 576-8108.
**Air Canada:** (416) 925-2311 in Toronto; (514) 393-3333 in Montreal;
(800) 565-3940 from Atlantic Canada; (800) 361-8620 from Quebec;
(800) 268-7240 from Ontario.
**Canadian Airlines International:** (800) 665-1177 from Canada;
(800) 426-7000 from the U.S.
**Hostelling International Canada:** (800) 444-6111.
**Parks Canada:** (800) 213-7275 (Atlantic provinces); (800) 463-6769
(Quebec); (613) 938-5866 (Ontario).
**Car Rentals (Canada):** Avis, (800) 879-2847; Budget, (800) 268-8900; Hertz,
(800) 263-0600; Thrifty, (800) 367-2277; Tilden, (800) 387-4747.
**Via Rail:** (800) 361-1235 from Ontario, (800) 361-5390 from Quebec,
(800) 561-3952 from the Maritimes, and (800) 561-3926 from Newfoundland.

**Area Codes**
Niagara Falls and the Niagara Peninsula — 905
Toronto — 416
Thousand Islands and Ottawa — 613
Montreal — 514
Quebec City, Charlevoix, Tadoussac, Gaspé — 418
New Brunswick — 506
Prince Edward Island — 902
Nova Scotia — 902
Newfoundland and Labrador — 709

# 1
# NIAGARA FALLS

Niagara Falls is billed as the Honeymoon Capital of the World. It is breathtaking in its aggressive garishness, especially on Clifton Hill, the tourist center of town. Fortunately, the Niagara Parkway and a wide expanse of the riverbank across from the falls themselves are on Niagara Parks Commission land and thus kept pleasantly green and unspoiled. The parklands extend from Lake Erie to Lake Ontario, parallel to the Niagara River on the Canadian side of the border; entry to the park is free. Be prepared for crowds. Niagara Falls, a city of 73,000, attracts somewhere between 10 million and 12 million visitors annually.

For the record, the Canadian Horseshoe Falls—the more spectacular of the two waterfalls—drops 52 meters (170 feet) into the Maid of the Mist pool, while the waters at the American Falls plunge between 21 and 34 meters (70 to 110 feet) onto a rocky slope at their base. More than 168,000 cubic meters (6 million cubic feet) of water go over the Horseshoe Falls crestline every minute; that's about a million bathtubs full of water every second. The torrents of waters are eroding the rock underneath at the estimated rate of 36 centimeters (about 14 inches) every 10 years. Some 12,000 years ago, the falls were 11 kilometers (7 miles) downstream from where they are now. But the erosion rate has actually slowed since the early 1950s, thanks to major water diversions for a generating plant and construction of something called an International Control Works, which spreads the flow more evenly over the entire crestline of Horseshoe Falls. ∎

# NIAGARA FALLS

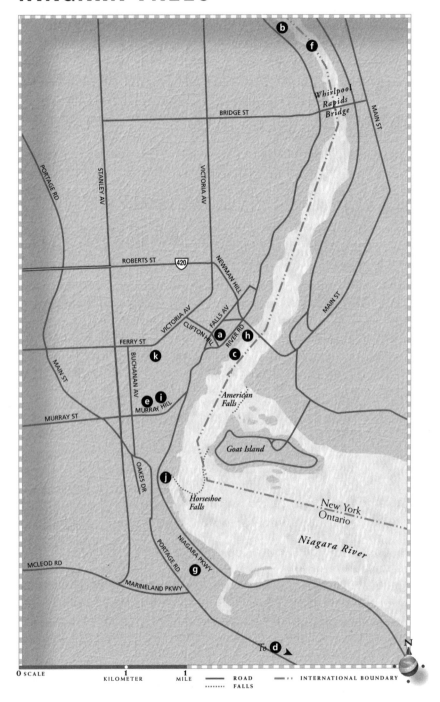

**Streets and labels on map:**

PORTAGE RD
STANLEY AV
VICTORIA AV
BRIDGE ST
MAIN ST
Whirlpool Rapids Bridge
ROBERTS ST
420
NEWMAN HILL
MAIN ST
VICTORIA AV
FALLS AV
CLIFTON HILL
RIVER RD
FERRY ST
BUCHANAN AV
MAIN ST
MURRAY ST
MURRAY HILL
American Falls
Goat Island
OAKES DR
Horseshoe Falls
New York
Ontario
Niagara River
MCLEOD RD
PORTAGE RD
NIAGARA PKWY
MARINELAND PKWY
To

N

O SCALE
1 KILOMETER
1 MILE
—— ROAD
········ FALLS
— · · — INTERNATIONAL BOUNDARY

## Sightseeing Highlights

ⓐ  Clifton Hill

ⓑ  Great Gorge Adventure

ⓒ  Maid of the Mist

ⓓ  Marineland

ⓔ  Niagara Falls IMAX Theater

ⓕ  Niagara Gorge Rapids

ⓖ  Niagara Parks Commission Greenhouse

ⓗ  Ride Niagara

ⓘ  Skylon Tower

ⓙ  Table Rock Scenic Tunnels

ⓚ  Tivoli Miniature World

## A PERFECT DAY AT NIAGARA FALLS

I like to get closer and closer to the falls as the day progresses. First I check out the IMAX show to bone up on the history of the falls. Then it's up to the top of the Skylon Tower for a panoramic view, followed by lunch at the Table Rock Restaurant, which sits right next to the falls. After touring the scenic tunnels, which bring you still closer to the torrent, it's on to the famous *Maid of the Mist* for an awesome closeup view.

## GETTING THERE AND AROUND

Arriving by road from the United States, the access points are four bridges across the Niagara River. Starting south of Niagara Falls, the Peace Bridge links Buffalo, New York, and Fort Erie, Ontario; after crossing the bridge, drive north on the Niagara Parkway for the scenic route or, for the fastest route, go north on the Queen Elizabeth Way highway (widely known as the QEW). Either way, the drive is only about 20 kilometers (12 miles). The Rainbow Bridge and the Whirlpool Rapids Bridge both link Niagara Falls, New York, with Niagara Falls, Ontario. North of Niagara Falls, travelers entering

Ontario via the Queenston–Lewiston Bridge can drive south on the Niagara Parkway. Arriving from Toronto, the most direct route is via the QEW, which links Toronto with Niagara Falls.

In Niagara Falls itself, the major attractions are within walking distance of each other. For instance, the scenic tunnels are about a 10-minute walk along the Niagara Parkway from the Skylon. Since none of the attractions except Ride Niagara involves sitting down a spell, you may want to get a pass for the Niagara Parks People Movers—buses that shunt back and forth all day among various attractions along the parkway and operate between May and October. The passes cost $3.50 for adults and $1.75 for children. If you have parked in the IMAX parking lot, you can also hitch a ride to the scenic tunnels on a double-decker bus that shuttles from the theater along the southern part of the parkway and back. The ride is free, and the bus looks just like a London doubledecker except that it's covered in coins, giving it a golden glitter.

## SIGHTSEEING HIGHLIGHTS

★★★ *Maid of the Mist* • It's almost a cliché, but it's also a must: if you have time to do nothing else in Niagara Falls, take the *Maid of the Mist* boat ride. *The Maid of the Mist* building is at the foot of Clifton Hill. You walk down a winding ramp and ride an elevator down still further to the base of the cliff. Passengers are handed oilskins before going out on the dock. On board the *Maid of the Mist*—there are actually several of them, operating from both the Canadian and American sides of the river—the best vantage point is the bow of the lower level. Otherwise, head for the front of the upper level. There is a recorded commentary, but you probably won't be able to hear it over the roar of the falls. The boat pauses briefly opposite the American Falls, then heads up into the Horseshoe Falls basin and hovers there, its powerful engines fighting the raging current. This is the closest you can get, and from here, it's awesome—a wall of water soaring into the sky. The cost is $9.55 for adults and $5.90 for children 6 to 12. Hours: From May through October, boats depart about every 15 minutes and the trip lasts roughly half an hour. Phone: (905) 358-5781. (1 hour)

★★★ **Niagara Falls IMAX Theater** • To learn about the falls and their history, stop first at the IMAX Theater, a pyramid-shaped building on Buchanan Avenue behind the Skylon Tower, to see the 45-minute film on a screen so enormous—six stories high, they say—that it makes you feel like you're right there. The movie, *Niagara: Miracles, Myths and Magic,* wondrously conveys the power and beauty of the falls, as well as their strange allure for assorted eccentric daredevils. The building also houses a display on the history of the falls, complete with some of the barrels and other contraptions in which people have gone over the edge. The film is shown daily on the hour, so stroll the exhibit either before or after viewing the movie. The exhibit takes about half an hour to see properly. Admission is $7.50 for adults, $6.75 for seniors 60 and up and youths 12 to 18, and $5.50 for kids. Parking is free. Hours: In summer, IMAX is open are 10:00 a.m. to 9:00 p.m., in spring and fall 11:00 a.m. to 8:00 p.m., seven days a week. From October to March, the hours are 2:00 and 3:00 p.m. weekdays, 11:00 a.m. to 8:00 p.m. Saturdays, and 11:00 a.m. to 4:00 p.m. Sundays. Phone: (905) 374-4629. (1½ hours)

☆☆☆ **Table Rock Scenic Tunnel**s • Well worth seeing, particularly since entrance fees are relatively low. After entering, you're given a cheap plastic raincape. You'll need it! Then you get on an elevator, descend about 38 meters (125 feet), and emerge into a long, damp tunnel filled with the dull roar of the falls. The tunnel leading away from the elevator ends on an open bluff jutting from the cliff next to Horseshoe Falls—hence the term Table Rock. Another tunnel to the right ends right under the falls; all that's visible is a thundering torrent of white water. For a drenching, get close to the railing. Entrance fees are $5.50 for adults and $2.75 for kids 6 to 12. Hours: Mid-June to early September, 9:00 a.m. to 10:30 p.m.; 9:00 a.m. to 5:00 p.m. the rest of the year. Phone: (905) 354-1551. (½ hour)

☆☆ **Skylon Tower** • It's next door to the IMAX Theater. Leave the car in the parking lot at the theater, walk across to the tower, and head up to the observation deck for a panoramic view of the falls, the river, and the entire surrounding area. On a really clear day, you can see Toronto across Lake Ontario. Entrance fees are $6.50 for adults, $3.95 for kids 12 and under, and $5.50 for seniors. There are souvenir shops aplenty, both on the ground level and at the observation deck level. (Up the road apiece, the Minolta Tower also offers panoramic views of the falls but isn't as tall as the Skylon.) Hours: The observation deck is open from 8:00 a.m. to 1:00 a.m. Phone: (905) 356-2651. (½ hour)

☆ **Clifton Hill** • At night Clifton Hill looks like Las Vegas, only the attractions are mainly kitschy "museums" instead of casinos. The

Guinness Book of World Records museum vies for attention with Ripley's Believe It or Not! museum, the Movieland Wax Museum, and other such attractions, which can be entertaining if you're in the right mood. Admission prices are fairly steep, running around $6 to $10 a person. If you do nothing else, absorb the atmosphere by strolling the length of the hill. It's only a couple of blocks. (1 hour)

☆ **Ride Niagara** • You've seen the falls; how about going over them in a space-age capsule? Ride Niagara is a simulator ride that takes you over the falls in safety and comfort. Like most simulator rides, it starts with a preamble, in this case a film, followed by an elevator ride to the "abandoned hydro tunnel" where "space-age shuttles" (actually motion simulators) await. Climb in and you are propelled through the tunnel system to emerge above the falls. You're surging toward the brink, and then . . . I won't give it away. Suffice it to say the ride has some surprises and some entertaining narration. The whole experience takes about 20 minutes, but the ride itself takes less than 5 minutes. To get there, take a People Mover shuttle bus or walk along the parkway to the Ride Niagara building under the Rainbow Bridge. Entrance is $7.95 for adults, $6.95 for seniors 55 and up, and $3.95 for kids 6 to 12. Hours: The show runs every half-hour between 10:15 a.m. and 8:00 p.m. daily. Phone: (905) 374-RIDE. (½ hour)

☆ **Tivoli Miniature World** • If you're traveling with young kids, this might be an evening alternative to the brassy lights of Clifton Hill. Miniature World is impossible to miss in its Victoria Avenue building fronted with massive Greek columns. Inside are miniature recreations of more than 90 landmarks and buildings from around the world. It's open until quite late in the evening, and the displays are floodlit. The Eiffel Tower is here, as are the Statue of Liberty, the Acropolis, the Kremlin, the pyramids, the White House, and so on. Some of the models look pretty slipshod, but others are magnificent. Most impressive of all is the re-creation of the Vatican, the last display before the exit. Miniature World is in an open-air compound, so don't go if it's raining. Admission is $10 for adults, $8 for seniors, and $4.27 for kids 5 to 12. (1 hour)

**Other Sights** • Besides the attractions highlighted here, there are literally dozens of others in and around Niagara Falls. Most are geared to families, such as the **Marineland** theme park, featuring assorted aquatic shows and midway rides (7657 Portage Road South), and the

Great Gorge Adventure (4330 River Road), a tunnel that leads to the edge of the lower Niagara Gorge Rapids. One lesser-known attraction worth checking out is the Niagara Parks Commission Greenhouse, where a flock of 50 Peruvian hummingbirds fly among the seasonal floral displays. Best of all, admission is free. The greenhouse is located just south of Horseshoe Falls on the Niagara Parkway. Year-round, it's open daily from 9:30 a.m.

Nor does Niagara Falls shut down in winter. From late November until mid-January, the Winter Festival of Lights is a miles-long lighting extravaganza centered on a "motion light" display from 5:30 p.m. to 11:30 p.m. each evening in Queen Victoria Park. Trees and buildings along the Niagara Parkway and in the city itself are also festooned with lights during the festival, which organizers say is the largest holiday lighting display in the world. The 7-week festival has a full calendar of family-oriented activities, including alcohol-free festivities on New Year's Eve, plus theater, symphonies, and craft shows.

For more information, call the Niagara and Mid-Western Ontario Travel Association at (800) 267-3399.

## FITNESS AND RECREATION

The Niagara Parks stretch for 56 kilometers (35 miles) from Fort Erie to Niagara-on-the-Lake, along the length of the Niagara River. A bicycle path runs through the park, offering dazzling views and plenty of picnic areas. You can rent bikes in Niagara Falls and head south to Fort Erie or north to Niagara-on-the-Lake.

## FOOD

Niagara Falls has dozens of restaurants of every variety. The ones that stand out are those with views of the falls, like the Table Rock Restaurant. A good choice for lunch, it's right next to Horseshoe Falls and has floor-to-ceiling windows. If you're traveling with kids, you might prefer to duck into the Table Rock Fast Food downstairs for burgers, pizza, or salads. Otherwise, try the Table Rock Restaurant upstairs for a more leisurely meal. You can get in without reservations during the off-season, but even then you may have to wait about 20 minutes. Prices are reasonable, given the dramatic location, and the food is quite good. Main dishes at lunch run from $7.95 to $10.95. The restaurant opens at 11:30 a.m. Phone (905) 354-3631 for reservations.

The Table Rock is operated by the Niagara Parks Commission,

# NIAGARA FALLS

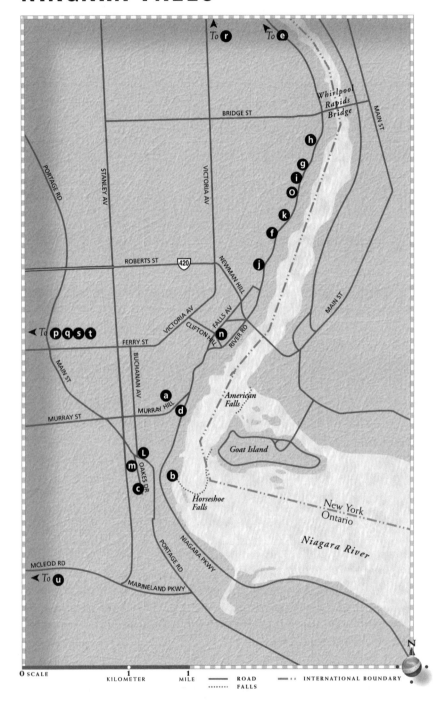

## Food

**ⓐ** Revolving Dining Room (Skylon Tower)

**ⓐ** Summit Suite Buffet Dining Room (Skylon Tower)

**ⓑ** Table Rock Restaurant

**ⓒ** Top of the Rainbow (Minolta Tower)

**ⓓ** Victoria Park Restaurant

**ⓔ** Whirlpool Restaurant

## Lodging

**ⓕ** A Rose and A Kangaroo

**ⓖ** Bed & Breakfast with Friends

**ⓗ** Bedham Hall

**ⓘ** Butterfly Manor

**ⓙ** Glen Mhor House

**ⓚ** Gretna Green

**ⓛ** Oakes Inn

**ⓕ** Rainbow Hospitality

**ⓜ** Sheraton Fallsview Hotel

**ⓝ** Skyline Foxhead Hotel

**ⓞ** White Night Inn

## Camping

**ⓔ** Campark Resorts

**ⓠ** Niagara Falls K.O.A.

**ⓡ** Niagara Glen-View Tent and Trailer Park

**ⓢ** Orchard Grove Tent & Trailer Park

**ⓣ** Scott's Tent and Trailer

**ⓤ** Yogi Bear's Jellystone Park Camp-Resort

*Note: Items with the same letter are located in the same place.*

which also runs a couple of other scenically situated eateries in the area. The **Victoria Park Restaurant** in Queen Victoria Park faces American Falls and is open for lunch and dinner. Phone (905) 356-2217 for reservations. The **Whirlpool Restaurant**, a short drive north along the Niagara Parkway, is next to a public golf course; you can watch golfers from your table. Phone (905) 356-7221.

If budget is irrelevant, try one of the restaurants in the Skylon Tower or the Minolta Tower. In the **Revolving Dining Room** at the top of the Skylon, for instance, luncheon main courses run from $12.95 to $17.50 and dinner main courses from $25.50 (for chicken *cordon bleu*) to $37.95 (lobster tails). A second Skylon restaurant, the **Summit Suite Buffet Dining Room**, is less pricey but still not cheap. For reservations in either establishment, phone (905) 356-2651. Or go to the **Top of the Rainbow** in the Minolta Tower, which overlooks Horseshoe Falls. For reservations, call (905) 356-1501.

## LODGING

Although Niagara Falls is often viewed as an expensive destination, accommodation costs vary depending on the season and even on the numbers of visitors, which in turn can depend on factors like the weather. Most hotels and inns have honeymoon suites with Jacuzzis. On the other hand, scores of establishments also offer packages for families that allow kids under 12 to stay and eat for free. Overall, there's a vast range of accommodations from which to choose. The *South Central Ontario Trip Planner*, published by Ontario Travel, lists some 90 hotels and motels and provides basic information on each. In June, July, and August, reserve ahead. The rest of the year, except for holiday weekends, just drive around and pick and choose.

At the budget end of things, the main motel strip is along Lundy's Lane. Generally, the farther you go from the center of town, the cheaper the rates. They begin around $40 a night in-season. I found a clean, basic motel room for $22 a night in early autumn, at the time only about $4 more than camping in a tent would have cost. The motel manager said that at the height of the season, the same room could run $80.

There are also numerous more expensive hotels in the downtown tourist core. Hotels offering rooms with views of the falls include the **Oakes Inn** at 6546 Buchanan Ave., 356-4514 locally or (800) 263-2577, and the **Sheraton Fallsview Hotel** at 6755 Oakes Drive, 374-1077 locally or (800) 267-8439. Both establishments are wheelchair accessible and both can provide babysitting services. Another hotel that overlooks the falls is the **Skyline Foxhead Hotel** at 5875 Falls Avenue, 374-4444 locally or (800) 263-7135; it is not, however, wheelchair accessible. Naturally, rooms with a view are among the priciest in town. Expect to pay $100 and up per night at such establishments.

There is a string of bed and breakfasts in Victorian-era houses along River Road, part of the Niagara Parkway that overlooks the Niagara River Gorge. Try **A Rose and A Kangaroo** at 5239 River Road, (905) 374-6999; Park Place B&B at 4851 River Road, (905) 358-0279; **Butterfly Manor** at 4917 River Road, (905) 358-8988; **White Night Inn** at 4939 River Road, (905) 374-8767; **Gretna Green** at 5077 River Road, (905) 357-2081; **Glen Mhor House** at 5381 River Road, (905) 354-2600; **Bed & Breakfast with Friends** at 4877 River Road, (905) 374-4776; **Rainbow Hospitality** at 5239 River Road, (905) 358-2861; or **Bedham Hall** at 4835 River Road, (905) 374-8515. Rates range from about $40 to $60.

It's also possible to reserve accommodations at selected hotels and resorts through Ontario's tourist information line at (800) ONTARIO.

## CAMPING

There are eight campgrounds in the immediate area, four of them on Lundy's Lane: **Campark Resorts** at 9387 Lundy's Lane, (905) 358-3873; **Niagara Falls K.O.A.** at 8625 Lundy's Lane, (905) 356-CAMP; **Orchard Grove Tent & Trailer Park** at 8123 Lundy's Lane, (905) 358-9883; and **Scott's Tent and Trailer** at 8845 Lundy's Lane, (905) 356-6988. Other campgrounds include **Niagara Glen-View Tent and Trailer Park** at 3950 Victoria Avenue, (905) 358-8689, and **Yogi Bear's Jellystone Park Camp-Resort** at 8676 Oakwood Drive, (905) 354-1432.

## HELPFUL HINTS

A particularly dramatic way to see the falls is by helicopter. It's expensive, but if you're game, call Niagara Helicopter Rides at (905) 357-5672 the day or evening before. Rates are $70 for adults, $130 for couples, and $25 for children 2 to 11.

# *Scenic Route:* The Niagara Parkway

Winston Churchill once described the **Niagara Parkway** as the
"prettiest Sunday-afternoon drive in the world." The parkway runs
lazily along the Niagara River and ends at Niagara-on-the-Lake. It's only
22 kilometers (13 miles) from Niagara Falls to Niagara-on-the-Lake,
but with the rolling, scenic parkland on either side you'll probably want
to take your time.

After strolling through pretty little Niagara-on-the-Lake, take a
tour of one of the many wineries on the Niagara Peninsula, which juts
into the southern tip of Lake Ontario. If you wish, you can follow the
signposted Winery Route.

A sleepy but historic village on the Canadian side of the
Queenston-Lewiston Bridge, **Queenston** is a stop mainly for history
buffs. Here, during the War of 1812 in which the Americans tried to
conquer British North America, Sir Isaac Brock routed the enemy in
the Battle of Queenston Heights. Today in **Queenston Heights Park**
there is a towering monument to Brock, the commander of the British
forces in Upper Canada, as Ontario was then called. Brock died in the
battle. Hours: Open daily from mid-May to Labor Day. On Partition
Street in Queenston, the **Laura Secord Homestead** honors a
Canadian heroine who saved the British from American attack at one
point in the same war. She walked 30 kilometers (18 miles), skirting
the enemy, to warn the British of an impending American attack.
Hours: 10:00 a.m. to 6:00 p.m. from the Victoria Day weekend in May
until Labor Day.

From 1791 to 1796, **Niagara-on-the-Lake** was Upper
Canada's first capital, then called Newark. Nowadays it has a preserved
nineteenth-century main street that the town modestly refers to as
"the prettiest street in the world," and back streets boasting 200-year-
old mansions. Niagara-on-the-Lake is home to the annual summer
Shaw Festival. It's also expensive. The 4-block stretch of Queen Street
that is the tourist hub of town is chockablock with trendy country-
style shops and restaurants. It is seriously crowded on most weekends
except in winter. Prices are pretty high but if the street's not too busy,
it's a lovely place to browse and window-shop. Chocoholics should
stop in at Renaissance, a shop and factory where workers make
chocolate on vast marble slabs behind the counter. For reasonably
priced food, get away from Queen Street, where a cup of coffee costs
$1.95. The tourist information office at 153 King Street can supply
information and brochures.

The **Shaw Festival**, running from April to October every year, highlights the plays of George Bernard Shaw and his contemporaries with daily performances in three theaters—the Festival Theater, the Royal George, and the Court House. Over the course of the 28-week season, ten plays are usually presented. Tickets range from $10 to $60, including GST. Phone: 468-2172 locally or (800) 267-4759.

The Niagara Peninsula is a major wine-growing area, thanks to its rich soil and temperate climate, and **winery tours** are one of the most popular draws for visitors to the region. In international competitions, Ontario wines frequently take top honors in the Sweet Wine and Chardonnay categories; their other output isn't bad either. Personally, I usually stop in at the Inniskillin Winery because I like some of their wines so much. The 45-minute guided tours, offered twice daily in the summer, conclude with free samplings of two wines. (Go easy on the tasting if you're driving.) There is also a nifty boutique with wine and wine paraphernalia housed in an attractive old barn that also showcases original art by Canadian painters. Inniskillin is on the Niagara Parkway a

# THE NIAGARA PARKWAY

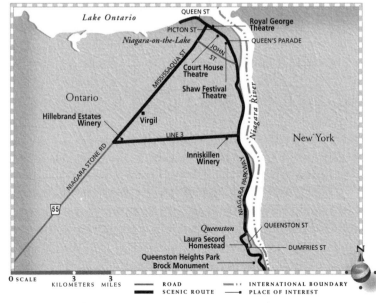

few kilometers south of Niagara-on-the-Lake. Watch for the sign on the left-hand side of the road as you drive north. Phone: (905) 468-3554.

Also recommended is Hillebrand Estates Winery on Highway 55 between Niagara-on-the-Lake and the QEW. It offers free tours and tastings 7 days a week, all summer long. Altogether, 19 wineries make up the wine route on the Niagara Peninsula; the provincial tourism department has a brochure called Wine Route, which describes all of them.

The Niagara Peninsula also offers forts, scenic riverside drives, canals and all manner of things to explore if you have the time. For more information, call the Niagara and Mid-Western Ontario Travel Association at (800) 267-3399.

(You can also head from here to Toronto. The distance from Niagara Falls to Toronto is only 130 kilometers [78 miles], so your traveling time depends on how often you stop to admire the sights en route.)

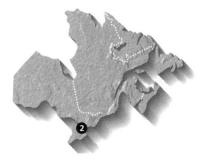

# 2
# TORONTO

Toronto, a sprawling city of 3.5 million perched on the north shore of Lake Ontario, lies farther south than most of Michigan and all of Minnesota, at the same latitude as the northern California border. The huge Lake Ontario keeps the climate temperate; summers are clear and hot, winters cool with little snow.

"Toronto" is the Huron Indian word for "meeting place," which is how American Indians used the site before a French fur-trading post was established here in 1750. The British colonized it in 1793 and named the town York, which later reverted to Toronto when the city was incorporated. During the War of 1812, an American force of ships raided York, burned the parliament buildings, and ransacked the village. In retribution, the British invaded Washington and tried to burn down the President's residence. The building remained intact, but its scorched outside walls had to be whitewashed—hence, the White House.

At Canada's Confederation in 1867, Toronto was the capital of Upper Canada, now Ontario. The seat of government is at Queen's Park, on land that was once used as an asylum for the mentally disturbed.

Over the years, Toronto has grown into a manufacturing and industrial powerhouse because of its proximity to natural resources, agricultural land, inexpensive energy, and the nearby markets of the American heartland. Banking and financial services are the biggest industries, followed by tourism, manufacturing, and communications. ◪

# TORONTO

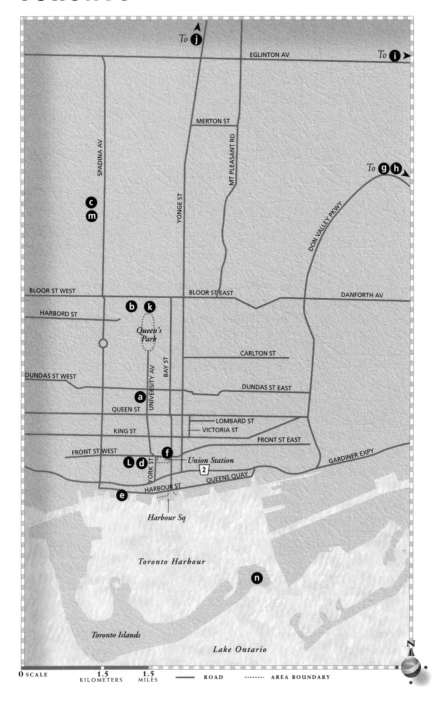

To **j**

EGLINTON AV

To **i** ▶

MERTON ST

MT PLEASANT RD

SPADINA AV

YONGE ST

To **g** **h** ▶

DON VALLEY PKWY

**c**
**m**

BLOOR ST WEST

BLOOR ST EAST

DANFORTH AV

HARBORD ST

**b** **k**

*Queen's Park*

CARLTON ST

UNIVERSITY AV

BAY ST

DUNDAS ST WEST

DUNDAS ST EAST

**a**

QUEEN ST

KING ST

LOMBARD ST

VICTORIA ST

FRONT ST EAST

FRONT ST WEST

**f**

GARDINER EXPY

**L** **d**

YORK ST

*Union Station*
2

QUEENS QUAY

HARBOUR ST

**e**

*Harbour Sq*

*Toronto Harbour*

**n**

N

*Toronto Islands*

*Lake Ontario*

0 SCALE     1.5 KILOMETERS     1.5 MILES    ── ROAD    ⋯⋯⋯ AREA BOUNDARY

## Sightseeing Highlights

- **a** The Art Gallery of Ontario
- **b** The Bata Shoe Museum
- **c** Casa Loma
- **d** CN Tower
- **e** Harbourfront
- **f** Hockey Hall of Fame
- **g** McMichael Canadian Art Collection
- **h** Metro Toronto Zoo
- **i** Ontario Science Center
- **j** Paramount Canada's Wonderland
- **k** The Royal Ontario Museum
- **l** The SkyDome
- **m** Spadina House
- **n** Ward's Island

## A PERFECT DAY IN TORONTO

The Toronto Islands, small oases that sit in the harbor practically within shouting distance of the downtown waterfront but seem a world away from the city bustle, are always worth a visit. By way of contrast afterwards, I like to wander through the heart of downtown to get in some serious window-shopping, followed by a dose of culture and history at the Royal Ontario Museum and the Bata Shoe Museum (strange though that may sound). Then it's off to The Beaches, a lively neighborhood east of downtown that boasts a 2-mile-long boardwalk along the beach and lots of restaurants, cafes, bars and boutiques.

## GETTING AROUND

Traffic is dense in metro Toronto and a nightmare at rush hour. Parking can be hard to find and expensive when you do find it. The city has a strict ticketing and tow-away policy. Leave your vehicle at the hotel and use the efficient public transit system of subway, buses, and streetcars—or walk. The major sights and activities are mostly downtown within walking distance of each other. If you get hungry, you can stop to buy a hot dog from the street vendors.

Toronto is laid out in a grid pattern and it's quite easy to orient yourself. Starting at the waterfront and moving north, the major east–west streets are Queens Quay, Front Street (CN Tower and the SkyDome), King Street, Queen Street and Dundas. Farther north, Bloor and Eglinton are big cross streets.

The major north-south artery is Yonge Street (pronounced Young), reputedly the world's longest street. It runs from the Toronto riverfront to Rainy River, Ontario, near James Bay, 1,900 kilometers (1,140 miles) away. Yonge also divides cross-street addresses into east and west. Bay Street (Canada's Wall Street), University, Spadina, and Bathurst are to the west of Yonge, Jarvis and Parliament to the east.

The main subway artery runs in an elongated U along Yonge Street and University Avenue, looping through Union Station, at the base of the U. The other line runs east–west along Bloor Street. Ticket costs for the subway, streetcars, and buses are $2 per ticket, $6.50 for a strip of five tickets, $13 for a strip of 10 tickets or $5 for a day pass which can be used after 9:30 a.m. Pick up a copy of the "Ride Guide" at subway entrances, or call the Toronto Transit Commission information line at (416) 393-INFO between 7:00 a.m. and 11:30 p.m. daily.

Pearson International Airport, the busiest in Canada, handles more than 35 airlines in three terminals. Terminal 3, with its soaring, atrium-like main hall, opened in early 1991. Pearson is connected to the city by airport bus every 20 minutes, taxi and limousine. The Toronto Island Airport in Toronto Harbor handles short-haul commuter flights and is minutes from downtown. Via and Amtrak trains stop in Union Station right downtown. Union Station, magnificently cavernous, is worth seeing even if you're not arriving by train.

## TORONTO LIFE

Toronto is sometimes called Toronto the Good, a nickname arising from the city's strict puritanism in the late nineteenth century. Perhaps out of envy, other Canadians still tend to view Toronto with some suspicion—it works too well, something must be wrong—and its residents as being uptight and driven, motivated mainly by the urge to make money.

In reality, Toronto has a thriving cultural life. For example, it has the third-largest theater industry in the English-speaking world, behind London and New York. It also has a panoply of ethnic communities to enliven things; in fact the United Nations deemed Toronto the most "ethnically diverse" city in the world in 1989. It was originally settled by English and Scottish immigrants, but today is home to more than 80 different ethnic groups speaking 100 different languages. It claims relations among the ethnic communities are good, but Toronto was the only Canadian city in which there was rioting and looting after the Los Angeles riots in 1992, and relations between police and ethnic communities are not the best. It has particularly large Italian, Chinese, Greek, Korean, and Portuguese populations, each with its own area—Little Italy, Chinatown, Little Athens, Koreatown, and Kensington (Portuguese and West Indian).

## SIGHTSEEING HIGHLIGHTS

★★★ **CN Tower** • Toronto's most famous landmark, the tallest free-standing structure in the world, provides a bird's eye view of the terrain for miles around. The very tip of the tower is 553 meters (1,815 feet) high—the equivalent of 187 stories—and the observation level is about three-quarters of the way up. The elevators go up and down the outside of the tower and naturally have glass walls. The ride up or down takes 58 seconds. From the outside observation deck, you can look straight down through something known, logically enough, as the Glass Floor. Trust me, this is not for people who don't like heights. From the inside observation deck, look for some of Toronto's more architecturally striking buildings, such as the wedding-cake-like Holiday Inn, the colorful CBC building, and the Royal Bank Plaza—the one that glints gold in the sunlight. Several million dollars' worth of gold flakes are embedded in its windowpanes. The gold acts as an insulator, reducing heating and cooling costs. Entrance to the CN Tower observation level costs $12 for adults, $9 for seniors, and $7 for children 4 to 12. That includes admission to the Eco-Dek, an interactive environmental attraction located on the observation deck. Address: 301 Front Street West. You can get to the tower from the street, or walk through the Skywalk from Union Station, a vast glass-encased walkway lined with shops on one side. For infor-mation or to make dining reservations at the Top of Toronto Revolving Restaurant, call (416) 360-8500. (1 hour)

✹✹✹ **The Royal Ontario Museum** • Take the subway to Museum, the stop (logically enough) for the Royal Ontario Museum, one of the five most popular museums in North America. It's Canada's largest, home to an enormous variety of treasures. The most-visited displays are the dinosaur hall and the bat cave, the latter being a dark, eerie, and quite fabulous exhibit in which the bats seem creepily alive. There is also a large gallery of life-sized animals, from musk ox and caribou to lions, tigers, and reptiles. All these exhibits are on the second floor. On the ground floor, the museum houses Chinese collections renowned for their range and quality. The third floor has a permanent display called Caravans and Clipper Ships which recounts the history of east–west trade, plus exhibits on the history of the Mediterranean world, from ancient Egypt to Islamic civilizations. There is a free self-guided audio tour. The entrance fee is $7 for adults, $4 for seniors and students, $3.50 for children, and $15 for families. Hours: 10:00 a.m. to 8:00 p.m. Tuesday, 10:00 a.m. to 6:00 p.m. Wednesday through Sunday. Closed Mondays between Labor Day and May 20. Address: 100 Queen's Park. Phone: (416) 586-8000. (2 hours)

✹✹ **The Art Gallery of Ontario** • Art lovers, stop in at the Art Gallery of Ontario. At any given time, about 10 percent of the gallery's collection of 16,000 works of Canadian and international art is on exhibit. Highlights include a wealth of Canadian works by the Group of Seven and others, the Henry Moore Sculpture Center, and a collection of Inuit art. The AGO, as it's commonly called, is now the tenth-largest public art gallery in North America following a massive renovation and expansion project; art and architecture critics alike lauded the results when the project was completed in 1993. Right next door is **The Grange**, an 1817 building which was the first home of the AGO and is now restored as a "gentleman's house" of the 1830s. It features costumed interpreters and a working kitchen. Admission is $7.50 for adults and $4 for seniors and children, except on Wednesday evenings, when admission is free. Address: 317 Dundas Street West, 2 blocks west of University Avenue. The nearest subway stop is St. Patrick. Phone: (416) 979-6648. (2 hours)

✹✹ **The Bata Shoe Museum** • A shoe museum? How bizarre. I thought so too until I saw it. It has some 10,000 shoes and related artifacts that provide remarkable insight into social history. Shoes, after all, are personal artifacts that reveal a great deal about the owner's social status, habits, culture, and religion. Spanning 4,500 years, the display includes platform boots worn by Elton John and space boots worn by astronauts back through to funereal shoes of the royal tombs of the pharaohs of Egypt and ancient sandals worn by Australian Aborigines. As the display explains, the Aborigines were always barefoot except when it came time to execute someone. Because footprints revealed one's identity, the executioner wore sandals in order to remain anonymous. The 5-story museum is the brainchild of Sonja Bata, wife of the owner of the Bata shoe manufacturing and retail empire. She has been scouring the world for shoes since the 1940s and they are all now in the museum, billed as unique in the Western hemisphere. Entrance is $6 for adults, $4 for seniors and students, and $12 for families. Admission is free on the first Tuesday of each month. Hours: 10:00 a.m. to 5:00 p.m., with longer hours on Thursdays and shorter ones on Sundays. Closed Mondys. Address: 327 Bloor Street West. The subway is St. George. Phone: (416) 979-7799 for information. (2 hours)

☆☆ **Casa Loma** • Toronto's spectacular "castle on a hill" was constructed at great cost by a wealthy entrepreneur who later had to give it up because, curiously, he couldn't afford the taxes. Sir Henry Pellatt built it as his dream home between 1911 and 1914, importing craftsmen from Europe to assist. With the economic downturn after the First World War, however, Sir Henry found himself in arrears on his city taxes. He was forced to turn the 98-room castle over to the city of Toronto. The building is still owned by the city and operated by the Kiwanis Club. The outstanding rooms are the Conservatory on the main floor and, on the second floor, Lady Pellatt's Wedgewood-blue suite next door to Sir Henry's suite. The shower in Sir Henry's bathroom is pretty remarkable, too. When first built, Casa Loma was the only castle in the world to have an electrically operated elevator and an indoor swimming pool. The pool is on the lower floor and was never actually completed, but original plans called for it to be surrounded by cloisters, marble arches, and gold swans. The lower floor also contains the entrance to the 450-meter (1,470-foot) tunnel that connects the castle with the stables, where the stalls are made of mahogany and the floors laid with Spanish tile. From the third floor of the castle there is access to some of the towers above. Seeing everything takes at least 90 minutes. Entrance fees are $8 for adults and $4.50 for seniors and children 6 to 16. Self-guided audio tours are provided. Hours: 10:00 a.m. to 4:00 p.m. daily, but you can wander around until 5:00 p.m. Address: 1 Austin Terrace, off Spadina between

Davenport and St. Clair Avenue West. The nearest subway stop is Dupont. Phone: (416) 923-1171. (2 hours)

☆☆ **Ontario Science Centre** • Consider a visit to the Ontario Science Centre, where hands-on displays will entrance children and adults, science fans and neophytes alike. Admission is $7.50 for adults, $5.50 for youths, and $3 for children and seniors. Hours: Daily 10:00 a.m. to 6:00 p.m. Address: 770 Don Mills Road, south of Eglinton Ave. E. Phone (416) 696-3127 for more information. (3 hours)

☆☆ **Spadina House** • Next door to Casa Loma is a gracious Victorian-Edwardian mansion that belonged to four generations of the Austin family. Built in 1866, the house is filled with preserved original furniture and a kitchen that was used until the last member of the Austin family moved out in the early 1980s. The surrounding six acres of beautifully restored Victorian gardens are truly glorious. It all makes for an interesting contrast to the ostentatious Casa Loma. Spadina House has been open to the public only for the last 10 years, since shortly after the property was given in part to the city by the Austin family. Admission is $5 for adults, $3.25 for seniors and youths, and $4 for children under 13. Address: 285 Spadina Road. Phone: (416) 392-6910 for information. (1 hour)

☆☆ **Ward's Island** • A series of interconnected islands in Toronto Harbor, the Toronto Islands are accessible by ferry year-round. On the island chain's western tip, at Hanlan's Point, the Toronto Island Airport serves commercial and private flights. Centre Island, with its small amusement park, picnic grounds, and bicycle rentals, is the most popular destination among the three islands.

My favorite spot is the charming Ward's Island at the eastern end of the islands. It remains relatively uncrowded even on summer weekends. About 300 people live in a tiny community of tiny old houses on Ward's Island. As you get off the ferry, you'll see small houses nestled in a clump to the left, dissected by tiny streets that are actually more like pathways but have street names. Some of the houses look pretty run-down, but in spring, summer, and fall there is so much greenery and so many flowers around most of them that they still look lovely. A beach and boardwalk are on the other side of the island.

Ward's Island also has lots of parkland and picnic tables, and ducks wandering around at will. It's like being in another world, yet just across the water is a magnificent view of the heart of Toronto.

The ferry terminal is next to the Harbour Castle Hotel; round-trip fares are $3 for adults, $1.50 for students and seniors, and $1 for kids under 15. Departures are frequent. (Call 416-392-8193 for ferry information.) (2 hours)

✸ **Harbourfront** • Harbourfront is a combined recreation and shopping area that stretches from the foot of York Street west to Bathurst Street. Walk from Union Station down to the ferry docks next to the Harbour Castle Hotel and then go 1 block west. Harbourfront encompasses craft studies, art galleries, an antique market and the Queen's Quay Terminal shopping complex of trendy boutiques. The waterside promenade hums with activity in summer. (2 hours)

✸ **Hockey Hall of Fame** • This attraction will have hockey fans in heaven. It's billed as the world's most comprehensive collection of hockey artifacts, displays, and memorabilia. Both King and Union Stations are connected underground to the Hall of Fame, whose entrance is in the concourse level of BCE Palace (at the corner of Yonge and Front streets). Admission is $8.50 for adults and $5.50 for seniors and children. Phone: (416) 360-7765 for more information. (1 hour)

✸ **McMichael Canadian Art Collection** • Although it isn't in central Toronto, the McMichael Canadian Art Collection in nearby Kleinburg is a must-see. The gallery features an impressive collection of works by the Group of Seven artists, the most famous landscape painters in Canada, with works by other Canadian artists and Indian and Inuit artists as well. Admission is $6 for adults, $3 for students and seniors, and $13 for families. Seniors get in free on Wednesdays. Hours: 10:00 a.m. to 5:00 p.m. daily April 1 to October 31; 10:00 a.m. to 4:30 p.m. Tuesday through Sunday the rest of the year. Address: The McMichael is in a woodland setting in Kleinberg, about half an hour north of downtown Toronto by car. Head up the Don Valley Parkway, which runs between the QEW and the 401 and turns into Highway 404 after it crosses the 401. Take Major Mackenzie Drive off the 404 and follow the signs. Phone (416) 893-1121 for information. (1 hour)

✸ **Metro Toronto Zoo** • If you're traveling with children, a visit to this highly rated zoo should keep them enthralled. It has more than 4,000 animals housed in six "zoogeographic" regions. Admission is $9.75 for adults, $7 for youths 12 to 17 and seniors, and $5 for

children 5 to 11. Open daily, mid-May to Labor Day, from 9:00 a.m. to
7:00 p.m. Address: In Scarborough on Highway 401 at Meadowvale
Road, 16 kilometers east of the Don Valley Parkway (exit 389 east-
bound, exit 392 westbound). Phone: (416) 392-5900. (4 hours)

✹ **Neighborhoods** • Toronto has some colorful, diverse neighborhoods that are well worth exploring. Chinatown is a hectically busy
enclave of small streets around the intersection of Dundas and Spadina.
The bustling bazaar of Kensington Market is centered on Kensington,
just west of Spadina. Queen Street West, Toronto's answer to
Greenwich Village, is lined with funky shops, offbeat restaurants, and
trendy bars. Cabbagetown, around Ontario and Berkeley south of
Carlton Street from Gerrard to Queen Street, is a gentrified area
replete with charming Victorian houses.

Little Italy, on College Street between Ossington and Euclid,
hums with trattorias, sidewalk cafés and boutiques. Greektown on the
Danforth features a wealth of restaurants and *tavernas*, most with a
sidewalk section. The Annex, west of Yorkville on Bloor Street, is populated with students, writers, and artists and consequently features
budget bookstores, specialty shops, and cafés. High Park is not so
much a neighborhood as a large oasis of rolling greenery located still
further west on Bloor Street.

All these neighborhoods are pretty much in the downtown-
midtown core of the city. To the east lies The Beaches, a former resort
community whose summer cottages have been converted to permanent
homes. Queen Street East in The Beaches has a lively nightlife and is
also a favorite area for brunch on the weekends. To get there, take the
"red rocket" streetcar along Queen Street East and get off just past
Woodbine.

✹ **Paramount Canada's Wonderland** • Another good possibility if
you're with children, Canada's Wonderland, located just north of
Toronto, features more than 50 rides and a waterslide theme area, plus
live shows and assorted other attractions. A day-pass covering all rides
costs $30.95 for ages 7 and up, $15.45 for children under 7, seniors,
and disabled guests and escorts. Hours: Open 10:00 a.m. to 10:00 p.m.
daily, late May to late September. Phone: (905) 832-7000. (All day)

✹ **The SkyDome** • The SkyDome is the only stadium in the world
with a fully retractable roof. The 32-story-high roof opens and closes
in about 20 minutes, at a cost of $500 per time. It's home to the

Toronto Argonauts, Toronto's football team, as well as the 1992 and 1993 World Series winners the Toronto Blue Jays. Seating is 53,000 for baseball, 54,000 for football, and up to 64,000 for other events. The SkyDome took three years to build and cost $550 million. You'll notice that the Skydome Hotel abuts the stadium, and some hotel rooms with big picture windows actually look out onto the playing field. Shortly after the complex opened in 1989, the hotel got more publicity than money can buy when a couple in one such two-level suite took time out from watching the game to play some games of their own on the bed upstairs. They neglected to draw the curtains, and the incident was all over the newspapers the next day. A guided tour of the stadium, available when events schedules permit, includes a film about its construction and visits to a dressing room, the press box, and a "Skybox." Hours: One-hour tours begin most days at 10:00 a.m.; the cost is $9 for adults and $6 for children and seniors. Address: Next door to the CN Tower. Phone: (416) 341-3663. (1 hour)

## FITNESS AND RECREATION

The Leslie Street Spit, which reaches out into the east end of the harbor, is a popular spot for cyclists and walkers. At the end of the spit there's a great view of the skyline. Toronto Islands Park offers bicycle rentals and bike paths. The boardwalk at The Beaches is a good place for jogging.

## FOOD

Toronto has more than 5,000 restaurants, serving every variety of food imaginable. Here are just a few recommendations. **Ohh Kitchen** serves Chinese food with entirely fresh ingredients, including Szechwan snapper or melon shrimp. It's at 23 Baldwin, phone (416) 977-1255. A highly recommended French restaurant is **Encore SVP**, serving moderate to expensive seafood, grilled meats, and other Continental dishes at 4 Front Street East; call (416) 947-0655. For steak and seafood, try **The Senator**, a retro-style diner and steakhouse at 249 Victoria Street, phone (416) 364-7517.

The **Bofinger Brasserie** is a tavern-style place at 1507 Yonge Street, (416) 923-2300. **North 44** serves a wide selection of dishes described as "new-world Italian with Californian-Asian undertones" at 2537 Yonge Street, (416) 487-4897. The menu at **Oliver's**, a Mediterranean-style bistro at 2433 Yonge Street, is likewise wide in

# TORONTO

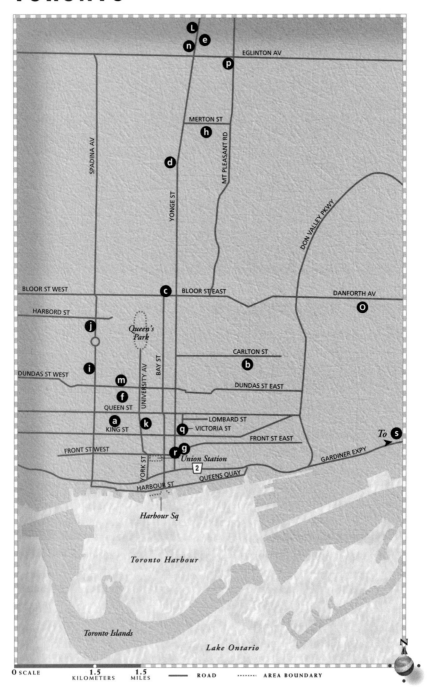

EGLINTON AV

MERTON ST

SPADINA AV

YONGE ST

MT PLEASANT RD

DON VALLEY PKWY

BLOOR ST WEST

BLOOR ST EAST

DANFORTH AV

HARBORD ST

*Queen's Park*

CARLTON ST

DUNDAS ST WEST

DUNDAS ST EAST

BAY ST

UNIVERSITY AV

QUEEN ST

LOMBARD ST

KING ST

VICTORIA ST

FRONT ST EAST

FRONT ST WEST

GARDINER EXPY

*To* **s**

YORK ST

*Union Station*

2

HARBOUR ST

QUEENS QUAY

*Harbour Sq*

*Toronto Harbour*

*Toronto Islands*

*Lake Ontario*

N

0 SCALE    1.5    1.5
        KILOMETERS  MILES        ━━━ ROAD    ········ AREA BOUNDARY

# Food

**ⓐ** Bamboo

**ⓑ** Baralo

**ⓒ** Bemelmans

**ⓓ** Bofinger Brasserie

**ⓔ** Centro Grill & Wine Bar

**ⓕ** Champion House

**ⓖ** Encore SVP

**ⓗ** La Grolla

**ⓘ** The Hunan Palace

**ⓙ** The Kensington Kitchen

**ⓚ** Movenpick

**ⓛ** North 44

**ⓜ** Ohh Kitchen

**ⓝ** Oliver's

**ⓞ** Ouzeri

**ⓟ** Pronto Ristorante

**ⓠ** The Senator

**ⓡ** Shopsy's Deli & Restaurant

**ⓢ** Whitlock's

scope, but at budget prices; call (416) 485-8047. **Bemelmans** at 83
Bloor Street West also serves a wide selection; phone (416) 960-0306.

**Whitlock's** restaurant at 1961 Queen Street East in The Beaches
serves a mix of Continental and Canadian dishes at moderate prices;
call (416) 691-8784. **The Kensington Kitchen** at 124 Harbord Street
is a popular place with a moderately priced menu and a rooftop patio
that gets crowded in summer; call (416) 961-3404.

**Shopsy's Deli & Restaurant** at 33 Yonge Street features 1930s
decor and has been a Toronto institution for some 70 years; phone
(416) 365-3333. **Movenpick** is a trendy cafeteria-style establishment
whose decor makes it unlike any other cafeteria you've ever seen. It
serves reasonably good food at reasonable prices, but you'll have to line
up. It is located at 165 York Street.

**Baralo** at 193 Carleton serves good Italian food in the moderate-
to-upper price range; call (416) 961-4747. **Pronto Ristorante** at 692
Mount Pleasant is a moderately priced Italian restaurant; call (416)
486-1111. **La Grolla** at 195 Merton is another Italian restaurant in the
mid-price range; call (416) 489-7227. For Italian nouveau cuisine at
higher prices, try **Centro Grill & Wine Bar** at 2472 Yonge Street,
(416) 483-2211.

**Ouzeri** is a lively Greek restaurant at 500a Danforth Avenue;
phone 778-0500.

**The Hunan Palace** at 412 Spadina Avenue is one of the more
popular Chinese restaurants in Chinatown; call (416) 593-9831. Also in
Chinatown, try **Champion House** at 480 Dundas Street West, (416)
977-8282.

**Bamboo** is a Caribbean place that's a good bet for lunch and also
has entertainment in the evenings. It's at 312 Queen Street West, (416)
593-5771.

## LODGING

Toronto is a big city, so staying downtown makes particular sense.
The tradeoff is that it's generally more expensive, although even
downtown lodging comes in all price ranges, from budget to deluxe.

Expensive but noteworthy hotels include the grand old **Royal
York Hotel** at 100 Front Street across from Union Station. The
Royal York recently underwent a multimillion-dollar renovation and
is looking better than ever. Room rates average $135 to $155 for dou-
bles; phone 368-2511 locally or (800) 441-1414. The **King Edward
Hotel** at 37 King Street East, a relatively small, luxurious European-

style hotel, has rooms from $160; phone 863-9700 locally or (800) 225-5843. Seventy of the **SkyDome Hotel's** 300-plus rooms, including 31 luxury suites, have stadium views. Rates begin at $109; call 341-7100 locally or (800) 441-1414. The upscale **Westin Harbour Castle** at 1 Harbour Square is right on the waterfront and has a revolving rooftop restaurant. Rates run around the $200 level; phone 869-1600 locally or (800) 228-3000. All four of these establishments, as well as most of the other upscale hotels in town, are wheelchair accessible.

More moderately priced downtown hotels include the **Quality Hotel** at 111 Lombard Street, between King and Queen Streets. Rates run from roughly $60 to $95; phone (416) 367-5555 or (800) 228-5151. A sister property, **Quality Hotel Midtown**, is at 280 Bloor Street West and offers rates from $79 to $120; call (416) 968-0010 or (800) 228-5151. Note that the Lombard Street location is wheelchair accessible, while the midtown property is not. **The Strathcona** at 60 York Street, 1 block from the SkyDome, is another of the few hotels in this price range to be wheelchair accessible. It offers rooms ranging from $59 to $80. Call (416) 363-3321 or (800) 268-8304. **Days Inn Toronto Downtown** has 536 rooms and rates running from $79 to $130. It's at 30 Carleton Street; call (416) 977-6655 or (800) 325-2525.

There are also various motels off some of the major highways into Toronto. Near the QEW, for instance, **Motel 27** at 650 Evans Avenue offers comfortable rooms starting around $40 for a double. Take exit 138 or 139 from the QEW. The phone number is (416) 255-3481.

Toronto has several hotel accommodation services that will book a room for you in your preferred area and price range. Try Accommodation Toronto at (905) 629-3800 or Econo-Lodging Services at (416) 494-0541. Both services are free and offer economy, moderate, and deluxe hotels. If you're calling the province's tourist information line (800-ONTARIO), ask about reserving lodging in Toronto.

Bed and breakfast registries include Bed and Breakfast Homes of Toronto, P.O. Box 46093, College Park Post Office, 444 Yonge Street, Toronto, Ont., Canada M5B 2L8, (416) 363-6362; A Downtown Toronto Association of Bed and Breakfast Guest Houses, P.O. Box 190, Station B, Toronto, Ont., Canada M5T 2W1, (416) 368-1420; and Metropolitan Bed and Breakfast of Toronto, at (416) 964-2566. If you're thinking B&B, one particularly attractive area is The Beaches, a mere ten minutes east of downtown but seemingly a world away.

# TORONTO

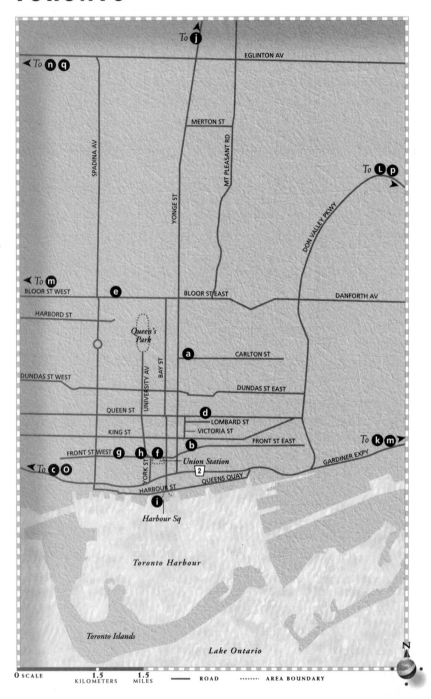

To **j**

EGLINTON AV

To **n** **q**

MERTON ST

MT PLEASANT RD

SPADINA AV

YONGE ST

To **L** **p**

DON VALLEY PKWY

To **m**
BLOOR ST WEST

**e**

BLOOR ST EAST

DANFORTH AV

HARBORD ST

*Queen's Park*

UNIVERSITY AV

BAY ST

**a**

CARLTON ST

DUNDAS ST WEST

DUNDAS ST EAST

QUEEN ST

**d**

LOMBARD ST

KING ST

VICTORIA ST

**b**

FRONT ST EAST

To **k** **m**

FRONT ST WEST **g** **h** **f**

YORK ST

*Union Station*
2

GARDINER EXPY

To **c** **O**

HARBOUR ST

QUEENS QUAY

**i**

*Harbour Sq*

*Toronto Harbour*

*Toronto Islands*

*Lake Ontario*

N

0 SCALE    1.5    1.5    —— ROAD    ······· AREA BOUNDARY
KILOMETERS    MILES

# Lodging

- **a** Days Inn Toronto Downtown
- **b** King Edward Hotel
- **c** Motel 27
- **d** Quality Hotel
- **e** Quality Hotel Midtown
- **f** Royal York Hotel
- **g** SkyDome Hotel
- **h** The Strathcona
- **i** Westin Harbour Castle

# Camping

- **j** Cedar Beach Park Ltd.
- **k** Glen Rouge Park
- **l** Grangeways Trailer Park
- **m** Heber Downs Conservation Area
- **n** Indian Line Tourist Campground
- **o** Milton Heights Campground
- **p** Ponderosa Campground
- **q** Toronto West KOA Kampground

## CAMPING

There are several campgrounds within 50 kilometers (about 30 miles) of Toronto. The closest is **Indian Line Tourist Campground** in Brampton, open from mid-May to mid-October (phone 905-678-1233). Alternatives include **Toronto West KOA Kampground** in Campbellville, open April to October, phone (905) 854-2495; the **Milton Heights Campground** in Milton at (905) 878-6781; **Grangeways Trailer Park** in Mount Albert, (905) 852-3260; **Ponderosa Campground**, also in Mount Albert, (905) 473-2607; **Glen Rouge Park** in Scarborough, (416) 392-2541; **Cedar Beach Park Ltd**. in Stouffeville, (905) 642-1700; and the **Heber Downs Conservation Area** in Whitby, (905) 655-3978.

## NIGHTLIFE

The first thing to know about the nightlife in Toronto is that the bars close at 1:00 a.m., which means last call is at 12:30 a.m. A tram-ride away from the center of the city, The Beaches at the eastern end of Queen Street East is a favorite area for people-watching, and on weekend nights the bars are hopping. The Queen Street West area is for the younger crowd, while Yorkville's bars attract an older, wealthier crowd. **The Hard Rock Café** near the Eaton Centre was the first in North America; it was opened by two Torontonians back in 1978. There is lots of live music in Toronto; for up-to-date listings, check one of Toronto's three daily newspapers (the Toronto *Star*, the *Globe & Mail*, or the Toronto *Sun*) or pick up a copy of *Now* or *Eye*, two free weekly news and entertainment guides.

In the last decade, Toronto has emerged as a world-class theater center. Lately there have been major restorations of several old theater buildings and the opening of a new venue. **The Pantages Theater**, which had been divided into a multiscreen theatre, was restored to its original opulence at a cost of $20 million. **The Elgin and Winter Garden Complex**, one of the few remaining "stacked" theaters (with one theater on top of the other), has also been restored. The Elgin is a large velvet-and-gilt theater, while the Winter Garden upstairs features tree trunks for pillars and foliage on the ceiling. **The Royal Alexandra Theater** frequently offers blockbuster productions such as *Phantom of the Opera*. A new entry on the theater scene, opened in 1993, is the **Princess of Wales Theater**, a 2,000-seat venue built especially for *Miss Saigon*. Many other, smaller theaters offer innovative performances of classical and contemporary plays. The city's theater district lies east of Union Station, girded by Front, Jarvis, King, and Parliament Streets. For discounts on same-day theater tickets, try the T.O. Tix booth outside the Eaton Centre at Yonge and Dundas streets. For concerts and musicals, **Roy Thomson Hall** is a circular building with state-of-the-art acoustics and a lobby that encircles the concert hall. It is home to the Toronto Symphony.

## SHOPPING

Toronto is one of those cities where you really could shop 'til you drop. **The Eaton Centre** on Yonge Street between Queen and Dundas has more than 350 boutiques, services, and restaurants on five levels, anchored by two department stores, Eaton's and The Bay. The nearest subway stops are Dundas or Queen. **Queen's Quay Terminal** on the waterfront is a renovated landmark building with some 100 specialty boutiques and restaurants that are open seven days a week. The nearest subway stop is Union.

If money is no object, check out the Yorkville-Bloor area, probably the most exclusive shopping area in the city. In the '60s, Yorkville was a rundown hippie haven, the Toronto equivalent to San Francisco's Haight-Ashbury at its peak; now it's home to tony shopping centers like **Hazelton Lanes** and the **Holt Renfrew Centre** (Holt Renfrew being a Canadian-owned chain of extremely upscale clothing stores). The nearest subway stop is Bay.

To soak up some atmosphere while shopping, visit the **Kensington Market**, a multiethnic bazaar of foodstuffs, clothes, and street vendors. Best time to go: Saturday morning. The nearest subway stops are St. Patrick and Queen's Park. **Queen Street West** has some offbeat shopping and restaurants. MuchMusic, the Canadian equivalent of MTV, is housed here in a building that's hard to miss. You can look through large street-level windows directly into the studio, and an old City TV news car literally juts out of the side of the building at about the third-story level. (MuchMusic is owned by the same people who own City TV.) The nearest subway stop to this area is Queen.

## HELPFUL HINTS

There are all manner of festivals and events in Toronto each year, but the most fun is Caribana, a two-week blowout in late July. Toronto's 300,000-strong West Indian community includes immigrants from all 25 Caribbean islands, and the carnival-like Caribana festival now draws more than a million visitors to the city each summer. Its highlight is a parade, usually held on August 1. For more traditional family-style entertainment, consider visiting the city during the last couple of weeks of August, when the annual Canadian National Exhibition takes place at the Canadian National Exhibition Grounds west of downtown. Amusement-park rides are the major attraction, but there are also lots of exhibits.

The Toronto International Film Festival, considered one of the best in the world, takes place in early September and is worth checking out.

Year-round, the Metropolitan Toronto Convention & Visitors Association operates a Visitor Information Centre on Yonge Street south of Dundas, outside the Eaton Centre. Seasonal visitor information centers are located throughout Toronto from late May to Labor Day. For travelers coming in to Toronto on Highway 401, there is a computerized tourist information center, the Shell Info Centre, on the 401 west of Winston Churchill Boulevard; or contact the association's main office in Toronto at (416) 203-2600 or (800) 363-1990. Ontario Travel has a travel center on level two in the Eaton Centre.

## SIDE TRIP FROM TORONTO: STRATFORD

Stratford, 90 minutes west of Toronto, is famous for its annual May to November Shakespeare Theater Festival. The festival features a dozen plays—from Shakespeare to contemporary works—on three stages, with tickets running $35 to $50. Book accommodations and theater tickets well ahead, no matter what time of year you plan to visit. For information, lodging reservations, and festival tickets, call (800) 561-SWAN, or 271-5140 in Stratford. From Toronto, take Highway 401 west to Kitchener; follow Highway 8 northeast to Stratford.

**3**

# THE THOUSAND ISLANDS

The Thousand Islands, a necklace of islands scattered along 80 kilometers (50 miles) of the St. Lawrence River from Kingston to Brockville, make for one of the most scenic stretches in all of Ontario. Picturesque, historic Kingston is less than 3 hours from Toronto by road, and Gananoque, (pronounced ga-na-naw-quai), the Canadian gateway to the Thousand Islands, is about 20 minutes farther on. A visit to historic Fort Henry, a drive along the Thousand Islands Parkway, and a cruise through the Thousand Islands are must-do activities. Weirdly fascinating Boldt Castle can be visited during the cruise. ◼

# THE THOUSAND ISLANDS

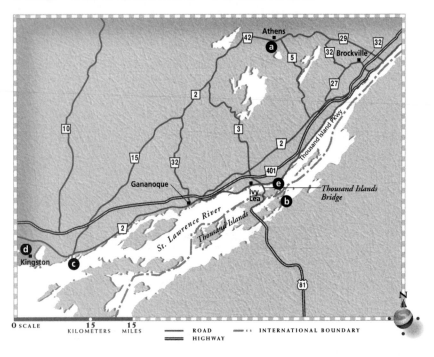

## Sightseeing Highlights

**ⓐ** Athens Murals

**ⓑ** Boldt Castle

**ⓒ** Fort Henry

**ⓓ** Kingston

**ⓔ** Thousand Islands Parkway

## A PERFECT DAY IN THE THOUSAND ISLANDS

In Kingston I'd have lunch at Chez Piggy—don't let the name put you off; the restaurant serves up delicious homestyle cooking. If you're willing to forgo seeing Boldt Castle up close, you can take a Thousand Islands cruise from the Kingston waterfront. But I find the castle so extraordinary that I prefer to take a cruise out of Gananoque, one that actually deposits passengers on Heart Island, site of Boldt Castle. The Thousand Islands Parkway between Kingston and Gananoque is well worth the drive. After the cruise, I'd stop off in the tiny town of Athens to see the colorful murals there.

## SIGHTSEEING HIGHLIGHTS

★★★ **Boldt Castle** • Boldt Castle, on Heart Island on the New York State side of the islands, is a massive monument to a monumental kind of love. In 1900, George Boldt, millionaire proprietor of the Waldorf Astoria hotel in New York City, decided to build a full-sized replica of a Rhineland castle for his wife, Louise. He bought heart-shaped Hart Island and renamed it Heart Island. Work was well under way on 11 buildings, with over U.S.$2.5 million invested in construction and furnishing costs, when Louise died suddenly in 1904. Grief-stricken, George Boldt ordered construction halted immediately, mid-hammer-strike, and for decades thereafter the castle was left open to the elements and to any people who cared to stop at the island.

Many of the castle's interior walls and even some of the ceilings are covered with graffiti. In 1977, the Thousand Island Bridge Authority assumed ownership of the badly deteriorated castle and began charging visitors to see the place, using all net revenues to gradually restore the castle. The idea is not to make it what it would have been, but to bring it back to the state it was in when the construction workers laid down their tools. The exteriors of most of the buildings have been largely restored, and they look magnificent from the outside. Inside is another story, and it's the contrast that's so compelling.

One of the most remarkable buildings is the Alster Tower, or the Play House, as the Boldts called it. They actually lived in this whimsical mini-castle for a time; once it is fully restored, complete with furnishings, it promises to be an amazing place. The architecture is so eccentric it defies description; go in, wander around, and see for yourself. Admission to Boldt Castle, which is not included in cruise prices, is U.S.$3.25 for adults and U.S.$1.75 for children 6 to 12. Phone: (800) 8-ISLAND for more information. (2 hours)

☆☆☆ **Kingston** • One-time capital of Canada and one of its oldest settlements, this attractive city on the banks of the St. Lawrence River is filled with 150-year-old buildings and cobblestone lanes that lead to cafés and restaurants. It has a university—Queen's—and more penitentiaries than anywhere else in Canada. The new Kingston Penitentiary Museum across from the brooding Kingston Penitentiary houses a collection of rare photographs, inmate hobbycrafts, homemade weapons, and escape paraphernalia. The university presence makes for some good bookstores and lively nightlife, and Kingston is well worth a few days if you have the time. If not, the best bet is to head for the central square on Ontario Street across from City Hall and take a Confederation Tour Train ride. The 50-minute trip, operating throughout the summer, takes in Queen's, Royal Military College, Fort Henry, the Marine Museum, and Bellevue House, an early home of Sir John A. Macdonald, Canada's first prime minister. The cost is $7.50 for adults and $5.50 for seniors and youths. Kingston's tourist information center is across from City Hall. (2 hours)

☆☆☆ **Thousand Islands** • There are, in fact, more than 1,000 islands—1,865 is one figure that's been bandied about. To be classified as an island, a piece of land here must have two trees and 6 square feet of soil. Hundreds of the islands are indeed that small, and many are just large enough to hold a small house, a couple of trees, and a dock. Still others, particularly along so-called Millionaire's Row, boast mansions or even castles. Most are privately owned.

On a steamer from Kingston to Montreal in 1842, Charles Dickens described the scene as "a picture fraught with uncommon interest and pleasure." Indeed. The best way to see the islands is to take a cruise, offered from Kingston, Gananoque, or Ivy Lea Village, from May to October. The Canada–U.S. border cuts right through the Thousand Islands, so part of the time on the cruise you're in the United States. Canadian and United States citizens need proper I.D., while citizens of other countries need passports and, if they're visiting Boldt Island, a U.S. visa.

From Kingston, Island Queen and Island Bell Cruises offers paddlewheeler cruises of 90 minutes or 3 hours. The trips, which do not visit Boldt Island, depart from #1 Brock Street on the waterfront, opposite City Hall. Rates for the 3-hour cruises are $15.95 for adults and half that for kids 4 to 12. The 90-minute harbor cruise is $9.34 for adults and half that for children. Phone: (613) 549-5544.

For a cruise that does visit the castle, take one that leaves from Gananoque or Ivy Lea instead. From Gananoque, Gananoque Boat Line offers regular 3-hour cruises at $15 for adults and $6 for children 7 to 12. (Phone 613-382-2144 or 613-382-2146.) These feature an unlimited stop at Boldt Castle, allowing you to get off, spend as long as you like, and take the next boat back. Cruises from Ivy Lea Village, about 11 kilometers (7 miles) east of Gananoque, also include stopovers at Boldt Castle. The cost is $12 for adults and $6 for children 4 to 12. Phone: Ivy Lea 1000 Islands Boat Tours at (613) 659-2293.

From Brockville, at the eastern end of the Thousand Islands, Brockville 1000 Islands Seaway Cruises offers cruises of various lengths at $10 to $15 for adults, $8.50 to $13 for seniors and youths, and $5 to $8 for kids. Phone: (613) 345-7333. (90 minutes to 3 hours, depending on the cruise)

✩✩ **Fort Henry** • The most famous landmark in Kingston is Fort Henry, the so-called Citadel of Upper Canada. It was constructed during the War of 1812 on a point of land overlooking the confluence of Lake Ontario and the St. Lawrence, but its guns have never been fired in anger. Nowadays the Fort Henry Guard recreates drills and marches for the public. Admission is $9.50 for adults, $7.15 for seniors, $6.75 for students, and $4.75 for children 6 to 12. Hours: From 10:00 a.m. daily, with the first tour departing at 10:15 a.m. One-hour tours are offered from mid-May to mid-October, departing every 15 minutes at the height of the season. Phone: (613) 542-7388. (1½ hours)

✩ **Athens Murals** • Athens is a tiny town about 25 minutes north of Highway 401; if you have time, make this side trip. Scattered throughout Athens are a number of large, eye-catching murals. Just park on the main street and wander. One mural is of the main street in the last century, another of a park scene. Another, on the side of the fire-department building, depicts the worst thing that ever happened in Athens: a big fire that the new truck couldn't fight because its hose was too short. A local hero climbed down a well within yards of the flaming building and passed up buckets of water, saving the day. My personal favorite is the mural that includes a depiction of the artist painting it. (½ hour)

## FITNESS AND RECREATION

There are riverside parks, beaches, playgrounds, bicycle paths, and walking trails all along the Thousand Islands Parkway; pack up the kids, the bicycles, and a picnic lunch, and enjoy.

## FOOD

Chez Piggy is one of my favorite eateries in Kingston. Housed in a restored limestone stable, with an off-street patio, it's at 68R Princess Street and is wheelchair accessible. **Sax Restaurant** at 288 Wellington Street specializes in Cajun food, while **Windmills Cafe** at 184 Princess Street is a great place for gourmet sandwiches. For pub fare, try the **Royal Oak Tavern** (613-542-3339), where the prices are reasonable. It's at 331 King Street East. Kingston also offers a wide array of family restaurants, including the **Red Lobster** at 410 Bath Road.

## LODGING

If you're overnighting in Kingston, the city offers a wealth of moderately priced hotels and motels. There are two **Comfort Inns**, for example, both charging between $65 and $90 for a room. However, the one at 55 Warne Crescent (613-546-9500 or 800-668-4200) is wheelchair accessible, while the one at 1454 Princess Street (613-549-5550 or 800-4-CHOICE) isn't. The **Desert Lake Family Resort**, with a beach and babysitting services, would be a good bet for families. It's also wheelchair accessible. Rooms range from $73 to $83. It's on Desert Lake Road; call (613) 374-2196. **Days Inn Kingston** is also wheelchair accessible; it's at 33 Benson Street, with access off Highway 401. Rates are $67-$85; call (613) 546-3661 or (800) 267-7888. The **Holiday Inn Kingston Waterfront** has all the amenities, including wheelchair accessibility and babysitting services, plus a good view, but at $114 to $145, you're paying for all that. Call (613) 549-8400 or (800) 465-4329. For sheer atmosphere, try the beautiful **Hochelaga Inn**, which blends antique furniture with modern amenities. Room rates run from $75 to more than $100, depending on the season; phone (613) 549-5534 or (800) 267-0525. If you want to go the B&B route, contact the Bed and Breakfast Registry at O'Brien House, which can book selected guest homes in the area starting at $48 for a double room. Write to 39 Glenaire Mews, Kingston, Ont. K7M 7L3, or phone (613) 545-1741.

# KINGSTON

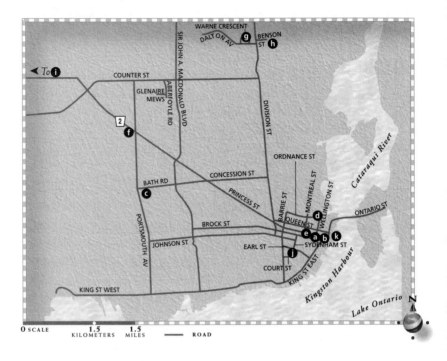

## Food

- **a** Chez Piggy
- **b** Royal Oak Tavern
- **c** Red Lobster
- **d** Sax Restaurant
- **e** Windmills Cafe

## Lodging

- **f** Comfort Inn-Princess Street
- **g** Comfort Inn-Warne Crescent
- **h** Days Inn Kingston
- **i** Desert Lake Family Resort
- **j** Hochelaga Inn
- **k** Holiday Inn Kingston Waterfront

For more lodging suggestions, see the *Eastern Ontario Trip Planner* from
Travel Ontario.

## HELPFUL HINTS

Kingston has an annual festival of music, comedy, and drama that
takes place at the Grand Theatre nightly throughout July and
August. The theater is at 218 Princess Street. To find out what's on,
call (613) 530-2050 or (800) 615-5666.

The Kingston Buskers Festival, held every summer, is also not to
be missed. More than 100 street performers from around the world
show up for it every year.

The Festival of the Islands is an annual event centered in
Gananoque that runs for 10 days in the middle of August. Waterfront
fireworks, sound-and-light shows, children's concerts, period costumes
and displays, and powerboat races are just some of the dozens of activities offered.

For more information on the Thousand Islands, contact the
Greater Kingston Tourist Information Office, 209 Ontario St.,
Kingston, Ont., Canada K7L 2Z1, (613) 548-4415; the Gananoque &
Area Chamber of Commerce, 2 King Street East, Gananoque, Ont.,
Canada K7G 1E6, (613) 382-3250 or (800) 561-1595; or, for
information on the entire eastern Ontario area, call (800) 567-3278.

# 4
# OTTAWA

Twenty years ago a federal cabinet minister was heard to declare that the best thing about Ottawa was the train to Montreal. Some people may still feel that way; but in truth the city has changed for the better, with improved dining, shopping, and nightlife. Several new major attractions have opened in the last few years, notably the National Gallery of Canada and the Canadian Museum of Civilization. Also relatively new to Ottawa is a National Hockey League team, the Senators.

With its miles of bicycle paths, generous amounts of green space, and the Rideau Canal snaking lazily through its heart, Ottawa is one of the prettiest capital cities anywhere. It reaches a picturesque peak during April and May, when millions of tulips burst into glorious blossom. During the Second World War, the Dutch royal family fled Holland and sought shelter in Ottawa. While there, then-Princess Juliana gave birth to Princess Margriet, but a problem arose because Dutch royalty must be born on Dutch soil, so the hospital room was declared to be part of the Netherlands. Every year since the end of the war, the grateful people of the Netherlands have shipped 10,000 tulip bulbs to Ottawa. ◣

# OTTAWA

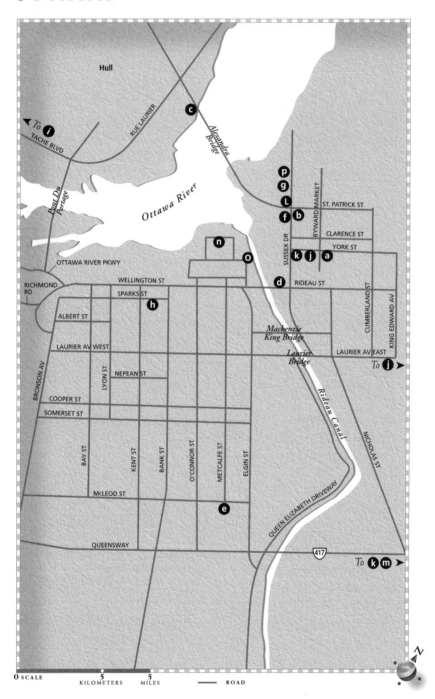

Hull

To **i**
TACHE BLVD

RUE LAURIER

Alexandra Bridge

**c**

Ottawa River

Pont Du Portage

**p**
**g**
**L**
ST. PATRICK ST
BYWARD MARKET
**f** **b**
SUSSEX DR
CLARENCE ST
YORK ST
**k** **j** **a**

**n**

**o**
OTTAWA RIVER PKWY

RICHMOND RD

WELLINGTON ST

**d** RIDEAU ST

CUMBERLAND ST

KING EDWARD AV

SPARKS ST

**h**

ALBERT ST

Mackenzie King Bridge

LAURIER AV WEST

Laurier Bridge

LAURIER AV EAST

To **j**

NEPEAN ST

BRONSON AV

LYON ST

COOPER ST

Rideau Canal

SOMERSET ST

BAY ST

KENT ST

BANK ST

O'CONNOR ST

METCALFE ST

ELGIN ST

NICHOLAS ST

McLEOD ST

**e**

QUEEN ELIZABETH DRIVEWAY

QUEENSWAY

417

To **k** **m**

N

O SCALE
5 KILOMETERS
5 MILES
ROAD

## Sightseeing Highlights

**ⓐ** Byward Market

**ⓑ** Canadian Museum of Caricature

**ⓒ** The Canadian Museum of Civilization

**ⓓ** The Canadian Museum of Contemporary Photography

**ⓔ** Canadian Museum of Nature

**ⓕ** Canadian Ski Museum

**ⓖ** Canadian War Museum

**ⓗ** Currency Museum

**ⓘ** Gatineau Park

**ⓙ** Laurier House

**ⓚ** National Aviation Museum

**ⓛ** The National Gallery of Canada

**ⓜ** National Museum of Science and Technology

**ⓝ** Parliament Hill

**ⓞ** Rideau Canal Promenade

**ⓟ** Royal Canadian Mint

## A PERFECT DAY IN OTTAWA

A visit to Parliament Hill is de rigueur for first-time visitors, but I've done it several times over the years and try to avoid it now. Instead, I head for the always-interesting photography museum and then on to the Byward Market area, where the cafés, restaurants, bars, and shops can provide hours of pleasurable wandering and socializing. If I want more culture, I head across Sussex Drive to the National Gallery of Canada. Dinnertime will likely find me at one of the Mexicali Rosa's outlets; I remember when the first one opened way back when, and what a delight it was at a time when restaurant choices in Ottawa were pretty limited, especially if you were on a budget.

## HISTORY

O
ttawa was not always a government town. After the first
Europeans arrived in 1613, in the form of French explorer
Samuel de Champlain, it became a trading center because of its location at the confluence of the Ottawa, Rideau, and Gatineau Rivers. By
the 1800s Ottawa and Hull, the settlement across the river, were brawl-
ing lumber towns. In 1857 Queen Victoria named Ottawa the capital
of the United Provinces of Canada, chiefly because it was centrally
located and politically acceptable to both Canada East and Canada
West. Or, as Sir Edmund Head, then governor general, put it, "I
believe that the least objectionable place is the city of Ottawa. Every
city is jealous of every other city except Ottawa."

## COLD CAPITAL

I
t must be noted that Ottawa is the coldest national capital in the
Western world (Ulan Bator, Mongolia, holds the world record). The
pain of making it through those snowy, subdued months is eased by
Winterlude, an annual February fête that draws a million people a year.
During Winterlude, locals and visitors alike throw themselves into
winter sports, chief among them skating on the Rideau Canal, trans-
formed each winter into the world's longest skating rink—7.8 kilometers (almost 5 miles) long. (Summer, however, is deliciously warm,
and autumn is the best time to check out Gatineau Park, a vast natural
reserve of lakes and forests behind Hull.)

## GETTING AROUND OTTAWA

W
ith a population of 304,000, Ottawa boasts the prime advantage
of a small city: the major hotels, most noteworthy sights, and
best shopping and dining are virtually all in the downtown area.
Confederation Square, the heart of the city, is actually a triangular
piece of land rimmed by Parliament Hill and the stately Chateau
Laurier hotel, the National Arts Center (Ottawa's showcase for per-
forming arts), and the Sparks Street Mall. The Byward Market, a lively
area of shops, bars, and restaurants, and the Rideau Centre, Ottawa's
largest shopping mall (with some 230 boutiques), lie below the
Château Laurier, while the National Gallery of Canada is down Sussex
Drive behind the hotel.
    Leave your car at the hotel and get around on foot or on city

buses. Weekdays, riding OC Transpo buses costs $2.10 in the peak periods between 6:00 a.m. and 8:30 a.m. and 3:00 p.m. to 5:30 p.m. The rest of the time, a single fare is $1.60. For more information, contact the OC Transpo offices at 294 Albert Street, or phone (613) 741-4370.

## SIGHTSEEING HIGHLIGHTS

✯✯✯ **Byward Market** • This formerly seedy section of town is now a quirky mix of pricey boutiques and second-hand stores, food markets, and yuppie bistros. The Market, as locals call it, is the oldest part of Ottawa; the city's first houses and taverns went up there, in what was then called Lower Town, 150 years ago. Over the last 25 years the 6-square-block area has been fully restored. But part of the Market has remained unchanged, with meat, fish, poultry, cheese, and produce shops that boast the freshest food and best prices in town. In summer, farmers set up outdoor stalls selling fruit, vegetables, and flowers. Ottawans do their marketing there in droves on weekends. There are also pubs, wine bars, live-music bars, French bistros, healthfood cafés, and restaurants. A takeout stand called Hooker's, at the corner of William and York, serves beaver tails—paddle-shaped yeasty dough, deep-fried. Sprinkle cinnamon and sugar on the puffy, soft confection and enjoy. (2 hours)

✯✯✯ **The Canadian Museum of Civilization** • This massive complex houses a world of wonders, including a unique, convertible IMAX-Omnimax theater and a History Hall featuring life-size buildings that represent historic Canadian scenes. For kids, there is a Children's Museum with hands-on activities designed to impart information about other cultures. Interactive computer terminals are located throughout the museum, allowing visitors to learn more about each exhibit. The museum is housed in a futuristic, undulating building across the Ottawa River from Parliament Hill. Museum admission is $5 for adults, $3.50 for youths and seniors, and $1 for children 12 and under. Admission to the IMAX-Omnimax theater, known as Cineplus, is $7 for adults and $5 for seniors, youths, and kids. Admission to both museum and theater is $11 for adults, $7.50 for youths and seniors, and $5.50 for children. Hours: Daily 9:00 a.m. to 8:00 p.m. on Thursdays; 9:00 a.m. to 6:00 p.m. the rest of the week. Closed on Mondays in winter. Address: 100 rue Laurier in Hull. Phone: (819) 776-7000. (3 hours)

★★★ **The Canadian Museum of Contemporary Photography •**
Canada's first photography museum opened in 1992 and houses an
impressive collection of some 158,000 images (not all on display at one
time!). Its boutique should delight photo buffs. Admission is free.
Hours: In summer, open daily from 11:00 a.m. to 5:00 p.m., except
Wednesday, when hours are 4:00 to 8:00 p.m., and Thursday, when
hours are 11:00 a.m. to 8:00 p.m. Hours are shorter the rest of the
year. Address: 1 Rideau Canal, between the Parliament Buildings and
the Château Laurier. Phone: (613) 993-4497. (2 hours)

★★★ **The National Gallery of Canada •** A luminous structure of
glass and granite, the National Gallery rises from a promontory about
a mile downstream from the Parliament buildings. Prominent
Canadian architect Moshe Safdie broke up the building by creating a
series of smaller pavilions to house the various permanent collections
and temporary exhibits, including what is billed as the world's most
comprehensive collection of Canadian art. One standout permanent
exhibit is the reconstructed interior of the Rideau Street Chapel, with
its neo-Gothic fan-vaulted ceiling. Public tours are offered daily, at
11:00 a.m. and 2:00 p.m. There are a bookstore, a gift shop, and two
restaurants. Admission to the permanent collection is free, but charges
apply to special exhibitions. Hours: In summer, 10:00 a.m. to 6:00 p.m.
(8:00 p.m. on Thursdays). In winter, hours are 10:00 a.m. to 5:00 p.m.
(8:00 p.m. on Thursdays). Closed Mondays. Address: 380 Sussex Drive.
Phone: (613) 990-1985. (2 hours)

★★★ **Parliament Hill •** The Parliament buildings stand on a cliff
overlooking the Ottawa River. In season, you should book same-day
free tours through Infotent on Parliament Hill. It operates from
9:00 a.m. to 5:00 p.m. from May 17 to June 30; 9:00 a.m. to 9:00 p.m.
weekdays, and 9:00 a.m. to 6:00 p.m. weekends from July 1 to 31;
9:00 a.m. to 8:30 p.m weekdays, and 9:00 a.m. to 6:00 p.m. weekends
from August 1 to September 7; closed on July 1, Canada Day. The rest
of the year, free tours are offered daily except on Christmas and New
Year's. The tours begin at the main entrance and last from 30 to 45
minutes. After each tour, except for the final one of the day, visitors are
free to take the elevator to the observation deck of the Peace Tower,
the central tower that rises 92 meters (300 feet) over Parliament Hill.
When Parliament is in session, visitors may obtain tickets to sit in the
public galleries of the Senate and the House of Commons and listen to
debate. If you're on Parliament Hill when the changing of the guard

happens, fine. Otherwise, don't sweat it. The Changing of the Guard takes place at 10:00 a.m. daily, weather permitting, from June 22 to August 30. Phone: (613) 996-0896. (2 hours)

★★★ **Rideau Canal Promenade** • This is a particularly scenic walk in a city filled with scenic walkways. The canal was designed and built after the War of 1812 to provide a protected military supply route from Montreal to the Great Lakes. It runs for 202 kilometers (121 miles) between the Ottawa River and Lake Ontario at Kingston. The part that goes through Ottawa has a promenade running along nearly 8 kilometers (5 miles) through downtown and beyond. Start next to Confederation Square and wander at will, or take a boat ride. Call Paul's Boat Lines at (613) 225-6781. Boat tours depart from near the National Arts Centre. (2 hours)

★★ **Canadian Museum of Nature** • This venerable establishment displays everything from insects to dinosaurs and is a good opportunity to lose the kids for a couple of hours, thanks to its hands-on exhibits, live animals, and mini-theater presentations. Admission is $4 for adults, $2 for seniors, $3 for students, and $2 for kids up to age 16. Family admission is $9. Hours: 9:30 a.m. to 8:00 p.m. Sunday, Monday, and Thursday, and 9:30 a.m. to 5:00 p.m. Tuesday, Wednesday, Friday, and Saturday. Address: McLeod Street at Metcalfe. Phone: (613) 996-3102. (2 hours)

★★ **Laurier House** • This century-old mansion was the residence of Canada's longest-serving prime minister, William Lyon Mackenzie King. He was also, as far as anyone knows, the most eccentric of our prime ministers. King seemed rather a colorless man during his prime-ministry, which ran for a total of nearly 22 years at various times in the '20s, '30s, and '40s. It has since been revealed that he believed in spirits and communed regularly with the dead, chief among them his mother. Among the goodies at Laurier House are King's crystal ball and an eerie portrait of his dear departed mother. Admission is $2.25 for adults, $1.75 for seniors, and $1.25 for kids 6 to 16. Address: 335 Laurier Avenue East. Phone: (613) 692-2581. (1 hour)

★★ **National Museum of Science and Technology** • This is a particularly good bet for children because of its hands-on exhibits. Admission is $5 for adults, $4 for students and seniors, and $1.75 for children 6 to 15. The family rate is $10. Hours: 9:00 a.m. to 5:00 p.m.

daily and 9:00 a.m. to 9:00 p.m. Thursday between May 1 and Sept. 6; and 9:00 a.m. to 5:00 p.m. Tuesday through Sunday the rest of the year. Address: 1867 St-Laurent Boulevard; take the Queensway to St-Laurent, exit south and follow your nose until you see a lighthouse on your left. Phone: 991-3044. (3 hours)

✸ **Canadian Museum of Caricature** • It has cartoons and caricatures spanning three centuries of Canadian history, but most of the exhibit dates from the 1950s to the present. It will (hopefully) make you laugh, and admission is free. Hours: 10:00 a.m. to 6:00 p.m. Saturday through Tuesday, 10:00 a.m. to 8:00 p.m. Wednesday through Friday. Address: 136 St. Patrick Street at Sussex Drive. Phone: (613) 995-3145. (½ hour)

✸ **Canadian Ski Museum** • This is for ski buffs only. The museum features ski memorabilia, including a 5,000-year-old cave drawing of men on skis. Admission is $1 for adults and 50 cents for children 12 and up. Hours: Tuesday through Sunday year-round, 11:00 a.m. to 4:00 p.m. from May through September and 12:00 noon to 4:00 p.m. the rest of the year. Address: 457A Sussex Drive. Phone: (613) 241-5832. (½ hour)

✸ **Canadian War Museum** • Right next door to the National Gallery of Canada, the Canadian War Museum houses a permanent collection of the history of the Canadian military. However, the most popular—and macabre—display is Adolf Hitler's 1940 Mercedes. Admission is $2.50 for adults, $1.25 for seniors and students, and free for kids under 16. Hours: 9:30 a.m. to 5:00 p.m. daily and 9:30 a.m. to 8:00 p.m. on Thursday; closed Mondays in the off-season. Address: 330 Sussex Drive. Phone: (613) 776-8600. (2 hours)

✸ **Currency Museum** • This small display in the Bank of Canada depicts the history of money in Canada by showcasing various kinds of cash that have been used over the years, including $3, $6, $7, and $8 bills. Admission is $2 per person, free for kids under 7, and $5 for families. On Tuesdays, everybody gets in free. Hours: Open year-round 10:30 a.m. to 5:00 p.m. Monday through Saturday and 1:00 p.m. to 5:00 p.m. Sunday. Address: 235 Sparks Street. Phone: (613) 782-8914. (½ hour)

✸ **Gatineau Park** • Nature-lovers will find Gatineau Park, across the river on the other side of Hull, well worth the 20-minute drive from

Ottawa. The park, spread over hundreds of acres of the gently rolling Gatineau Hills, boasts endless kilometers of nature trails. Kingsmere, the country estate of the late, eccentric prime minister, William Lyon Mackenzie King, is also located in the park and is open to visitors. To get to Gatineau Park, follow Tache Boulevard west from Hull and turn north onto the Gatineau Parkway. Open year-round; free admission. Phone: (819) 827-2020. (2 hours)

☆ **National Aviation Museum** • This museum boasts an impressive collection of vintage and modern planes and related artifacts. Admission is $5 for adults, $4 for seniors and students, and $1.75 for children 6 to 15. The family rate is $10. Hours: 9:00 a.m. to 5:00 p.m. daily and 9:00 a.m. to 9:00 p.m. Thursday from May 1 to Sept. 6, and 9:00 a.m. to 5:00 p.m. Tuesday through Sunday the rest of the year. Address: Rockcliffe Airport. Phone: (613) 993-4243. (2 hours)

☆ **Royal Canadian Mint** • If you want to know how Canada makes its money, visit the Royal Canadian Mint. Hours: Open 8:30 to 11:00 a.m. and 12:30 p.m. to 2:30 p.m. from May through August, weekdays only. Address: 320 Sussex Drive. Phone: (613) 993-8990 to reserve space on a tour.

## FITNESS AND RECREATION

Long before cycling became such a popular, environmentally correct activity, Ottawa was renowned for its kilometers of bicycle paths that wind along the picturesque Rideau Canal and through the greenest parts of the city. Bicycle rentals are available downtown; check at tourist information for details. Hikers, meanwhile, can head for the hills—the hills of Gatineau Park across the river, that is.

## FOOD

The range and quality of restaurants in Ottawa has improved dramatically in recent years; following is a sampling of the best of what's available in various price ranges.

For designer pasta dishes, the Ritz chain of Italian restaurants is a good bet. They don't take reservations and are very busy around 7:00 p.m., which seems to be Ottawa's peak dining hour, so try to arrive earlier or later than that. The **Ritz Canal**, which provides a view of skating in winter and boating in summer, is at 375 Queen Elizabeth

# OTTAWA

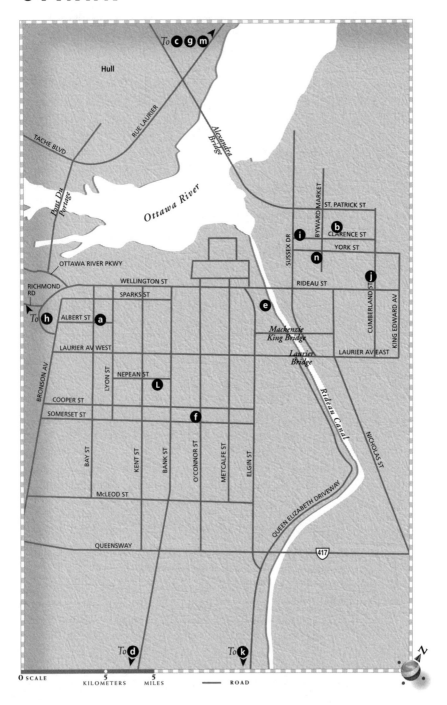

Hull

*To* **c** **g** **m**

RUE LAURIER

*Alexandra Bridge*

TACHE BLVD

*Pont Du Portage*

*Ottawa River*

ST. PATRICK ST

BYWARD MARKET

**i** SUSSEX DR

**b** CLARENCE ST

YORK ST

**n**

OTTAWA RIVER PKWY

RICHMOND RD

*To* **h**

WELLINGTON ST

SPARKS ST

ALBERT ST **a**

RIDEAU ST

CUMBERLAND ST

KING EDWARD AV

**j**

**e**

*Mackenzie King Bridge*

LAURIER AV WEST

*Laurier Bridge*

LAURIER AV EAST

BRONSON AV

LYON ST

NEPEAN ST

**L**

COOPER ST

SOMERSET ST

**f**

*Rideau Canal*

BAY ST

KENT ST

BANK ST

O'CONNOR ST

METCALFE ST

ELGIN ST

NICHOLAS ST

McLEOD ST

QUEEN ELIZABETH DRIVEWAY

QUEENSWAY

417

*To* **d**

*To* **k**

N

0 SCALE    5
KILOMETERS    5
MILES    ——— ROAD

# Food

- ⓐ Bay Street Bistro
- ⓑ Blue Cactus Bar and Grill
- ⓒ Café Henry Burger
- ⓓ Chahaya Malaysia
- ⓔ Le Café
- ⓕ Le Metro
- ⓖ Le Pied de Cochon
- ⓗ Lindenhof
- ⓘ Memories
- ⓙ Mexicali Rosa's
- ⓚ Ritz Canal
- ⓛ Ritz Uptown
- ⓜ Thai Kitchen
- ⓝ Zak's Diner

Driveway. **Ritz Uptown** is at 226 Nepean. Other Ritz restaurants are at 15 Clarence Street in the Market; at 1665 Bank Street; and at 274 Elgin Street. For affordable fish, chicken, and meat dishes plus gourmet pasta and pizza, try the **Bay Street Bistro** (613-234-1111), an indoor-outdoor bistro-café at 160 Bay Street at the corner of Albert.

**Mexicali Rosa's** is a chain that started out as a single small establishment on Bank Street and has now spread to other locations in Ottawa as well as other Canadian cities. The reason for their success is the reasonably priced Mexican food and casual atmosphere. You'll probably have to line up. A few addresses: 895 Bank Street; 1001 Queen Elizabeth Drive; and 207 Rideau Street.

In the Byward Market, check out **Zak's Diner**, a retro kind of place with jukeboxes and formica at 14 Byward at the corner of York. Zak's is a particularly good bet if you're with kids or teenagers. **Memories**, at 7 Clarence Street in the Market, is the local dessert place, while the **Blue Cactus Bar and Grill** at 2 Byward on the corner of Clarence serves Cajun, Southwest, and Texan dishes.

There's a Malaysian restaurant, **Chahaya Malaysia**, at 749 Bank St., that has a good reputation; call (613) 237-4304. For Thai food, try the **Thai Kitchen**, a small, unpretentious place at 144 Maisonneuve Boulevard in Hull; call (819) 595-3505. For traditional German fare, there's **Lindenhof** at 965 Richmond Road; call (613) 725-3481.

For French dining, **Le Metro** is highly recommended for both its ambiance and its food. It's at 315 Somerset Street West; call (613) 230-8123 for reservations. Other (pricey) French restaurants include the **Café Henry Burger** at 69 rue Laurier in Hull (819-777-5646) and **Le Pied de Cochon** at 248 Montcalm in Hull. (Literally translated, "pig's foot," but don't let that put you off; call 819-777-5805.)

At the National Arts Center, the canal-side **Le Café** serves delicious Canadian fare like caribou and northern pike—(613) 594-5127.

# LODGING

At the high end of Ottawa's accommodations spectrum, room rates at several hotels begin around $120 a night for a double, but hotels also offer periodic specials or weekend rates. The **Château Laurier** at 1 Rideau Street, down a slope from Parliament Hill, is a landmark in itself; phone (613) 241-1414 or (800) 441-1414 . Other centrally located and expensive hotels include the luxury **Westin Hotel**

**Ottawa** next to the Rideau Centre ($100 to $165, 613-560-7000 or 800-228-3000) and the **Minto Place Suite Hotel** at 433 Laurier Avenue West (regular $120 and up, special rates $93 and up, 613-232-2200 or 800-267-3377). All three establishments are wheelchair accessible and offer babysitting services.

In the moderate range near the city center, **Quality Hotel** at 290 Rideau Street is wheelchair accessible and charges from $97 to $112 a night (789-7511 locally or 800-4-CHOICE). The grand old **Lord Elgin Hotel** at 100 Elgin Street has lately been renovated and offers rooms from $81 to $141 (613-235-3333 or 800-267-4298). It, too, is wheelchair accessible and also offers babysitting services. The **Novotel Hotel** at 33 Nicholas Street has rooms for from $85 to $99 and is wheelchair accessible (613-230-3033 or 800-NOVOTEL). **Welcominns** at 1220 Michael Street charges from $77 to $90 (613-748-7800 or 800-387-4381).

The **Doral Inn**, at 486 Albert Street near Bay Street, is not right downtown but is central enough and, being both small and relatively inexpensive, worth checking out. Regular rates for two begin at $69, special rates at $65. Call (613) 230-8055 or (800) 26-DORAL.

The local B&B referral service, Ottawa Bed and Breakfast, is at 488 Cooper, Ottawa, Ont., Canada K1R 5H9, (613) 563-0161 or (800) 461-7889. Singles begin around $40 a night, doubles around $50. Or consider the **Australis Guest House**, a B&B in residential Sandy Hill that comes highly recommended by people who have stayed there. Double rooms are $55 and the address is 35 Marlborough Avenue, Ottawa, Ont. K1N 8E6, phone (613) 235-8461.

For a rather eerie experience, try the **Ottawa International Hostel** at 75 Nicholas. It served as the Nicholas Street Jail for more than 100 years before being converted into a hostel. Accommodation is provided in the refurbished cells. Call (613) 235-2595 for reservations or just for a tour of the place.

The Visitor Information Centre at the National Arts Centre runs a free summertime booking service for hotels, motels, and bed and breakfasts; call (613) 237-5158 or (800) 465-1867. You can also reserve at selected hotels through Ontario's tourist information line, (800) ONTARIO.

# OTTAWA

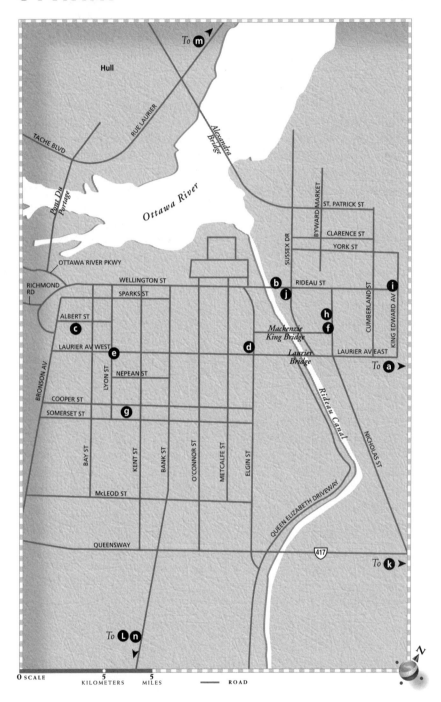

Hull

To **m**

RUE LAURIER

TACHE BLVD

Pont Du Portage

Alexandra Bridge

*Ottawa River*

OTTAWA RIVER PKWY

BYWARD MARKET

ST. PATRICK ST

CLARENCE ST

YORK ST

SUSSEX DR

RICHMOND RD

WELLINGTON ST

**b**    RIDEAU ST

**j**

CUMBERLAND ST

KING EDWARD AV

**i**

SPARKS ST

ALBERT ST

**c**

**h**

*Mackenzie King Bridge*

**f**

LAURIER AV WEST

**e**

**d**

*Laurier Bridge*

LAURIER AV EAST

To **a**

BRONSON AV

LYON ST

NEPEAN ST

COOPER ST

SOMERSET ST

**g**

BAY ST

KENT ST

BANK ST

O'CONNOR ST

METCALFE ST

ELGIN ST

McLEOD ST

*Rideau Canal*

NICHOLAS ST

QUEEN ELIZABETH DRIVEWAY

QUEENSWAY

417

To **k**

To **L** **n**

0 SCALE    5          5
      KILOMETERS  MILES         ROAD

# Lodging

**ⓐ** Australis Guest House

**ⓑ** Château Laurier

**ⓒ** Doral Inn

**ⓓ** Lord Elgin Hotel

**ⓔ** Minto Place Suite Hotel

**ⓕ** Novotel Hotel

**ⓖ** Ottawa Bed and Breakfast

**ⓗ** Ottawa International Hostel

**ⓘ** Quality Hotel

**ⓙ** Westin Hotel Ottawa

**ⓚ** Welcominns

# Camping

**ⓛ** Camp Hither Hills

**ⓜ** Lac Philippe Family Campground

**ⓝ** Poplar Grove Campground

## CAMPING

Of four National Capital Commission campgrounds in the area, Lac Philippe Family Campground in Gatineau has the most facilities. The rate per site is $16. You can make reservations by mail from early April by writing to NCC Campgrounds, 161 Laurier Avenue West, Ottawa, Ont., Canada K1P 6J6, and by telephone after early June by calling (819) 456-3016. Among other campgrounds in the area, Poplar Grove Campground has the most facilities, including tennis courts, a playground, a store, and a beach. It's 13 kilometers (8 miles) south of the city, off Highway 31. Phone (613) 821-2973. Also off Highway 31, but closer to the city, is Camp Hither Hills, with a beach and playground but no store. Call (613) 822-0509.

## NIGHTLIFE

For nightlife, try the Byward Market area or the clump of bars along Elgin Street, which runs up to the Parliament buildings. The Chateau Laurier's exquisitely restful lounge, Zoe's, overlooking Confederation Square, is one of the best places in town for a quiet drink after a long afternoon of sightseeing.

To find out what's on at the National Arts Centre, phone (613) 996-5051, ext. 375, or check the listings in the Ottawa *Citizen*, the Ottawa *Sun*, or the weekly Ottawa *X-Press*.

## HELPFUL HINTS

Ottawa is the national capital, and 24 Sussex Drive is the Canadian version of 1600 Pennsylvania Avenue or 10 Downing Street. The prime minister's residence is set back from the street behind walls and shrubbery, and you can't see much of the house. Nearby, however, is Rideau Hall, the governor-general's residence, with lush grounds which are open to the public in summer.

For more information on Ottawa, call the Ottawa Tourism and Convention Authority at (613) 237-54158. Visitor information centers are located in the National Arts Centre at 65 Elgin Street and 14 Metcalfe Street across from Parliament Hill. Other sources of information include Canada's Capital Information Center at (613) 239-5000 or (800) 465-1867.

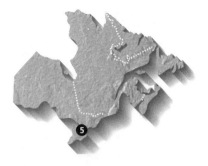

# 5
# MONTREAL

A h, Montreal. The Paris of North America, known for its *joie de vivre*, cosmopolitan atmosphere, and European flavor. I happened to wander through old Montreal recently, just a day after returning from Europe, and briefly felt confused as to which continent I was on. Montreal has much to offer—history, festivals, Old Montreal, drinking, and eating, all set against the background of a culture that's an odd hybrid of European and North American. It ought to be one of this continent's tourist Meccas, but it's not. Of course, the uncertainty surrounding the issue of separation doesn't help tourism. But visitors are unaffected by such issues, so visit Montreal and be smug in the knowledge that you're onto a place a lot of travelers miss. ◣

# MONTREAL

N

St. Lawrence River

PIERRE DE COUBERTIN AV

NOTRE DAME ST

125

SHERBROOKE ST

134

Jacques Cartier Bridge

Île Ste-Hélène

MOUNT-ROYAL AV

DULUTH AV

ROY ST

BERRI ST

STE-CATHERINE ST

RENÉ-LÉVESQUE BLVD

VIGER ST

ST. DENIS ST

ST-PAUL ST

Concordia Bridge

Old Port

Parc des Îles

Notre Dame
Island

LAURIER
BLVD

ST-LAURENT ST

PRINCE ARTHUR ST

AYLMER

METCALFE ST

GAUCHETIÈRE ST

ST-ANTOINE ST

ST-URBAIN ST

PARK AV

FAIRMONT ST

UNIVERSITY ST

ST-JACQUES ST

ST-VIATEUR WEST

Mt. Royal Park

MAISONNEUVE BLVD

STANLEY ST

PEEL ST

112

Victoria Bridge

BONAVENTURE

CÔTE-DES-NEIGES

ATWATER AV

DU FORT ST

GUY ST

MACKAY ST

BISHOP ST

CRESCENT ST

DE LA MONTAGNE ST

SHERBROOKE ST

Lachine Canal

QUEEN
MARY
RD

0 SCALE

1.5
KILOMETERS

1.5
MILES

——— ROAD

═══ HIGHWAY

········· AREA BOUNDARY

# Sightseeing Highlights

**ⓐ** Alcan House

**ⓑ** Biodome

**ⓒ** The Biosphere

**ⓓ** The Canadian Centre for Architecture

**ⓔ** The Château Ramezay Museum

**ⓕ** The International Museum of Humor

**ⓖ** McGill University

**ⓗ** Montreal Botanical Gardens

**ⓘ** Montreal Museum of Contemporary Art

**ⓙ** Montreal Museum of Fine Arts

**ⓚ** Montreal World Trade Centre

**ⓛ** Mount Royal Lookout

**ⓜ** Notre-Dame Basilica

**ⓝ** The Old Port

**ⓞ** Olympic Stadium

**ⓟ** Parc des Îles

**ⓠ** Place Jacques Cartier

**ⓡ** Pointe-à-Callière, Museum of Archeology and History

**ⓢ** St- Joseph's Oratory

## A PERFECT DAY IN MONTREAL

My perfect day in Montreal starts off with brunch in an outdoor café—on St-Denis Street, perhaps, or, if it's raining, at Beauty's on Mount Royal. Then it's off to the east end of the city in search of nature at the Biodome and the Botanical Gardens. A stroll through Old Montreal and along the waterfront promenade at the Old Port, with a drink at one of the outdoor terraces on Jacques Cartier Square, would cap off the afternoon. Deciding where to have dinner can be a problem because there is such an embarrassment of choices, but I love Thai food so I'd probably go for Chao Phraya, a Thai restaurant on St-Denis Street. Then I'd head over to the pedestrian mall of Prince Arthur Street and, late into the night, do some serious people-watching from one of the sidewalk cafés there.

## FRENCH CANADA

In 1535 French explorer Jacques Cartier, searching for a passage to India, became the first known white man to set foot on the island that would become Montreal. It was then the site of Hochelaga, an Iroquois village. Cartier named the mountain Mount Royal. In 1611 another French explorer, Samuel de Champlain, founder of New France, arrived and set up a fortified settlement, Place Royale. In 1642 a small group of French colonists established a settlement called Ville Marie at the Pointe-à-Callière; later they moved to higher ground in the heart of what is now Old Montreal. Initially a mission to convert the natives, the settlement quickly became a busy trading center thanks to its location at the confluence of the St. Lawrence, Ottawa, and Richelieu Rivers. In 1760 the British conquered New France. British soldiers and a handful of British colonists were left to build a British Canada among a French population of some 60,000. To do it sanely, Britain gradually confirmed the right of French Canadians to retain their Roman Catholic faith, their language, and their legal code.

For some 200 years the powerful English minority ran the province's economy. In the 1960s a separatist movement began to grow among French Quebecers, and in 1976 the Parti Québecois, whose main platform plank was independence, was voted into power. A provincial referendum on independence was narrowly defeated four years later, and the PQ themselves lost the next election to the Liberals. But the sovereignty question remained unresolved. In October 1992, a national referendum was held on a new constitutional agreement that would have brought Quebec, the only province that had not signed a previous agreement, into the Canadian fold. The vote was a resounding "no!" in most parts of the country—in Quebec because Quebecers thought they weren't getting enough, and in some other provinces because people thought Quebec was getting too much. The Parti Québecois returned to power in 1994 and on October 30, 1995 held another provincial referendum on independence. The result was a squeaker—slightly more than one percentage point divided the two sides—that left Canada intact but the Quebec population deeply divided. Another referendum looms inevitably in Quebec's future.

I have lived in Quebec most of my life and the debate has continued for as long as I can remember. My feeling is it might never end, but meanwhile life goes on much as usual. English-speaking Montrealers make up about 14 percent of the city's 3.1 million residents, and many francophones are bilingual, so visitors get the best of both worlds—a distinct French flavor, but with plenty of people around who can speak English. A word of warning, however: Most traffic and commercial signs are in French only. When driving, try to remember that *est* means east, *ouest* means west, *sud* means south, and *nord* means north. When shopping, you might keep an eye out for stickers in store windows that say "F/E," which indicate merchants will serve you in French or English, whichever you prefer.

While in Montreal, you may hear references to not just anglophones and francophones, but "allophones." Allophones are residents whose mother tongue is neither French nor English. Altogether, more than a million of the province's 7 million residents speak English or languages other than French at home.

## GETTING TO AND AROUND MONTREAL

Montreal has two international airports: Dorval, about 20 minutes from downtown, and Mirabel, an hour north of the city. Domestic and transborder flights come into Dorval, while huge Mirabel, widely known as a white elephant, serves international flights and is never busy. Via Rail trains arrive at Central Station next to the Queen Elizabeth Hotel downtown, while intercity buses come into the Voyageur bus station on Berri Street east of downtown.

Sherbrooke Street is the major artery running east-west through Montreal. The next streets south are de Maisonneuve Boulevard, Ste-Catherine Street, and René-Lévesque Boulevard, in that order. North

of Sherbrooke Street, at least in the downtown area, the slopes of
Mount Royal begin. South of René-Lévesque, the major streets are
St-Antoine, St-Jacques, and Notre-Dame, while de la Commune fronts
the St. Lawrence River. The major cross-streets from west to east are
Atwater, Guy, Crescent, de la Montagne, Peel, and University. Eight
blocks east of University, St. Lawrence Street, alias St-Laurent, alias
The Main, divides the city into east and west.

Old Montreal is southeast of downtown, near the waterfront,
spreading east from the corner of University and St-Jacques and south
toward the river. The Olympic Stadium, the Biodome, and the
Botanical Gardens are in a clump in the east end, about 15 minutes by
subway from downtown.

Parking downtown is hard to find, and driving in Montreal can be
nerve-wracking for people who aren't accustomed to it. Drivers and
pedestrians are constantly at war. Montrealers jaywalk all the time.
Occasionally police decide to crack down and start handing out fines
for jaywalking. It never lasts very long and nobody takes it seriously.
Drivers aren't much better, frequently changing lanes without signal-
ing, racing through yellow lights as they turn red and honking impa-
tiently if the car in front doesn't move fast enough. Drive—and
walk—defensively in Montreal.

Better yet, abandon your car at your hotel and get around on the
public transit system. In this case that means chiefly the clean, efficient,
and relatively crime-free subway, the métro. One of the subway lines
runs right along Ste-Catherine and out past the Olympic Stadium in
the east end of the city; another goes past the edge of old Montreal.
Single tickets for bus or métro cost $1.75, while a strip of six tickets
costs $7.75. For information, call AUTOBUS (288-6287).

The major tourist information center is Centre Infotouriste at
1001 Dorchester Square Street, in the block bordered by Ste-
Catherine, René-Lévesque, Peel, and Metcalfe Streets (nearest métro
stop is Peel). There is also an information kiosk at 174 Notre-Dame
Street East on Place Jacques Cartier in Old Montreal.

## SIGHTSEEING HIGHLIGHTS

★★★ **Biodome** • The Biodome, a strange combination of zoo, aquarium, botanical garden, and museum, became one of Montreal's most-
visited tourist attractions as soon as it opened in 1992. The Biodome's
display of four different ecosystems is aimed at making visitors more

aware of the planet's fragility. The environments, spread over 10,000 square meters, are a tropical rain forest, Quebec's Laurentian forestlands, the St. Lawrence River's marine world, and the polar worlds of the Arctic and Antarctic. Re-created with both authentic and artificial flora and fauna, the rain forest area is filled with suffocating heat, screeching birds, and chattering monkeys. The Laurentian woodland surrounds a huge beaver dam, while the centerpiece of the St. Lawrence River exhibit is a massive tank filled with cod, halibut, striped bass, even sharks, with northern gannets swimming on the surface.

Because of the distinct temperature changes as you move from ecosystem to ecosystem through laser-prompted glass doors, officials recommend you wear something lightweight but carry a sweater or coat. Admission is $9.50 for adults, $4.75 for children 6 to 17, $6.75 for seniors, and free for children under 6. Joint tickets to the Biodome and the nearby Botanical Gardens are also available. Hours: Open daily year-round, 9:00 a.m. to 6:00 p.m. (8:00 p.m. in summer). Address: 4777 Pierre-de-Coubertin Avenue. The nearest subway station is Viau. Phone: (514) 868-3000. (2½ hours)

★★★ **Montreal Museum of Fine Arts** • Founded in 1860, the oldest art museum in Canada is now made up of two buildings facing each other across Sherbrooke Street. The original is a magnificent neoclassical structure on the north side of the street; the new extension across from it was designed by Moshe Safdie, architect of the National Gallery of Canada in Ottawa. Permanent collections include prints, drawings, sculpture, paintings by both old masters and contemporary artists, furniture, and silver. There's a gift shop, too. The museum usually brings some sort of blockbuster show to Montreal each summer. Admission to the permanent collection is $12 for adults, $7 for students or seniors, and $3 for children 12 and under. Entrance to temporary exhibitions generally costs more and includes entrance to permanent exhibits. Hours: Tuesday to Sunday from 11:00 a.m. to 6:00 p.m., Saturday 11:00 a.m. to 9:00 p.m. Address: 1379-80 Sherbrooke Street West. Phone: (514) 285-1600. (2 hours)

★★★ **Notre-Dame Basilica** • One of the largest and most beautiful churches in North America, the basilica is ornate and quite magnificent. Its huge, 7,000-pipe organ has to be seen to be believed. Wander in and look around. Contrary to popular belief, the basilica design was not inspired by the cathedral of the same name in Paris

but by two churches in London, Westminster Abbey and St.
Martin's-in-the-Fields. Address: 110 Notre-Dame Street West on
Place d'Armes. Place d'Armes is the nearest Métro stop. (½ hour)

★★★ **The Old Port** • After years of mouldering, the waterfront area
in Old Montreal has recently received a multimillion-dollar facelift
(the New Old Port, the promoters call it). Wander the esplanade that
runs along de la Commune Street and check out historic buildings that
now house various exhibitions, an IMAX theater, and a flea market.
The IMAX-Expotec complex on the King Edward Pier at the base of
St-Laurent Street includes the theater with its 7-story screen (call 514-
496-4629 to find out what's playing) and Expotec, an interactive exhibit
whose themes change from season to season. Images du Futur, one of
the oldest exhibitions in the Old Port, boasts holograms, computer ani-
mations, virtual reality-style interactive exhibits, and assorted other
mind-boggling audiovisual displays. It's tucked away at the end of King
Edward Pier.

The Old Port also features boat shuttles, picnicking, organized
activities for children, live performances, cruises, excursions, and a
yacht harbor. You can rent pedal boats; ride a replica of an eighteenth-
century Mississippi steamboat on a lunch or dinner cruise (514-842-
7655); take a 90-minute cruise on the Bateau-Mouche, a climate-
controlled boat with a glassed-in observation deck (514-849-9952); ride
the Amphibus, a bizarre half-boat, half-bus vehicle that takes you on a
cruise and a drive of the Old Port area; or ride the Lachine Rapids on a
jet-boat (514-284-9607). For information on port activities in general,
call (514) 496-PORT. (3 hours)

★★★ **Place Jacques Cartier** • In the very heart of Old Montreal, this
cobblestoned square is where you'll find lively cafés, bars, and restaurants and, on summer days, live entertainment by buskers. The imposing white building across the street from the top of the square is City
Hall. (2 hours)

★★★ **Pointe-à-Callière, Museum of Archeology and History** •
Unique and entertaining, this museum stands on the same spot where
the city was founded 350 years earlier. The modern building houses
vestiges of Montreal's past discovered in archeological digs begun in
1980 at Place Royale and Pointe-à-Callière. The complex has three
sites—the Eperon building, with archeological artifacts and the
remains of Montreal's first cemetery; the archeological crypt beneath

Place Royale, containing old stone foundations and artifacts; and the Old Customs House. There is also a multiscreen film about the history of Montreal, plus computer-activated holograms. To visit this museum is to take a walk through the city's foundations, in all senses. Admission is $7 for adults, $5 for seniors, $4 for students, $2 for children 6 to 12, and free for children under 6. Free entry for all after 5:00 p.m. Wednesdays. Hours: 10:00 a.m. to 5:00 p.m., Wednesdays until 8:00 p.m.; closed Mondays. Address: 350 Place Royale. Phone: (514) 872-9150. (2 hours)

★★ **The Canadian Centre for Architecture** • The CCA, devoted to architecture and its history, incorporates the landmark Shaughnessy House into its striking modern structure. The center was funded almost entirely by Phyllis Lambert, an architect who also happens to be one of the millionaire Bronfmans. The unique collection includes thousands of drawings and print, books, and photographs. The CAA is a must for any architectural tour or aficionado. Adults $5, students $3, free for children 12 and under. Hours: Wednesday and Friday 11:00 a.m. to 6:00 p.m., Thursday 11:00 a.m. to 8:00 p.m., Saturday and Sunday 11:00 a.m. to 5:00 p.m. Closed Monday and Tuesday. Address: The building fronts René Lévesque Boulevard, but the entrance is on the other side at 1920 Baile Street. Phone: (514) 939-7026. (1½ hours)

★★ **Montreal Botanical Gardens** • The second-largest botanical gardens in the world contain some 10 greenhouses and 30 theme gardens, including Chinese and Japanese gardens and pavilions. Also on the grounds is the Insectarium, with everything from butterflies to beetles, some live, some mounted. Housed in a building that looks like a stylized bug, the Insectarium is billed as unique in North America. The botanical gardens may be a place to avoid on weekends, when wedding parties galore are having photographs taken. Between mid-May and mid-October, admission to the gardens, greenhouses, and the insectarium is $7 for adults, $5 for seniors, $3.50 for students, and children under 6 get in free. Admission fees are slightly lower in the off-season. Hours: Daily from 9:00 a.m. to 6:00 p.m. Address: 4101 Sherbrooke Street East, Pix-IX métro stop. Phone: (514) 872-1400. (2 hours)

★★ **Montreal Museum of Contemporary Art** • Newly housed in Place des Arts, the museum has a permanent collection of 3,000 works by Quebec, Canadian, and international artists, from Jean-Paul

Riopelle to Andy Warhol. Admission is $5 for adults, $4 for seniors, $3 for students 12 and up, and $12 for families. Hours: Tuesday to Sunday, 11:00 a.m. to 6:00 p.m. Address: 185 Ste-Catherine Street W. Phone: (514) 847-6212. (1½ hours)

★★ **Mount Royal Lookout** • The lower slopes of Mount Royal are layered with mansions, many of which now belong to McGill University. When they were privately owned, the homes formed part of the Golden Square Mile between Sherbrooke, the mountain, Côte-des-Neiges, and Avenue du Parc. At the turn of the century it was estimated that 70 percent of Canada's wealth was controlled by about 100 people who lived in this area. The upper part of the mountain has been preserved as a 200-hectare green space overlooking the city. This is one area it's best to use the car to see. Head north on Guy Street, which becomes Côte-des-Neiges, and follow it until you see signs for Mount Royal. There are two lookouts. From the Mount Royal Chalet Lookout, you can see Westmount and downtown, the islands of Île Ste-Hélène and Île Notre-Dame in the river and, beyond them, the hills of the Eastern Townships. The other lookout, further along the same road, provides a view of the Olympic Stadium and the east end. (½ hour)

★★ **Olympic Stadium** • The $1.2-billion stadium was built for the 1976 Summer Olympic Games at monstrous cost overruns; hence its nickname, The Big Owe. Its landmark tower wasn't completed, nor its retractable roof installed and made workable, until nearly 15 years later. Now, finally, it boasts the world's tallest inclined tower, the top of which provides a panorama of the city and Mount Royal. Guided tours of the stadium complex are available.

   Admission to the tower is $7 for adults, $6 for seniors, and $5.50 for children. Hours: September to April from 10:00 a.m. to 6:00 p.m. daily and May to August from 10:00 a.m. to 11:00 p.m. daily; closed from mid-January to mid-February. Address: 4141 Pierre de Coubertin Avenue. The nearest métro station is Viau. Phone: (514) 252-TOUR. In summer there is a free shuttle from Viau station to the Olympic Park (with the stadium and the Biodome) and the botanical gardens across Sherbrooke Street from the stadium. (1 hour)

★ **Alcan House** • Stop in at the Maison Alcan, on the south side of Sherbrooke Street at the corner of Stanley Street, just to look around. The pleasing modern architecture artfully combines old building facades and airy spaces to attractive effect. A restaurant in the building, La Tulipe Noire, serves incredible chocolate desserts and sells divine chocolates at the counter. (15 minutes)

✶ **The Biosphere** • This interactive ecomuseum is housed in the one-time U.S. pavilion at Expo '67, a dramatic geodesic dome designed by Buckminster Fuller. After Expo, the dome was given to the city of Montreal. In 1976 a stray spark from a welder's torch set fire to the transparent plastic skin covering the dome, and the skeleton of the building remained a scorched landmark until it was reborn as the Biosphere in 1995. The exhibits are about water and the St. Lawrence River basin, focusing on its origins, chemistry, usage, and climate. Throughout, computers serve as interactive fonts of information about water. Admission is $6.50 for adults, $5 for seniors and students, and $4 for kids 7 to 17. Hours: In peak season daily from 10:00 a.m. to 8:00 p.m., closed Mondays in winter. The Biosphere is on Île Ste-Hélène, and the real St. Lawrence flows past less than 200 meters away. The nearest subway stop is Île Ste-Hélène. Phone: (514) 283-5000. (1½ hours)

✶ **The Chateau Ramezay Museum** • This mansion is a prime example of eighteenth-century architecture, with period furniture, engravings, paintings, and costumes typical of the French Regime. Admission is $5 for adults, $3 for students and seniors, and $10 for families. Hours: Tuesday to Sunday from 10:00 a.m. to 4:30 p.m. Address: 280 Notre-Dame Street East in Old Montreal. Phone: (514) 861-3708. (1 hour)

✶ **The International Museum of Humor** • The permanent exhibition in this one-of-a-kind museum is titled Laughing Matters—Humor Through the Ages. There are also a documentation center, a hall of fame, a cabaret-theater, a restaurant, and a boutique. Admission is $5. Hours: 1:00 p.m. to 8:00 p.m., Tuesday to Sunday. Address: 2111 St-Laurent Boulevard. Phone: (514) 845-4000. (1½ hours)

✶ **McGill University** • The gates to the university are on Sherbrooke at the top of McGill College Avenue. Founded in 1821, the university grounds contain imposing old buildings and the Redpath Museum of animal groups, fossils, Egyptian antiquities, gems, crystals, and rocks. Temporary exhibits often have an ecological theme. Admission is free. Afterwards, stroll down McGill College Avenue and check out an intriguing sculpture called *Illuminated Crowd* outside the BNP head-quarters. You can't miss it; it portrays a crowd of people gawking off into the distance. (1 hour)

⭐ **Montreal World Trade Centre** • In Old Montreal, even the newest buildings find a way to incorporate history. The atrium of the World Trade Centre runs along the old Ruelle des Fortifications where city walls used to stand, between St-Jacques and St-Antoine Streets. Beneath soaring glass, a suspended walkway connects the turreted tower of the Inter-Continental Hotel to the Nordheimer, an 1888 building at 363 St-Jacques West that has been richly restored to its original Victorian grandeur and contains the hotel's meeting rooms. Beneath the Nordheimer lie 200-year-old stone vaults that may once have been used to store ammunition but now house an oyster bar and a wine bar. (½ hour)

⭐ **Parc des Îles** • These are the one-time Expo islands in the St. Lawrence River between Montreal and the so-called south shore. Île Notre-Dame has a floral park open from mid-June to September, as well as the city's only beach. It is also the site of a casino. Neighboring Île Ste-Hélène is home to La Ronde, the amusement park left over from Expo '67, and the new Biosphere museum (see above). Admission to La Ronde is $21.50 for adults, $10.75 for children under 12, or $48.00 for families. A cheaper ticket, for $9.50, provides access to the grounds and four rides only. Phone: (514) 872-6222. La Ronde is also a good vantage point from which to watch the fireworks during the fireworks festival. Both islands have lots of green space and make for enjoyable strolling or cycling. The subway stop is Île Ste-Hélène. (3 hours)

⭐ **St-Joseph's Oratory** • This massively imposing basilica on a Mount Royal slope above Queen Mary Road is a renowned pilgrimage site, and in fact you may see a few people making their way on their knees up the impossibly long flight of outside stairs. Brother André, one of Quebec's most popular religious figures, founded the oratory. Functionally illiterate, he never advanced beyond lowly positions within his religious order, but he was also a faith healer, with St-Joseph as his patron. Although his work scandalized much of the established church, thousands of people attributed their miraculous healings to him, and in 1904 some of his fans helped him build a small oratory in honor of Joseph on the slopes of Mount Royal. Eventually the church got involved and a basilica was built on the site. The *Oratoire* also provides a lookout over the city. The nearest subway stop is Côte-des-Neiges. (1 hour)

## FITNESS AND RECREATION

Cycling and in-line skating seem to be the most popular sports in Montreal these days. You can rent bikes and skates at the Old Port and then wheel along the Lachine Canal bike path or head out to the Parc des Îles. Mount Royal is always a good place for a brisk walk. For a change of pace, you can go ice-skating at any time of the year on the rink on the ground floor of Le 1000 de la Gauchetiere building downtown, between the Bonaventure and Chateau Champlain Hotels. The rink is called Amphitheatre Bell. No need to tote your own skates, either; skate rentals are available on site. For information, call (514) 395-0555.

Speaking of skating, if you happen to visit Montreal in the winter you should know that there are more than 100 outdoor skating loops, ovals, and rinks inside a 7-kilometer radius of downtown. All are free and many offer rentals as well as heated changing areas.

The city is also within about an hour or so of ski hills in two directions—the Laurentians to the north, and the Eastern Townships to the southeast.

## FOOD

On a summer night in Montreal, one of the best things to do is try any of the restaurants along Prince Arthur or Duluth Streets. Prince Arthur, a lively, 3-block pedestrian mall of bars, cafés, and restaurants off St-Laurent a few blocks north of Sherbrooke, is a great place to eat, linger, people-watch, and party in the summer. Duluth, several blocks north of Prince Arthur, is not a pedestrian mall and so not as lively, but it has some good restaurants. For example, the **Jardin de Panos**, a Greek restaurant at 529 Duluth Street East, has a wonderful open-air terrace out back that seats 350 and is usually crowded; the phone number is (514) 521-4206.

The great thing about the restaurants on Prince Arthur and Duluth is that most are bring-your-own-wine establishments. As long as you remember to buy a bottle before getting there, this one small factor makes eating out markedly cheaper. Most of the restaurants on both streets are crowded most evenings, and most don't take reservations, so you may have to line up.

There are a zillion other restaurants in Montreal. My personal favorites include **Biddles,** which serves up ribs and live jazz at 2060 Aylmer (514-842-8656); **L'Express** at 3927 St-Denis, a French bistro-style place with affordable prices that remains steadfastly trendy and popular (514-845-5333); **La Louisiane,** which also specializes in Cajun and Creole cuisine but is a little cheaper, a 10-minute cab ride from downtown at 5850 Sherbrooke St. West (514-369-3073); **Chao Phraya,** a fine Thai restaurant at 4088 St-Denis (514-843-4194); **Curry House,** one of the best Indian restaurants in town and very reasonably priced, at 1433 Bishop Street (514-845-0326); and **Fusion,** a small tapas-and-bistro place at 1237 Guy Street (514-939-5990).

Several places around town tend to attract lots of tourists. **The Bar-B-Barn** at 1201 Guy Street (514-931-3811) features excellent ribs but serves you so quickly and hustles you out so fast it becomes an eat-and-run experience. For a not-bad deal in touristy Old Montreal, try **Le Jardin Nelson** on Place Jacques Cartier, which offers crepes, sandwiches, and salads on its courtyard terrace (514-861-5731).

At the high end are **Les Halles** at 1450 Crescent (514-844-2328), a French restaurant that is one of the most expensive establishments in town and worth it; the **Katsura** at 2170 de la Montagne (514-849-1172), among the best Japanese restaurants in town; and the **Pavilion de l'Atlantique** at the corner of Sherbrooke and Stanley Streets (514-285-1636) for expensive seafood in the Maison Alcan.

In the cheap-but-lots-of-atmosphere category are **Ben's Delicatessen**, a landmark establishment at 990 de Maisonneuve West at the corner of Mackay, right downtown, and **Schwartz's,** at 3895 St-Laurent. The latter is pretty small and often has long lines. Both establishments are known for smoked-meat sandwiches.

Numerous restaurants throughout the city offer Sunday brunch. **Beauty's** at 93 Mount-Royal Avenue is one of my favorite brunch spots.

Many Montrealers claim that Montreal bagels are better than New York bagels. Find out for yourself at either of two well-known bakeries where you can watch the bagels being cooked in huge wood-burning ovens—the **Fairmount Bagel Bakery** at 74 Fairmount Street West or the **St-Viateur Bagel Shop** at 263 St-Viateur West.

Finally, there is one place in Montreal where afternoon tea is still a grand tradition—the **Jardin du Ritz,** an exquisite garden cafe in a courtyard of the Ritz-Carlton. Open only in summer, at 1228 Sherbrooke Street West (514-842-4212).

## LODGING

If money is no object, try the **Ritz-Carlton** ($190 and up; 1228
Sherbrooke Street West, 514-842-4212, 800-363-0366 from
Canada, 800-426-3135 from U.S.), next door to the tony Holt Renfrew
department store and just up the street from the Montreal Museum of
Fine Arts; the **Westin Mount-Royal** ($155 and up, 1050 Sherbrooke
Street West, 514-284-1110); the **Inter-Continental** ($119 and up,
360 St-Antoine West, 514-987-9900 or 800-361-3600), part of the
new World Trade Centre complex at the edge of Old Montreal; or
**Hotel Vogue** ($135 and up, 1425 de la Montagne, 514-285-5555 or
800-465-6654), a relatively small, "European-style" establishment that
features a "designer floor" with futuristic, black-and-gray furnishings.

The venerable old **Queen Elizabeth Hotel** was recently renovated. People still sometimes leave flowers at the door of suite 1742,
where John Lennon and Yoko Ono held a bed-in in 1969 ($110 and up;
900 René Lévesque Boulevard West, 514-861-3511 or 800-441-1414).
Other central hotels include **Bonaventure Hilton** ($139 and up; 1
Place Bonaventure, 514-878-2332 or 800-HILTONS), which has a
heated outdoor pool on its rooftop; **Hotel du Fort** ($99 and up; 1390
du Fort Street, 514-938-8333 or 800-565-6333), another "boutique"
hotel; the **Holiday Inn Centre-Ville** ($105 and up; 99 Viger Street
West, 514-878-9888 or 800-HOLIDAY), at the edge of Chinatown and
Old Montreal; the **Radisson Gouverneurs Montreal** ($115 and up;
777 University Street, 514-879-1370 or 800-333-3333), midway
between downtown and Old Montreal; and **Château Versailles**, in a
beautiful old building on Sherbrooke Street West near the corner of
Guy ($99 and up; 1659 Sherbrooke Street West, 514-933-3611 or
800-361-7199).

More moderately, the downtown **Quality Hotel** at 3440 Park
Avenue (avenue du Parc) offers rooms priced between $90 and $105
(514-849-1413 or 800-228-5151). The **Comfort Suites Hotel** at 1214
Crescent charges from $82 and $99 (514-878-2711), while rooms at
the no-frills **Hotel Travelodge** (50 René-Lévesque Boulevard West,
514-578-7878 or 800-363-6535) range from $52 to $79. The **Novotel**
at 1180 rue de la Montagne charges between $89 and $160 per room
and is wheelchair accessible (514-861-6000 or 800-NOVOTEL).
Fourteen of the smaller rooms at the **Hotel de Paris**, housed in an old
mansion at 901 Sherbrooke Street East, were designed specifically for
budget travelers, with peak-season rates beginning at only $50 a room.

# MONTREAL

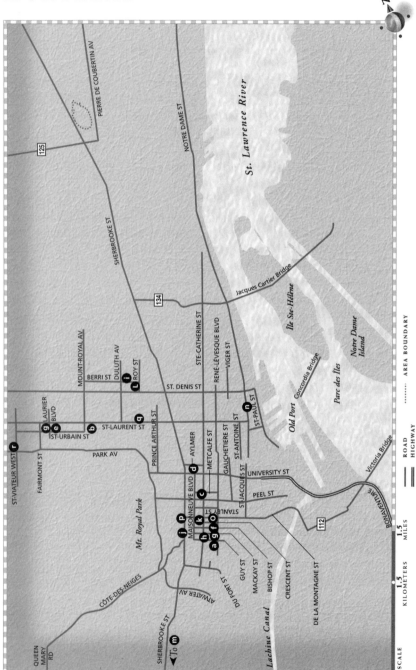

St. Lawrence River

Île Ste-Hélène

Notre Dame Island

Parc des Îles

Old Port

Jacques Cartier Bridge

Concordia Bridge

Victoria Bridge

PIERRE DE COUBERTIN AV

NOTRE DAME ST

SHERBROOKE ST

125

134

STE-CATHERINE ST

RENÉ-LÉVESQUE BLVD

VIGER ST

ST-PAUL ST

ST-ANTOINE ST

MOUNT-ROYAL AV

DULUTH AV

BERRI ST

ROY ST

ST. DENIS ST

LAURIER BLVD

ST-LAURENT ST

ST-URBAIN ST

FAIRMONT ST

PARK AV

PRINCE ARTHUR ST

ST-VIATEUR WEST

Mt. Royal Park

AYLMER

METCALFE ST

GAUCHETIÈRE ST

ST-JACQUES ST

UNIVERSITY ST

PEEL ST

STANLEY ST

MAISONNEUVE BLVD

GUY ST

MACKAY ST

BISHOP ST

CRESCENT ST

DE LA MONTAGNE ST

DU FORT ST

ATWATER AV

CÔTE-DES-NEIGES

QUEEN MARY RD

SHERBROOKE ST

Lachine Canal

BONAVENTURE

112

To

Mt. Royal Park

r

g e

b

q

i

L

n

d

c

j p

k

h

a g f o

m

N

O SCALE

1.5 KILOMETERS

1.5 MILES

—— ROAD

═══ HIGHWAY

·········· AREA BOUNDARY

# Food

**ⓐ** The Bar-B-Barn

**ⓑ** Beauty's

**ⓒ** Ben's Delicatessen

**ⓓ** Biddles

**ⓔ** Chao Phraya

**ⓕ** Curry House

**ⓖ** Fairmount Bagel Bakery

**ⓗ** Fusion

**ⓘ** Jardin de Panos

**ⓙ** Jardin du Ritz

**ⓚ** Katsura

**ⓛ** L'Express

**ⓜ** La Louisiane

**ⓝ** Le Jardin Nelson

**ⓞ** Les Halles

**ⓟ** Pavilion de l'Atlantique

**ⓠ** Schwartz's

**ⓡ** St-Viateur Bagel Shop

The hotel also has 15 other rooms in the standard and deluxe categories (514-522-6861 or 800-567-7217).

For B&Bs (*gîtes*, in French), the largest networks include Bed & Breakfast Downtown Network, offering rooms from $35 (write to Bob Finkelstein, 3458 Laval Avenue, Montreal, Que., Canada H2X 3C8, or phone 514-289-9749 or 800-267-5180); Bed & Breakfast à Montreal, with rooms starting around $50 (C.P. 575, succ. Snowdon, Montreal, Que., Canada H3X 3T8, 514-738-9410); and Network Hospitality Montreal, offering rooms at $40 and up (3977 Laval Avenue, Montreal, Que., Canada H2W 2H9, 514-287-9635 or 800-363-9635).

## CAMPING

There are several campgrounds within an hour of Montreal on the South Shore, across the St. Lawrence River. All have sites with water, sewage disposal, and electricity, at prices running around $20. Other sites cost from $12 to $17 nightly. The choices include **Camp Alouette** in Beloeil, (514) 464-1661; **Camping Pointe-des-Cascades** in Pointe-des-Cascades, (514) 455-2501; in St-Philippe, **Camping Bon Air**, (514) 659-8868; and **Camping KOA Montreal Sud**, (514) 659-8626; and **Camping D'aoust** in Vaudreuil, (514) 458-7301.

## NIGHTLIFE

There's lots of it. Try the aforementioned **Prince Arthur Street; St-Laurent**, mainly north of Prince Arthur; **Crescent Street**, still famous after all these years and still something of an English enclave, or neighboring **Bishop Street**; or **St-Denis Street**, the so-called "Latin Quarter."

Also, Montreal now has a casino. Run by Loto-Quebec, the provincial government's lottery corporation, it is on Île Notre-Dame and is always crowded during its opening hours of 11:00 a.m. to 3:00 a.m. Admission is free and so is parking, but the parking lots fill up rapidly; it's best to get there by taxi (5 minutes from downtown) or subway and bus (Île Notre-Dame subway stop, bus 167 to the casino). Children are not admitted; you must be 18 or over to enter. Dress is generally casual, but no T-shirts, jeans, or sneakers are allowed. For more information, phone 514-392-2746 or (800) 665-2274 from elsewhere.

The city has a handful of English-language theaters, namely **The**

Centaur (453 St-Francois-Xavier Street, 514-288-3161), **The Saidye Bronfman Centre** (5170 Côte-Ste-Catherine Road, 514-739-7944 or 514-739-4816), **Theatre 1774** (3964 St-Laurent Boulevard, 514-987-1774; plays are bilingual); and **Bulldog Productions**, 5723 Park Ave., 514-272-4290 (tickets), 514-933-6292 (information).

In summer, there are Shakespeare-in-the-park performances at several parks around town. Check the *Gazette*, the city's only English-language daily, for dates and times. Take a blanket or folding chair if you go to one of the performances.

Montreal is home base of the Cirque du Soleil, the magically theatrical circus troupe that started out in the '80s as a ragtag band of street performers and eventually went on to far-reaching fame. They're usually off touring the world, but occasionally they alight for a stint at home. If they're in town, get tickets; it's a must, no matter what your age.

For up-to-date entertainment listings, check the *Gazette* or pick up copies of the *Mirror* or the *Hour*, weekly independent newspapers that are distributed free.

## SHOPPING

The best shopping is downtown. The main shopping strip runs along Ste-Catherine Street from **Faubourg Ste-Catherine**, a trendy market-like shopping center on the south side of the street at the corner of Guy (nearest métro stop is Guy-Concordia), all the way east to St-Laurent.

## THE UNDERGROUND CITY

Some visitors are disappointed by Montreal's vaunted underground city, 29 kilometers (18 miles) of corridors lined with shops, restaurants, and movie theaters. Even if it doesn't look impressive, it sure makes life easier on blustery winter days. It's possible to stay at downtown hotels that connect with the underground city and eat, shop, and party for days at a time—without ever stepping outside.

## FESTIVALS

Summer in Montreal means almost wall-to-wall festivals. The season gets off to an explosive start in June with the International Fireworks Competition, wherein countries show off their pyrotechnic

# MONTREAL

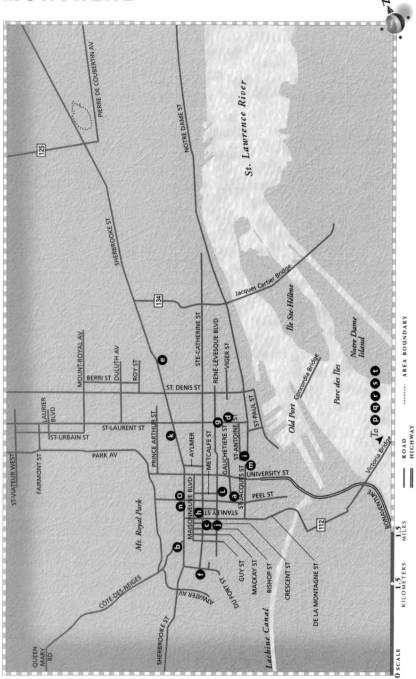

## Lodging

**ⓐ** Bonaventure Hilton

**ⓑ** Château Versailles

**ⓒ** Comfort Suites Hotel

**ⓓ** Holiday Inn Centre-Ville

**ⓔ** Hotel de Paris

**ⓕ** Hotel du Fort

**ⓖ** Hotel Travelodge

**ⓗ** Hotel Vogue

**ⓘ** Inter-Continental

**ⓙ** Novotel

**ⓚ** Quality Hotel

**ⓛ** Queen Elizabeth Hotel

**ⓜ** Radisson Gouverneurs Montreal

**ⓝ** Ritz-Carlton

**ⓞ** Westin Mount-Royal

## Camping

**ⓟ** Camp Alouette

**ⓠ** Camping Bon Air

**ⓡ** Camping D'aoust

**ⓢ** Camping KOA Montreal Sud

**ⓣ** Camping Pointe-des-Cascades

prowess in the skies over La Ronde, the amusement park on Île Ste-Hélène. Next up is the 10-day Montreal International Jazz Festival, with dozens of free concerts staged outdoors in an area around Place des Arts, Montreal's premiere concert hall. The "jazz village" is bordered by Ste-Catherine Street, Jeanne-Mance Street, de Maisonneuve Boulevard, and St-Urbain Street. Around the end of the first week of July, the Just for Laughs international comedy festival begins. It started out as a tiny, French-only affair in the mid-1980s but is now big and bilingual, with an English gala, a French gala, and dozens of shows in both languages by comedians from Quebec, the rest of Canada, and around the world. After that there's a pause until late August, when the glamorous and gaudy Montreal World Film Festival begins. In between are myriad lesser-known events and art exhibits; Infotouriste can supply information.

## HELPFUL HINTS

Museum lovers should note that a Montreal Museum Pass is now available, providing entrance to 17 museums around the city. A one-day pass costs $12 for adults or $24 for families, while a three-day pass costs $25 for adults and $50 for families. The passes are on sale at participating museums, Infotouriste, and numerous hotels.

Drop in at the Centre Infotouriste at 1001 Dorchester Square Street between Peel and Metcalfe. Infotouriste is open daily from 8:30 a.m. to 7:30 p.m. from May to October, and 9:00 a.m. to 6:00 p.m. the rest of the year. There is also an information kiosk at 174 Notre-Dame Street East on Place Jacques Cartier in Old Montreal. Otherwise, call (514) 873-2015 or (800) 363-7777 from elsewhere for more information on Montreal and the province.

## DAY TRIPS FROM MONTREAL

Both the Laurentians and the Eastern Townships (*Estrie*) are dotted with attractive towns and villages set amidst rolling hills. With plenty of lakes as well as ski hills, the two regions are popular cottage areas and tourist draws. The Townships, particularly Knowlton (also known as *Lac Brome*) and Sutton, still have substantial English populations. Infotouriste can supply information booklets on each area.

Canada produces almost 70 percent of the world's maple syrup supply, with Quebec accounting for 90 percent of that. So if you're in Montreal in the spring, try to find time to attend that great Quebec tradition, a "sugaring off." From mid-March to mid-April, sugar shacks in the countryside around Montreal convert the sap from maple trees into Quebec's fabled maple syrup, and many establishments open to the public in this period. You can watch the process by which the sap becomes maple syrup and then sit down for a huge meal of Quebecois fare like baked beans, *tourtière* (meat pie), and pancakes, all smothered in maple syrup. Ask for the names of some *établières* (sugar shacks) at Infotouriste.

# 6
# QUEBEC CITY

O ld Quebec *(Vieux-Québec)* is on UNESCO's World Heritage List, and deservedly so. With a population of 645,000, greater Quebec City sprawls over a sizable area, but the most interesting part for visitors is definitely Old Quebec, a section of the city perched above the edge of the St. Lawrence River. Entering Old Quebec through the St-Louis Gate is like going through a time warp.

The first known European in the area was French explorer Jacques Cartier, who arrived in the Algonquin village of Stadacona, high on a cape above the river, in 1534. Samuel de Champlain, founder of New France, settled in "Kebec" ("where the rivers meet," in the Algonquin language) in 1608. Because they considered it the gateway to the continent, the English kept trying to conquer the area.

In 1774, the Quebec Act allowed French Canadians to retain their right to practice their Roman Catholic religion (then banned in England) and to preserve their language and customs. In 1775, American rebels, trying to get all of British North America to join their movement, stormed the city but were badly defeated. That was the last battle at Quebec City, although the British later completed the fortifications that make Old Quebec one of the few walled cities in the world. ◣

# QUEBEC CITY

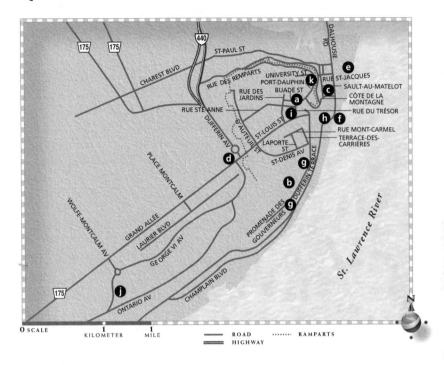

## Sightseeing Highlights

**a** Basilique-cathédrale Notre-Dame-de-Québec

**b** The Citadel

**c** Civilization Museum

**d** Hôtel du Parlement

**e** Old Port of Quebec

**f** Place Royale

**g** Promenade des Gouverneurs and Dufferin Terrace

**h** Quartier du Petit-Champlain

**i** Quebec Experience

**j** Quebec Museum

**k** Seminary Museum

## A PERFECT DAY IN QUEBEC CITY

I like to explore Upper Town first, especially the Plains of Abraham, so historic and attractive. Then it's down into Old Quebec, where the highlights include the unbelievably quaint Petit-Champlain neighborhood and the Old Port. For me, getting there is half the fun. It involves walking along the promenade from the Citadel to Dufferin Terrace behind the Château Frontenac. The view out over the St. Lawrence River is stunning. At the end of the day, I'd probably have dinner at Au Café Suisse, a block from the Château Frontenac. It specializes in a favorite of mine, fondues. But many out-of-towners might want to try Les Anciens Canadiens at 34 St-Louis, a cozy (but expensive) place specializing in traditional French Canadian dishes such as pea soup and maple syrup pies.

## GETTING AROUND QUEBEC CITY

Old Quebec is made up of Lower Town, which runs along the riverfront and includes the Old Port and Quartier Petit-Champlain, and Upper Town, atop Cape Diamond. Upper Town includes the Plains of Abraham, also known as Parc des Champs de Batailles (Battlefields Park); the provincial legislature, Grande-Allée; and the walled part of the city. Grande-Allée runs straight up to Porte St-Louis (St-Louis Gate), an entrance to the walled part of the city, after which it becomes St-Louis Street. Follow St-Louis a few blocks and you're at the Château Frontenac, set on a cliff above Lower Town and Quartier du Petit-Champlain, the oldest commercial quarter in North America. You can take a funicular from the Château down into Petit-Champlain, whose narrow, sloped streets are lined with boutiques, art galleries, bistros, and restaurants. Or you can walk down the steep set of stairs. Dufferin Terrace, behind the hotel, becomes Promenade des Gouverneurs and runs along the clifftop past the Citadel (or *Citadelle*), providing a magnificent view of the harbor and the St. Lawrence River.

The Quebec City Airport is in suburban Ancienne-Lorette, northwest of the city. The bus terminal is at 225 Charest Boulevard East in the center of the city, while the railway station, Gare du Palais, is at 450 rue de la Gare-du-Palais in Lower Town.

The city's tourist information bureau is at 60 D'Auteuil Street.; turn left onto D'Auteuil, the first street you come to after entering the walled city through the Porte St-Louis. From early June to Labor Day, the bureau is open daily from 8:30 a.m. to 8:00 p.m. The provincial tourism bureau is at 12 Ste-Anne Street, across from the Château Frontenac, open from 8:30 a.m. to 7:30 p.m., June through Labor Day.

Walking is the best way to get around Quebec City. For information about city buses, call the municipal bus information line at (418) 627-2511. Daily passes are available.

## SIGHTSEEING HIGHLIGHTS

☆☆☆ **Civilization Museum** • This imaginative museum houses assorted interactive, multimedia, and other traditional exhibits focused on such themes as language, natural resources, society, and the human body. Anything from clothing to sculptures might be on display at any given time. The museum is a blend of historic and new structures designed by the ubiquitous architect Moshe Safdie. Admission is $6 for adults, $3 for students, $5 for seniors, and free for children under 16. Free admission on Tuesdays. Hours: 10:00 a.m. to 7:00 p.m. from June 24 to Labor Day and 10:00 a.m. to 5:00 p.m. Tuesday to Sunday the rest of the year. Address: 85 Dalhousie Road in the heart of the Old Port, near Place Royale. Phone: (418) 643-2158. (3 hours)

☆☆☆ **Old Port of Quebec** • Le Vieux-Port has a market, an amphitheater, and the Old Port of Quebec National Historic Site, an interpretation center that explains the shipbuilding and lumber industries, historically the main industries centered on the port. Admission to the interpretive center is $2.25 for adults, $1.50 for seniors, and $1 for children 5 to 15. Hours: From June 24 to Labor Day, 1:00 to 5:00 p.m. on Mondays and 10:00 a.m. to 5:00 p.m. Tuesday through Sunday; hours are shorter the rest of the year, varying seasonally. Phone: (418) 648-3300. (1 hour)

☆☆☆ **Promenade des Gouverneurs and Dufferin Terrace** • Promenade des Gouverneurs (Governors' Walk) begins near the southwest corner of The Citadel and leads along the clifftops to Dufferin Terrace behind the Château Frontenac. A stroll along here provides a magnificent panorama of Lower Town, the Old Port, and the river. (½ hour)

☆☆☆ **Quartier du Petit-Champlain** • For $1 per passenger, the funicular, whose entrance is on Dufferin Terrace at the Chateau Frontenac, takes you to the foot of the cliff to the Petit-Champlain neighborhood, the oldest commercial quarter in North America. Its narrow, sloped streets are lined with boutiques, art galleries, bistros, bars, and restaurants, housed in restored seventeenth- and eighteenth-century buildings. This is an area to wander at will. (3 hours)

⁂ **The Citadel** • A star-shaped fortress with more than two dozen buildings, this is the largest fortified group of buildings in North America still occupied by troops—the Royal 22nd Regiment, or the Van-Doos (from *vingt-deux*, or 22 in French) as they are known in Quebec. Buildings include the Governor General's summer residence, the officers' mess, and the Royal 22nd Regiment Museum. Guided tours last 55 minutes, but military history buffs could probably happily spend all day here. Admission is $4.50 for adults, $4 for seniors, $2 for children 7 to 17, and free for children under 7. From mid-June to Labor Day there is a daily changing-of-the-guard at 10:00 a.m., weather permitting. Phone: (418) 648-3563. (2 hours)

⁂ **Place Royale** • A charming cobblestone square near the waterfront, Place Royale is where the first French settlers landed. There are an interpretation center about its development (entrance is free), an exhibition that traces the history of Place Royale and Lower Town (also free), and an information center that is also the departure point for guided tours. In summer, Place Royale is the setting for an array of outdoor plays and shows. (½ hour)

⁂ **Quebec Museum** • The Musée du Québec is in the middle of the Plains of Abraham, a historic battlefield that is now 250 acres of woodlands and gardens. The museum features Quebec art dating from earliest European life in the province to the present. Admission is $4.75 for adults, $3.75 for seniors, $2.75 for students 16 and up, and free for children under 16. Free admission on Wednesdays. A museum annex houses the National Battlefields Park Interpretation Center, a high-tech presentation about the history of the Plains of Abraham; admission is free. Hours: 10:00 a.m to 5:45 p.m. Thursday to Tuesday, and until 9:45 p.m. Wednesday, from May 24 to Labor Day; closed Mondays the rest of the year. Address: 1 Wolfe-Montcalm Avenue. Phone: (418) 643-2150. (2 hours)

⁂ **Basilique-cathédrale Notre-Dame-de-Québec** • First opened in 1650 and the oldest parish on the continent north of Mexico, this richly ornate edifice is replete with stained-glass windows, assorted artwork, a throned dais, a majestic organ, and a lamp that was a gift from Louis XIV. Numerous Quebec bishops and governors of New France are buried in the crypt. In the evenings, there are showings of a 46-minute multimedia history production, *Act of Faith*, beginning at 6:30 p.m.; admission is $5. Address: 16 Buade Street, a couple of blocks from the Château Frontenac. (½ hour, discounting *Act of Faith*)

☆ **Hôtel du Parlement** • This imposing Renaissance-style building off Grande-Allée East at Dufferin Avenue houses Quebec's legislature, known as the National Assembly. Free guided tours are available. Opposite Hôtel du Parliament on Grande-Allée, you'll notice a rather ugly concrete complex that houses the premier's offices and is known semi-affectionately as The Bunker. (½ hour)

☆ **Quebec Experience** • And you thought three-dimensional movies weren't made anymore! This is an entertaining half-hour journey through Quebec City's past, worth seeing for the three-dimensional experience as well as the history lesson. There are showings in English and in French. Admission is $6.50 per person, except for students and seniors, who get in for $4.50. Children under 6 are admitted for free. Address: 8 rue du Trésor, in Old Quebec. Phone: (418) 694-4000. (½ hour)

☆ **Seminary Museum** • The Musée de Seminaire is a history museum with a vast collection that focuses mainly on French North America. It houses everything from an Egyptian mummy to paintings by Canadian and European artists. Admission is $3 for adults, $2 for seniors and students, $1 for children 16 and under, or $6 for families. Hours: 10:00 a.m. to 5:30 p.m. from June 1 to September 30, closed Mondays the rest of the year. Address: 9 University Street, a block or two from Notre-Dame Basilica. Phone: (418) 692-2843. (2 hours)

## FITNESS AND RECREATION

There is a 200-kilometer network of mountain biking trails at Station Mont-Sainte-Anne in Beaupré, 40 kilometers east of the city. Rentals are available on-site. The Cap Tourmente National Wildlife Area, 50 kilometers east of the city, boasts 14 hiking trails. Hiking, mountain biking, rock climbing, canoeing, kayaking, and rafting are all available at Parc de la Jacques-Cartier, 30 minutes north of the city. Fishermen should head for the Parc des Laurentides,

# QUEBEC CITY

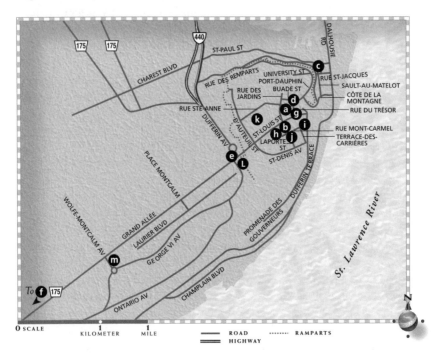

## Food

- **a** Au Café Suisse
- **b** Aux Anciens Canadiens
- **c** L'Echaudé
- **d** Le D'Orsay
- **e** Restaurant Le Louis Hébert

## Camping

- **f** Camping Aéroport

## Lodging

- **g** Auberge de la Place d'Armes
- **h** Auberge St-Louis
- **i** Château Frontenac
- **j** Hôtel Château Bellevue
- **k** Hôtellerie Fleur-de-lys
- **l** Hôtel Manoir Lafayette
- **m** Loews Le Concorde

northeast of the city, for its divine rainbow trout. As a setting for jogging or walking in the city, the Promendade des Gouverneurs can't be beat, and the Plains of Abraham aren't bad either.

## FOOD

For memorable French dining, try **Restaurant Le Louis Hébert** at 668 Grande-Allée East (Grande-Allée est), (418) 525-7812. The food is wonderful, and you can eat it in the Sun Room abutting the main restaurant. The Sun Room is filled with natural light, wicker furniture, and plants, making for a summery setting even during Quebec City's severe winters. The inn is upstairs.

Another favorite French restaurant is **L'Échaudé** (literally translated, "scalded person") at 73 Sault-au-Matelot, a narrow street in Lower Town. Call (418) 692-1299. **Aux Anciens Canadiens**, at 34 St-Louis a block from the Château Frontenac, serves Quebec specialties such as smoked sturgeon, Lac-St-Jean meat pie, hare civet, and maple syrup pie. Call (418) 692-1627. At **Au Café Suisse** at 32 Ste-Anne (also a block from the Château), fondues and raclettes are the specialties of the house; phone (418) 694-1320. For a pub-style atmosphere, try **Le D'Orsay** at 65 Buade Street, another street near the Chateau, (418) 694-1582.

For a more complete listing of restaurants to suit every mood and budget, pick up a copy of the restaurant guide published by the Greater Quebec Area Tourism and Convention Bureau.

## LODGING

Everything from B&Bs through small inns to luxury high-rise hotels is available, but in Old Quebec the emphasis is on inns (or *auberges*). The major exception is the magnificent **Château Frontenac**, which sits atop a cliff in the heart of Old Quebec, overlooking the old town below and the river beyond. It's a tourist attraction as well as a hotel. Even if you don't stay there, it's the place to start a walking tour, take the funicular down the cliff, or wander along Dufferin Terrace. A hundred years old in 1993, the landmark, copper-roofed hotel has recently undergone major renovations and is one of the most photographed hotels in Canada. With room rates beginning around $185, it's also more expensive than most other establishments in the area. Wheelchair accessible. Call (418) 692-3861 or (800) 441-1414.

**Loews Le Concorde**, another big luxury hotel ($155 and up), has the only rooftop revolving restaurant in the city. The hotel is wheel-chair accessible and is at 1225 Place Montcalm, off Grande-Allée; call (418) 647-2222 or (800) 223-0888.

The inns scattered around Old Quebec offer both moderate rates and lots of atmosphere. Try **Hôtellerie Fleur-de-lys** 1990 at 115 rue Ste-Anne (wheelchair accessible with assistance), (418) 694-0106; **Auberge St-Louis** at 48 St-Louis, (418) 692-2424 or (800) 663-7878; **Auberge de la Place d'Armes** ($60–$100) at 24 Ste-Anne, (418) 694-9485; **Hôtel Manoir Lafayette** ($60–$125) at 665 Grande-Allée East (they allow pets and also offer baby-sitting), (800) 363-8203; or **Hotel Château Bellevue** ($54–$94) at 16 Laporte Street (baby-sitting services available), (800) 463-2617.

For bed and breakfasts, try Bed and Breakfast Bonjour Québec, which represents 11 homes within a few minutes' drive of Old Quebec. Write to Denise and Raymond Blanchet, 3765 Monaco Boulevard, Quebec, Que. G1P 3J3, or phone (418) 527-1465. Another B&B reservation service, run by Therese Tellier and representing more than 30 homes in the city and surrounding area, is Gîte Québec Bed & Breakfast, 3729 avenue Le Corbusier, Ste-Foy, Que. G1W 4R8, (418) 651-1860.

There is a motel strip along Laurier Boulevard just after you come off Pierre Laporte Bridge into the city, but generally rooms here aren't much cheaper than in Old Quebec.

## CAMPING

Camping **Aéroport** in suburban Ste-Foy is among the most conve-niently located of the campgrounds in the area. It has 145 sites and extensive facilities including a restaurant, is wheelchair accessible, and allows pets. Rates are $21 and up. The campground is on Route 138 off Highway 73. Phone (418) 871-1574. Numerous other campgrounds in the area around the city are all listed in the Greater Quebec Area Accommodation Guide, a supplement to the regional tourist guide available from either the municipal or the provincial tourist boards.

## NIGHTLIFE

Quebec's nightlife is chiefly along **Grande-Allée East** between the Loews Le Concorde hotel and Place George V. Particularly in summer, this area is jammed with people because most of the restau-rants and bars have street-side terraces. The tourism promoters like to refer to Grande-Allée as the Champs Elysée of Quebec City, although it's nowhere near as long or wide as the real thing.

## SHOPPING

A 2-block section at the eastern end of St-Paul Street in Lower Town is home to virtually all the city's antique shops and makes for a fine area to browse. St-Paul and Sault-au-Matelot streets also have enticing neighborhood cafés, bistros, and restaurants, most of them budget-priced.

## FESTIVALS

The annual Quebec International Summer Festival, usually running the second and third week of July, offers a vast assortment of entertainment in the streets and parks of the city, especially Old Quebec. With more than 1,000 performers from around the world participating, it's billed as the biggest French-language cultural festival in North America.

The International Jazz and Blues Festival is usually the last two weeks of June. In late July and early August, Les Grands Feux Loto-Quebec, an international fireworks competition, takes place at Montmorency Falls outside the city. In August, the Quebec Medieval Festival, or *les Mediévals*, celebrates the Renaissance and the Middle Ages.

In winter—and Quebec City winters are brutally cold—locals and visitors warm up with a winter carnival (called *Carnaval*) billed as the largest in the world. The 10-day blowout, usually in early February, is centered around a massive ice palace that is a glittering wonder to behold. The ice and snow sculptures—there's a big competition every year—are also remarkable. Another star attraction is Bonhomme Carnaval, the jolly snowman-like festival mascot. During Carnaval, tradition calls for drinking a strong alcoholic concoction called Caribou out of hollow plastic canes.

## HELPFUL HINTS

For more information on Quebec City, contact the Greater Quebec Area Tourism and Convention Bureau, 60, rue D'Auteuil, Quebec, Que., Canada G1R 4C4, or phone (418) 692-2471. The offices are open daily from 8:30 a.m. to 8:00 p.m. between early June and Labor

Day; from 8:30 a.m. to 5:30 p.m. daily between Labor Day and mid-October; Monday to Friday, 9:00 a.m. to 5:00 p.m., from mid-October to mid-April; and 8:30 a.m to 5:30 p.m., Monday through Friday, from mid-April to early June. For information on Quebec City and the rest of the province, contact Tourisme Quebec at (800) 363-7777 or drop by the information center at 12 Ste-Anne Street in Quebec City, across from the Château Frontenac.

# 7

# CHARLEVOIX AND TADOUSSAC

C harlevoix County, with its starkly arresting scenery, has been
attracting tourists since holiday-making began in Canada in the
late eighteenth century. In Charlevoix, the Laurentian hills slope down
to the north shore of the St. Lawrence. The Laurentians are part of
the vast Canadian Shield, a continental crust so old that its "mountains" are now little more than round, gently sloping hills. Repeated
advances and retreats of ice sheets have left the shield strewn with
countless lakes, rivers, and ponds. (It is said that in Quebec alone, there
are 6 million lakes, but nobody knows for sure; they've never all been
counted.)

Highway 138 skirts the north shore of the St. Lawrence River
between Quebec City and Tadoussac. The 206-kilometer (123-mile)
drive can be done in a few hours if your time is limited. Ideally, however, give it at least a day so you can stop here and there to savor the
beauty of this region.

At the end of the route, a short ferry ride across the Saguenay
River, lies Tadoussac. A small but busy summer resort on the Saguenay
where it meets the St. Lawrence, Tadoussac has for decades hosted
vacationers drawn to the wild beauty of the Saguenay River. But starting about 15 years ago, growing numbers of visitors came to see the
whales who congregate in summer at the confluence of the two rivers.
It's estimated that the number of tourists has mushroomed to 200,000
from 20,000 in the early 1980s. So if you're planning to stay overnight,
book early. ◼

# CHARLEVOIX REGION

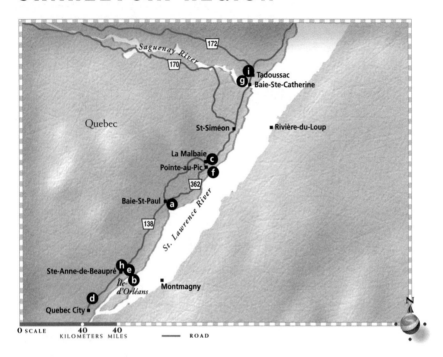

## Sightseeing Highlights

**a** Baie-St-Paul

**b** Ile d'Orleans

**c** La Malbaie

**d** Montmorency Falls

**e** Museum of the Bee

**f** Pointe-au-Pic

**g** The Saguenay Fjord

**h** Ste-Anne-de-Beaupre

**i** Whale Interpretation Center (Tadoussac)

## A PERFECT DAY IN CHARLEVOIX AND TADOUSSAC

I'd spend a couple of hours on Île d'Orléans, a designated historic district, then meander on to picturesque Baie-St-Paul for lunch and a wander. In Pointe-au-Pic, I'd stop at the Manoir Richelieu not to gamble—though there's a casino there—but to have afternoon tea on the terrace, with its glorious view of the St. Lawrence River. Then it would be on to Baie-Ste-Catherine to catch the ferry across the Saguenay River to Tadoussac. With any luck, I'd see some whales during that ferry trip. In Tadoussac, I'd follow one of the trails to a lookout point over the Saguenay, then wrap up the day with dinner at the venerable Hotel Tadoussac.

## SIGHTSEEING HIGHLIGHTS

★★★ **Île d'Orléans** • A mere 15-minute drive from Old Quebec is the Pont de L'Île, which connects verdant Île d'Orléans to the mainland. When explorer Jacques Cartier came across the island in 1535, he named it Île Bacchus because of its abundant wild vines, but it was soon renamed after the Duke of Orleans. One road, the Chemin Royal (Royal Road), rings the island, which measures 34 kilometers by 8 kilometers. Rich anglophones from Quebec City used to summer on Île d'Orléans in the last century, and many of their summer residences still stand along the Chemin Royal. Today the island is made up of six parishes. If you're stopping for lunch, consider La Goeliche, an inn just off the main road in Ste-Petronille parish. Dining on the inn's verandah offers wonderful views of Quebec City and the south shore of the St. Lawrence.

★★★ **The Saguenay Fjord** • The majestic, stark beauty of the glacier-carved Saguenay River is compelling by anyone's standards, except maybe for those who live on the fjords of Norway. The river, which issues from Lac-St-Jean in the Laurentian highlands, is lined with soaring cliffs averaging 300 meters (980 feet) in height, accentuated by coves and bays. For most of its length the water runs deep and swift and never really warms up, even at the height of summer. But the waters where the fresh-water Saguenay joins the salt-water St. Lawrence are shallow, with an abundance of aquatic flora and fauna—and hence a rich feeding ground for whales.

The Saguenay estuary has a resident population of beluga whales, a variety of white arctic porpoise. For assorted reasons, most having to do with humankind's greed, the beluga population is today severely depleted and has been declared endangered. One study concluded that the 500 beluga living in the heavily polluted St. Lawrence are among the world's sickest whales, in the sense that more than half of all the tumors reported in whales and dolphins around the world have been found in the St. Lawrence beluga. The federal and provincial governments are spending $110 million to clean up the whales' habitat, so there's still hope for the beluga. In summer, the feeding grounds at the mouth of the river may also attract blue whales, humpbacks, fin-backs, and assorted other whale species.

From Tadoussac or Baie Ste-Catherine, whale-watching cruises and boat rides on the Saguenay are available from about mid-May through September on everything from four-passenger Zodiacs to ships that carry 300 people. The cruises last anywhere from 90 minutes to 4 hours. They average between $10 and $15 per hour for adults and half that for kids. These cruises are popular; try to make reservations ahead of time. It's a good idea to take warm clothing to wear on board. Companies offering whale-watching cruises from Tadoussac and-or Baie Ste-Catherine include Croisière Navimex (418-237-4274 in season, 418-692-4643 in Quebec City the rest of the year); Compagnie de la Baie de Tadoussac (418-235-4548); and Croisière Express (418-235-4770). Hotel Tadoussac also runs 3-hour cruises both up the river and to whale-watch; prices are $30 for adults and $15 for kids. Call (418) 827-5711 or (800) 463-5250.

✩✩ **Baie-St-Paul** • Nestled in a scenic valley, the town of Baie-St-Paul is known as an artists' colony that draws not just painters but performers. In the 1970s street performers in Baie-St-Paul formed a loose group that later became the Cirque du Soleil, the acclaimed Montreal-based circus. Baie-St-Paul's narrow streets are lined with boutiques, outdoor cafés, and, naturally, art galleries. Visit the Centre d'art at 4 Ambroise-Fafard Street for a taste of local art. A tourist information counter can be found at the art center. (2 hours)

✩✩ **Pointe-au-Pic** • The tourism people claim this village was the birthplace of tourism in Canada. Traditionally it drew the affluent from Montreal, Quebec, and even New York City, but these days it is more democratic. To get a taste of how the other half lived, though, stop off at the Manoir Richelieu, a grand old hotel on a bluff overlooking the river. If you're interested in staying there, call (418) 665-3703 or (800) 463-2613 toll-free. Room rates run from $80 to $160; with breakfast and supper, it's about $200 to $250. One of the buildings on the Manoir grounds is now a casino. (1 hour)

✴ **La Malbaie** • The administrative center of the Charlevoix region, La Malbaie stands at the base of a lovely bay. Samuel de Champlain's ship ran aground here back in 1608 and Champlain reportedly described it in French as "la malbaie"—bad bay. A promenade runs along the waterfront. (½ hour)

✴ **Montmorency Falls** • At 83 meters (270 feet), Montmorency is 1½ times higher than Niagara Falls, although nowhere near as wide and somehow not as impressive. An information center, lookouts, picnic tables, trails, and a vast parking area are all open to the public in-season, with access clearly marked from the highway. If you're not taking time to stop, the falls are clearly visible from the highway. (½ hour)

✴ **Museum of the Bee** • The highlight of this attraction on Highway 138 just outside Ste-Anne-de-Beaupré is the apiary, where there's only a screen between you and 300,000 bees. Elsewhere, bilingual beekeepers demonstrate their craft with eight working hives. The museum also houses a mead winery. Admission is free, but be forewarned that tours end in a gift shop where every conceivable bee product is for sale, from royal jelly to honey ice cream. Hours: 9:00 a.m. to 6:00 p.m. May to October, 9 a.m. to 5 p.m. November to April. Phone: (418) 824-4411. (½ hour)

✴ **Ste-Anne-de-Beaupré** • More than 1.5 million pilgrims a year make their way to the famous Catholic shrine in Ste-Anne-de-Beaupré. Legend has it that Ste. Anne, the mother of the Virgin Mary, saved shipwrecked sailors off Cap Tourmante after they prayed to her, and modern pilgrims similarly hope for miracles by coming to Ste-Anne-de-Beaupré. The original wooden chapel dedicated to the saint was built in 1658 and later replaced by a stone church which was destroyed by fire in 1922. The present-day stone basilica, a massive structure visible from far down the highway, went up in 1923. Admission is free. (½ hour)

✴ **Whale Interpretation Center** • At the marine interpretation center, 108 de la Cale-Sèche Street in Tadoussac, you can learn all about St. Lawrence whales (baleines in French). It features interactive displays that test your knowledge of whales and let you listen to their songs. Kids can play a video game in which the aim is to help Delphi the beluga whale

hunt her daily ration of 12 kilograms (26 pounds) of food. Hours: 10:00
a.m. to 8:00 p.m., mid-May to mid-October. (1 hour)

## FITNESS AND RECREATION

B oth Île d'Orléans and Baie-St-Paul are laced with bicycle paths.
Bicycle rentals are available in both places, and in Baie-St-Paul
you can also rent a canoe. For the more adventurous, there is white-
water rafting on Malbaie River; call Descente Malbaie at (418) 439-
2265. There are pony rides for children and horseback riding for adults
at the Ranch du Fjord in Baie-Ste-Catherine; call (418) 237-4230.

The nature trails that lead to the river from Tadoussac are no
more than about 2 kilometers (just over 1 mile) round-trip, so a
before- or after-dinner stroll may be in order. One trail leads to
Colline de l'Anse a l'Eau, a good vantage point to see the majestic
Saguenay fjords, the St. Lawrence, and the village; the path skirting
Pointe de l'Islet offers two lookouts towards the St. Lawrence; and two
new trails, the Fjord Trail and the Anse à la Barque trail, lead toward
the cliffs of the Saguenay.

Golfers can play a round at the Hotel Tadoussac golf club for $24
on weekdays and $28 on weekends; equipment rental is available. Club
equestre de Tadoussac offers horseback outings across the sand dunes
in the Parc du Saguenay; call (418) 235-4630.

## FOOD

L e Bateau, at 246 rue des Forgerons (235-4427), serves up regional
specialties such as meat stew and features a panoramic view of the
two rivers. The large **Café du Fjord** at 154 rue du Bateau-Passeur
(235-4626) offers a seafood buffet. The menu at **Le Chant Martin** at
412 rue du Bateau-Passeur has a bit of everything, from seafood to
Italian to steak. And the **Crêperie La Bolée** at 164 rue Morin serves
up—naturally enough—crêpes.

## LODGING

T he historic (c. 1864) **Hotel Tadoussac** is a prime place to stay if
there's room and you can afford it. Rates for two people run from
$200 to $260 per room (including breakfast) in peak season. The hotel
offers many outdoor activities, such as tennis, swimming, and golf. Call
(418) 235-4421 or (800) 463-5250.

# TADOUSSAC

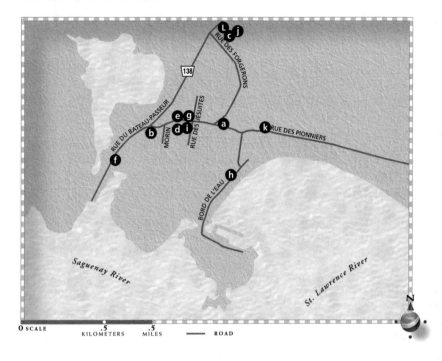

## Food

**a** Le Bateau

**b** Café du Fjord

**c** Le ChantMartin

**d** Crêperie La Bolée

## Lodging

**e** Auberge du Lac

**f** Hôtel-Motel Georges

**g** Hôtel-Motel Le Beluga

**h** Hotel Tadoussac

**i** Maison Clauphi Motel

**j** Motel Chantmartin

**k** Le Pionnier

## Camping

**L** Camping Tadoussac

Tadoussac has plenty of inns, motels, and B&Bs. In season it's best to reserve well ahead. Some contact numbers: **Hôtel-Motel Georges**, near a golf course, from $45 to $90 depending on the season, (418) 235-4393; **Auberge du Lac**, near both golf and horseback riding, from $50 to $92 depending on the season, (418) 235-4737; **Motel Chantmartin**, about $70 for two, (418) 235-4242; **Le Pionnier**, from $45 to $110, (418) 235-4666; **Maison Clauphi Motel**, from $41 to $78, (418) 235-4303; and **Hôtel-Motel Le Beluga**, from $55 to $97, (418) 235-4784.

## CAMPING

C amping Tadoussac is on Highway 138, also known as rue du Bateau-Passeur, at the edge of town. Rates for serviced sites are $24 maximum, plus power. Pets are welcome. Call (418) 235-4501.

## HELPFUL HINTS

R emember to reserve space ahead of time on the car ferry from Baie-Ste-Catherine to Tadoussac, particularly if you're traveling in summer. The ferry runs year-round; in summer, the service is every 20 minutes between 8:00 a.m. and 8:00 p.m., every 40 minutes between 8:00 p.m. and midnight, and once an hour between midnight and 8:00 a.m. To reserve, call (418) 235-4395.

Most of the route from Quebec City to Baie-Ste-Catherine is covered in Tourisme Quebec's Charlevoix guide, while information on Tadoussac can be found in the North Shore (or Côte-Nord) guide. Get copies of both from (800) 363-7777. Tourist information offices are open year-round at 4 Ambroise-Fafard Street in Baie-St-Paul and at 166 de Comporte Boulevard in La Malbaie. In Tadoussac, the tourist information office at 196 des Pionniers Street is open in-season from 8:00 a.m. to 8:00 p.m. daily.

# 8
# THE GASPÉ

The Gaspé Peninsula is one of the most scenic regions in the province. The coast road is a panoply of rolling hills, craggy cliffs, and picturesque villages with whimsical names. Cap-Chat? Cape Cat was reportedly so named because of a rock near the lighthouse that resembles a crouching cat. Anse-Pleureuse? The winds in Crying Cove sound like people wailing. Cap-aux-Os? Cape Bones was named after the whale bones people used to find there.

The Gaspé Peninsula, one of the oldest land masses on earth, is sparsely populated (235,000 residents on the whole peninsula, the vast majority living along the coast). Thankfully, its wild beauty remains largely unspoiled despite its popularity as a tourist destination. One of the highlights is Forillon National Park, a dramatic product of erosion. Others include the famous Percé Rock, one of the most popular tourist draws in Quebec, and Île de Bonaventure, a sanctuary a few kilometers offshore from Percé that attracts thousands of birds from dozens of species.

The Micmacs (or Mi'Kmaq, as it's also spelled), or "Indians of the Sea," have lived in the Gaspé for more than 2,500 years. In fact, the name Gaspé probably comes from a Micmac word meaning "land's end." Over the years, myriad European ethnic groups and Loyalists (refugees from the American Revolution) also settled on the peninsula, making for a multicultural mix that continues to this day.

The major industries in the Gaspé are fishing, forestry, and, increasingly, tourism. You will not only see superb scenery here, you'll be providing a badly needed shot in the arm to the local economy. ◣

# THE GASPÉ

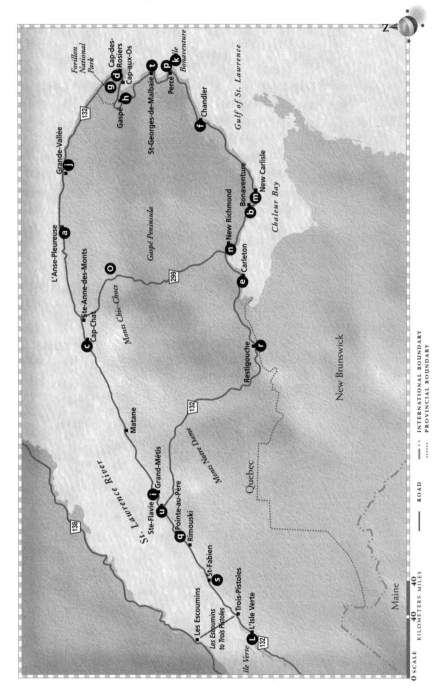

# Sightseeing Highlights

- **a** Anse-Pleureuse

- **b** Bonaventure

- **c** Cap-Chat

- **d** Cap-des-Rosiers

- **e** Carleton

- **f** Chandler

- **g** Forillon National Park

- **h** Gaspé

- **i** Grand-Métis

- **j** Grande-Vallée

- **k** Île Bonaventure

- **l** Île Verte

- **m** New Carlisle

- **n** New Richmond

- **o** Parc de la Gaspésie

- **p** Percé Rock

- **q** Pointe-au-Père

- **r** Restigouche

- **s** St-Fabien

- **t** St-Georges-de-Malbaie

- **u** Ste-Flavie

## A PERFECT DAY IN THE GASPÉ

I t's difficult to pin down what I like best about the Gaspé, but several things stand out. All of them, come to think of it, are rather eerie. For starters, there's the *Grand Rassemblement*, or the Great Gathering, a powerful work of art along the shore of Ste-Flavie wherein ghostly figures rise from the swirling gray water. It's the work of a local artist who spent several years on the project, and it's an amazing sight. Then there's the famous Percé Rock, another rather eerie offshore spectacle. I also like to stop in Anse-Pleureuse to listen to the haunting sound of the winds there.

## GETTING THERE

T here are car ferries across the St. Lawrence from St-Siméon, 33 kilometers (20 miles) southwest of Baie-Ste-Catherine on Highway 138, or from Les Escoumins, 39 kilometers (23 miles) northeast of Tadoussac on Highway 138. The ferry from Les Escoumins crosses to Trois-Pistoles, thereby saving about 50 kilometers of driving once you're across the river. From St-Siméon, the ferry crosses to Rivière-du-Loup. Either crossing takes 1¼ hours. The St-Siméon ferry begins running in April; find out exact crossing times and make a reservation by calling (418) 862-5094. The ferry between Les Escoumins and Trois-Pistoles runs from June 1 to October 31; for information and reservations, phone (418) 233-2202 in Les Escoumins or (418) 851-4676 in Trois-Pistoles.

From Rivière-du-Loup, take Highway 20 East, which becomes Highway 132. From Trois-Pistoles, get directly onto the 132 east. The 132 loops all the way around the peninsula. You'll need at least two days to tour the Gaspé.

## SIGHTSEEING HIGHLIGHTS

★★★ **Forillon National Park** • Located on a small peninsula at the easternmost tip of the Gaspé Peninsula, Forillon Park has rugged, hilly forests inland that are framed on the coast by soaring limestone cliffs, pebble beaches, small sandy coves, and rocks sculpted by the pounding sea. From offshore, the park has the strangest appearance—like a huge, jagged-edged block emerging at an angle from the sea, with one side sloping gently down to the water and the cliffside dropping precipitously. In summer, thousands of birds nest on the cliffs. Wildlife includes deer, moose, lynx, black bear, and red fox, and you might see whales and seals from coastal cliffs. There is also an unusually wide cross-section of plant life, given the relatively small size of the park (245 square kilometers). The theme of the park is harmony among humanity, earth, and ocean. Phone: (418) 368-5505. (3 hours)

★★★ Île Bonaventure • An estimated 220,000 birds nest every year on windswept Bonaventure Island, a conservation park a few kilometers offshore from Percé. The colony of gannets alone is 50,000 strong. The island is also rife with wildflowers, mosses, and mushrooms. You can take a boat excursion to Île Bonaventure from Percé. Check in at the interpretation center, the Centre d'interprétation du Parc de l'Île-Bonaventure-et-du-Rocher-Percé, for information. (2 hours)

★★★ Percé Rock • An enigmatic, arresting presence, this monolith sits just offshore, brooding over the town of Percé. It was once attached to the shoreline, and at low tide you can still reach it on foot. It is 510 meters long, 100 meters wide and 70 meters high (roughly 1,670 by 330 by 230 feet). It is named Percé because the sea has "pierced" holes in it to form archways. Way back in the mists of time, there were reputedly four such arches, but now there is just one large opening some 30 meters (98 feet) wide. Together, Percé Rock and Île Bonaventure make up the Parc de l'Île-Bonaventure-et-du-Rocher-Percé. Phone: (418) 782-2721. (1 hour)

★★★ Ste-Flavie • Ste-Flavie is called the "gateway to the Gaspé," but the reason you must stop here has nothing to do with that. Ste-Flavie is home to an outdoor art exhibit known as le Grand Rassemblement, or Great Gathering. It's made up of more than 80 life-size figures created from firewood and bark by local artist Marcel Gagnon. Dozens of the sculpted human forms seem to file solemnly toward the shore, where other figures stand. Still more human forms bob on seven rafts offshore. It is a strange and compelling sight. Some have compared the work to the sculptures of Easter Island, others to the standing stones of Brittany and Ireland. You can also visit the artist's gallery at 564 route de la Mer, which is Highway 132. (1 hour)

★★ Grand-Métis • Stop in Grand-Métis to see the enchanting Jardins de Métis (Metis Gardens), featuring six different ornamental gardens surrounding a luxurious villa. Now owned by the Quebec government, the estate once belonged to the niece of Lord Mount Stephen, the first president of Canadian Pacific Railroad. The niece, Elsie Reford, was an avid gardener. The mansion now houses a museum, a restaurant, and a crafts shop. Admission is $6 for adults, $2 for kids 8 to 14, free for children under 8, $5.50 for students and seniors, and $14 for families. The Jardins de Métis are open from June to September, from 8:30 a.m. to 8:00 p.m. daily. Phone: (418) 775-2221.

✿✿ **Parc de la Gaspésie** • At Ste-Anne-des-Monts, turn south on Highway 299; the park entrance is 15 kilometers down the 299. The mountainous park is the only place in the province where moose, wood caribou, and Virginia deer all live in the same territory. The park's Chic-Chocs are among the highest mountains in eastern Canada, with Mont Jacques-Cartier the loftiest at 1,268 meters (4,145 feet). The summit of another mountain, Mont Albert, is a 30-square-kilometer plateau boasting mosses, lichens, and shrubs that are normally found only in the far north. There are several lodging facilities in the park, which also features some 120 kilometers of hiking trails. The reception center is open from early June until Labor Day. (minimum 3 hours)

✿ **Anse-Pleureuse** • Listen to the wind in the trees in this coastal village. It's a haunting sound that according to local legend is the moans of the ghosts of two little girls, the sobs of a man who was murdered, and/or the cries of shipwrecked sailors. (15 minutes)

✿ **Bonaventure** • The Acadians, the predominantly French-speaking, Roman Catholic settlers of eastern Canada, were deported from Nova Scotia in the mid-1700s by the British, who were struggling with the French for control of North America. Some went to Gaspé after avoiding the deportation campaign. As an Acadian stronghold, Bonaventure is home to the Musée acadien du Québec, featuring antiques, period photos, and a slide show on the history of Acadians in Quebec (some 1 million Quebecers are of Acadian descent). Bilingual guided tours are available. Admission is $3.50 for adults, $2.50 for students and seniors, and $7.50 for families. Hours: 9:00 a.m. to 9:00 p.m. daily from late June until early September and shorter hours the rest of the year. Address: 97 Port-Royal Avenue. Phone: (418) 534-4000. (1 hour)

✿ **Cap-Chat** • Cap-Chat is where the St. Lawrence River officially becomes the Gulf of St. Lawrence. Cap-Chat also boasts the biggest and

most powerful vertical-axis wind tower in the world, 3 kilometers west
of the Cap-Chat bridge. There is a bilingual multimedia show about the
wind tower and life in the region at the Centre d'interpretation du vent
et de la mer (Wind and Sea Interpretation Center). (½ hour)

✵ **Cap-des-Rosiers** • Named by Samuel de Champlain for the wild
roses that grow on its cliffs, Cap-des-Rosiers features a lighthouse atop
a 37-meter (120-foot) cliff, making it the highest site for a Canadian
lighthouse. The village is also considered the gateway to Forillon
National Park. (½ hour)

✵ **Carleton** • This Acadian stronghold boasts a magnificent setting
between the sea and the mountains. From the top of Mont St-Joseph,
just north of town and accessible by car, there is a panoramic view of
the bay, the Gaspé coast, and the coast of New Brunswick across the
Baie-des-Chaleurs. (½ hour)

✵ **Chandler** • The wreck of the Peruvian freighter *Unisol* lies off
Chandler and is visible from shore. The ship didn't sink when it hit
some rocks there in 1983; it got wedged between the rocks and half of
it sticks out of the water at an angle, so that it looks eerily as if it is in
the process of going down. (½ hour)

✵ **Gaspé** • Gaspé, the administrative center for the area, is one of the
oldest settlements in North America. Jacques Cartier took possession
of Canada on behalf of the king of France and placed a cross on this
location in 1534. If you're interested in the history of the peninsula,
stop in at Musée de la Gaspésie at 80 Gaspé Boulevard. The permanent exhibition is titled Un peuple de la mer, or people of the sea. The
museum also houses temporary exhibits of artwork from the region.
Admission is $3.50 for adults, $2.50 for students and seniors, and $1.50
for children 6 to 11. Hours: 9:00 a.m. to 8:30 p.m. from June 24 to
Labor Day; 9:00 a.m. to 12:00 noon and 1:00 to 5:00 p.m. Monday to
Friday and 2:00 to 5:00 p.m. Saturday and Sunday during the rest of
the year. Phone: (418) 368-5710. (1 hour)

✵ **Grande-Vallée** • Outside Grande-Vallée is a roadside rest area that
offers a magnificent view of the village and valley. A covered bridge in
the middle of the village adds a nice touch to the quaint, peaceful
nature of the scene. (15 minutes)

★ **Île Verte** • "Green Island" is the only one in the region inhabited year-round. Forty people live there. There's a ferry service from L'Île-Verte on the mainland. The bucolic island also boasts the oldest light-house on the river; built in 1809, it provides a good vantage point for whale-watching. (1½ hours)

★ **New Carlisle** • This is a largely English-speaking village, populated mainly by descendants of Loyalist families—American colonists who supported the British cause during the American Revolution and came to Canada in great waves in 1783 and 1784. It's also the birthplace of the late René Lévesque, founder and leader of the Parti Québécois, champion of the separatist movement, and premier of the province in the late 1970s and early 1980s. Just recently, the white frame house where he grew up was recognized as a historic site by the Quebec government, but it's not yet open to the public. (½ hour)

★ **New Richmond** • Founded by the Loyalists, New Richmond has a living-history museum that re-creates the Loyalist era, complete with houses, period furniture, and bilingual guided tours. The Centre de l'Heritage britannique de la Gaspésie is at 351 Perron Blvd. W, open early June to Labor Day, 9:00 a.m. to 6:00 p.m. daily. Admission is $4 for adults, $3 for seniors and kids 12 and up, and $8 for families. Phone: (418) 392-4487. (2½ hours)

★ **Pointe-au-Père** • If you want to know more about the social history of the area, take Père Nouvel St. toward the river to the Musée de la mer et lieu historique national de Pointe-au-Père. This national historic site contains exhibitions and interpretations of regional history and marine life, plus a lighthouse. Admission is $3 for adults, $2.50 for students and seniors, and $1.25 for children 6 and up. (1 hour)

★ **Restigouche** • The largest Micmac reservation on the peninsula is in Restigouche. Stop in at the Centre d'interprétation de la culture Micmac to learn how the Micmacs have lived in Gaspé through the centuries. The Micmacs fished and hunted an area that spread from the coast of Nova Scotia across the Gaspé Peninsula. Admission is $3 for adults, $2 for seniors and students, $1 for children, and $5 for families. Hours: 9:00 a.m. to 7:00 p.m. daily from June to September, shorter hours the rest of the year. Address: 4 Riverside West. (1 hour)

✷ **St-Fabien** • More beaches and summer cottages, along with the only octagonal barn in the region. The barn, built in 1888, is in the center of the village. (½ hour)

✷ **St-Georges-de-Malbaie** • Just south of the village of St-Georges-de-Malbaie, there is a superb vista of Forillon on one side and Île Bonaventure and Percé Rock on the other. (15 minutes)

## FITNESS AND RECREATION

There are diving shops in Cap-aux-Os and Percé. Horseback riding is available in several towns, including Matane and Bonaventure. For hiking, there are the two parks—Gaspésie in the center of the peninsula, and Forillon at the eastern tip. You can swim off many parts of the coast, but you may want to save the swimming for the south coast of the peninsula, where the waters in the Baie des Chaleurs are relatively warm.

## FOOD

Any restaurant serving seafood should be fine; the seafood will be as fresh as the catch of the day. In the town of Gaspé, try the **Bistro-Bar Brise Bize** for moderately priced fare (2 Côte Charter, 418-368-1456). The food is fancier and the prices higher at the **Cafe-Restaurant La Belle Hélène**, billed as one of the region's best restaurants (135-A rue de la Reine in Gaspé, 418-368-1455). In Sainte-Flavie, **Le Capitaine Homard** at 180 Route de la Mer specializes in fresh lobster (418-775-8046). At Sainte-Flavie's **Les Portes de la Mer** you can get steak as well as seafood (418-775-8460). In Matane, **Le Vieux Rafiot Restaurant-Pub** serves up seafood and beef at 1415 avenue du Phare (418-562-8080). At the **Jardins de Métis** in Grand-Métis, you can eat on-site in the restaurant in the Reford Villa (418-775-3165). In Percé, **Le Matelot** is a restaurant-bar specializing in fresh seafood at 7 rue de l'Église (418-782-2569).

## LODGING

Motels and inns abound around the Gaspé coast. In Cap-Chat, the **Motel Fleur de Lys**, 184 Notre-Dame Street East, is wheelchair accessible and charges from $35 to $60 per room (418-786-5518). Sainte-Flavie's **Motel Le Gaspésiana** at 460 route de la Mer is a

# THE GASPÉ

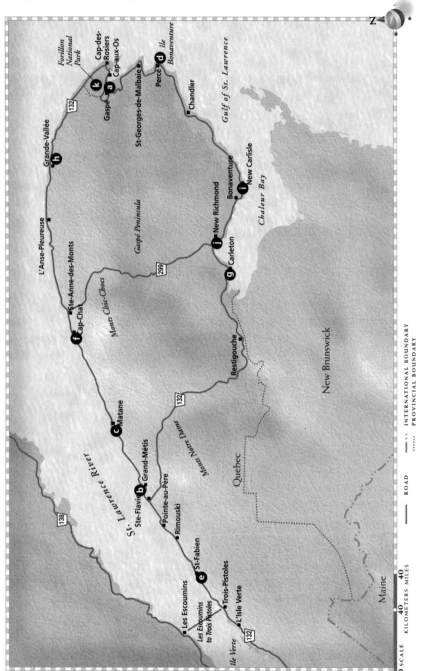

Forillon National Park
Cap-des-Rosiers
Cap-aux-Os
k
a
Gaspé
Grande-Vallée
h
L'Anse-Pleureuse
Ste-Anne-des-Monts
Cap-Chat
f
Monts Chic-Chocs
Gaspé Peninsula
St-Georges-de-Malbaie
Percé
d
Bonaventure île
Chandler
Gulf of St. Lawrence
New Carlisle
i
Bonaventure
New Richmond
j
Carleton
g
Chaleur Bay
Restigouche
New Brunswick
299
132
Matane
c
Grand-Métis
Ste-Flavie
b
Pointe-au-Père
Rimouski
Monts Notre Dame
Quebec
St. Lawrence River
138
St-Fabien
e
Trois-Pistoles
Les Escoumins
Les Escoumins to Trois Pistoles
L'Isle Verte
Île Verte
132
Maine

N

0 SCALE  40  40
KILOMETERS MILES

—— ROAD
‥‥ INTERNATIONAL BOUNDARY
····· PROVINCIAL BOUNDARY

# Food

- ⓐ Bistro-Bar Brise Bize
- ⓐ Cafe-Restaurant La Belle Hélène
- ⓑ Le Capitaine Homard
- ⓒ Jardins de Métis-Reford Villa
- ⓓ Le Matelot
- ⓔ Les Portes de la Mer
- ⓔ Le Vieux Rafiot Restaurant-Pub

# Lodging

- ⓓ Auberge au Pirate
- ⓖ Auberge La Visite Surprise
- ⓙ Auberge Le Cachet
- ⓗ Auberge-Motel Richard
- ⓓ La Maison Tommi
- ⓙ l'Étoile de Mer
- ⓔ Gîte Aux Chutes
- ⓓ Gîte Le Rendezvous
- ⓓ Gîte L'Extravagante
- ⓘ Motel Baie-des-Chaleurs
- ⓘ Motel Bellevue
- ⓕ Motel Fleur de Lys
- ⓔ Motel Le Gaspésiana

# Camping

- ⓕ Camping au Bord de la Mer
- ⓚ Camping Cap Bon-Ami
- ⓔ Camping Capitaine Homard
- ⓘ Camping Maison Hamilton
- ⓚ Camping Petit-Gaspé
- ⓚ Camping des Rosiers
- ⓗ Camping au Soleil Couchant

*Note: Items with the same letter are located in the same town or area.*

three-star facility that charges between $55 and $95 a night
(418-775-7233) and is wheelchair accessible. In the town of Percé,
**Auberge au Pirate** at 1 Promenade Bord de Mer charges from $55 to
$100 a night, but for that you get bed and breakfast in a historic build-
ing that looks out towards Percé rock (418-782-5055). In Carleton, the
**Auberge La Visite Surprise**, 527 Perron Boulevard, is wheelchair
accessible and charges about $50 a night (418-364-6553). In New
Carlisle, **Motel Baie-des-Chaleurs** at 104 rue Principale has room
rates of between $50 and $90 (418-752-3305), while **Motel Bellevue**
on Route 132 is slightly cheaper (418-752-3612). **Auberge Le Cachet**
at 185 Perron Boulevard West in New Richmond offers cabins with
kitchenettes for between $50 and $65 (418-392-4121). In Grande-
Vallée, the **Auberge-Motel Richard** at 36 rue Pinciple charges
between $30 and $50 a night (418-393-2670). If you prefer bed and
breakfasts, most charge between $45 and $60 for a room for two. In
Sainte-Flavie, **Gîte Aux Chutes** is a non-smoking establishment at 571
de la Mer (418-775-9432). In Percé, several B&Bs are right on Route
132, including **La Maison Tommi** (418-782-5104), **Gîte Le
Rendezvous** (418-782-5152) and **Gîte L'Extravagante** (418-782-
2102). In New Richmond, try **l'Étoile de Mer** at 256 rue Perron
(418-392-6246).

## CAMPING

Numerous campgrounds dot the coast, most charging from $12
and up per night. There are several campgrounds inside Forillon
National Park, including **Camping Cap Bon-Ami**, (418) 368-6050.
In Sainte-Flavie, **Camping Capitaine Homard** at 180 route de la Mer
has a restaurant if you don't feel like cooking (418-775-8046). In Cap-
Chat, **Camping au Bord de la Mer** on Route 132 has a convenience
store and a restaurant (418-786-2251). **Camping Maison Hamilton**
on Route 132 in New Carlisle has a laundromat (418-752-7048).
In Grande Vallée, **Camping au Soleil Couchant** at 73 Saint-François-
Xavier has a store, restaurant, laundromat and picnic tables
(418-393-2646).

## HELPFUL HINTS

A summer ferry service links Carleton with Cap-aux-Meules on the
Magdalen Islands (Îles-de-la-Madeleine). Though the Magdalens
are part of Quebec, they are closer to Prince Edward Island and Nova

Scotia than to the Quebec mainland; that's why this ferry service, aboard the John Hamilton Gray, takes 14 hours one way. The fee for a car is $125 one way and passenger fares are $60 for adults and $30 for children 5 to 12. The only other car ferry to the intriguing, windswept islands is from Prince Edward Island (see that chapter). It's worth noting that the ferry allows you to make a circuit through the Gaspé, the Magdalens, and Prince Edward Island in one go. For information on the service, phone (418) 364-6213.

Via Rail offers an overnight train, the Chaleur, between Montreal and the town of Gaspé. The train runs along the south shore from Montreal to Lévis, Rivière du Loup, Rimouski, and Mont Joli, then down the Matapedia Valley to Matapedia, east along the south Gaspé coast through New Carlisle and Percé, and finally to Gaspé. It takes 17 hours, and in both directions the sector between Matapedia and Gaspé is in daylight (at least in summer), allowing passengers to take in the spectacular scenery along the south Gaspé coast. If you're tired of driving, consider this trip instead. The Chaleur has comfortable coach cars, a dining car complete with a bar lounge, and sleeper cars with showers. Reserve well ahead for summer travel. For information, contact Via or see a travel agent.

For more information on the places along the route, use Tourisme Quebec's Bas St-Laurent and Gaspésie booklets. Phone (800) 363-7777. For still more information, contact the Association Touristique du Bas-St-Laurent at 189, rue Hôtel-de-Ville, Rivière-du-Loup, Que., G5R 4C3, (418) 867-3015; and the Association Touristique de la Gaspésie, 357 route de la Mer, Ste-Flavie, Que., G0J 2L0, (418) 775-2223. In person, drop in to the Ste-Flavie office, open year-round. Ste-Flavie, between Pointe-au-Père and Grand-Métis, is known as the gateway to the Gaspé Peninsula. There are also seasonal tourist information offices in 12 different towns and villages along Highway 132, including Gaspé, Percé, New Carlisle, Bonaventure, and New Richmond. Having completed the Gaspé circuit, cross over into northern New Brunswick. There is a bridge to Cambellton, N.B., from near Restigouche.

# 9
# FREDERICTON

M y favorite thing about Fredericton, the capital of New
Brunswick, is its many beautiful old Victorian houses. On a summer day, strolling the streets lined with these houses is just the ticket.
You may notice elm trees everywhere; Fredericton, a small, attractive
city of 45,000 in south-central New Brunswick, is known as "the city of
stately elms." It may be the capital, but by virtue of its size and perhaps
the character of its residents, it has a small-town, laid-back feel.

Fredericton sits astride the Saint John River and was originally
settled by the French. Eventually the British took control of what was
then a tiny trading post and small numbers of British settlers came to
the area. Some 2,000 Loyalists who arrived at the end of the American
Revolution spent a very rough first winter huddled in tents. The sur-
vivors helped build what became Fredericton. It was named the capital
in 1785 chiefly because of its location on a river—accessible, yet distant
enough from both the sea and the U.S. border that it was less prone to
attack than Saint John, the largest city in the province. ◣

# FREDERICTON

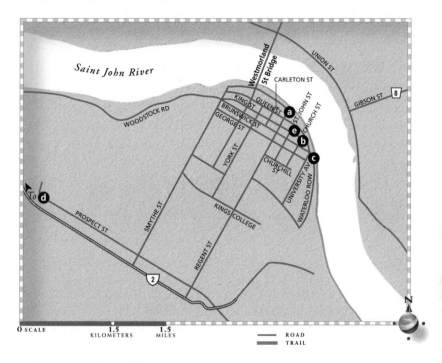

## Sightseeing Highlights

**a** Beaverbrook Art Gallery

**b** Christ Church Cathedral

**c** The Green and Waterloo Row

**d** Kings Landing

**e** Legislative Assembly Building

## A PERFECT DAY IN FREDERICTON

First I take a stroll through town to admire the houses. I also make sure to stop in at the Beaverbrook Art Gallery on Queen Street; the collection includes works by Gainsborough, Hogarth, and Reynolds. After an early lunch at La Vie en Rose, I spend the entire afternoon at Kings Landing Historical Settlement, a re-created Loyalist village outside Fredericton. It takes hours to see the entire village, which, with its costumed "residents," is a delight to explore.

## A WORD ABOUT NEW BRUNSWICK

New Brunswick, which lies east of Maine and south of Quebec, covers some 73,000 square kilometers (28,000 square miles, making it slightly smaller than Maine) and is bordered on the north by the Baie des Chaleurs, on the east by the Northumberland Strait, and on the south by the Bay of Fundy. The entire province has a population of 724,000, a mix of French- and English-speaking people of varying ethnic backgrounds. New Brunswick is the only officially bilingual province in Canada (Quebec is officially French, the other provinces English). For its size, the province's geography is diverse, with cliffs and rocky shores on some parts of the coast and sandy beaches and salt dunes on other parts. Inland, there is a mix of river valleys, farmland, forests, and wilderness.

Jacques Cartier and Samuel de Champlain were the earliest European explorers of New Brunswick, then populated by Micmac and Melcite Indians. When Cartier sailed into New Brunswick in 1534, he was so impressed by its beauty and the warmth of the waters that he named the area Baie des Chaleurs (Bay of Warmth). The first European settlers were French-speaking Acadians. Later, Loyalists also settled in New Brunswick.

## GETTING AROUND FREDERICTON

The city core is so compact that the only sensible way to tour Fredericton is on foot; just about everything you want to see is in within a few square blocks downtown.

Fredericton has a program whereby visitors can park for free when they put a special ticket in their windshield. This comes in handy if you're staying outside the center of town. Check in at the Tourist Information Center at City Hall on the corner of Queen and York streets, or call them at (506) 452-9500. The center is open daily from 8:00 a.m. to 8:00 p.m. from May 15 to Labor Day and from 8:00 a.m. to 4:30 p.m. the rest of the year. The tourism people can also provide you with a Fredericton Visitor Guide that includes a helpful suggested 5-block walking tour.

## SIGHTSEEING HIGHLIGHTS

★★★ **Beaverbrook Art Gallery** • Across Queen Street from the Legislative Assembly Building, this art gallery, while small, houses a remarkable collection of British paintings spanning the sixteenth to twentieth centuries, including works by Thomas Gainsborough, Sir Joshua Reynolds, and John Constable, among others. The Canadian collection covers the years from the early nineteenth century to the present, including works by the Group of Seven. The first painting you see on entering the building is Salvador Dali's massive masterpiece, *Santiago el Grande*. A bench faces the painting; sit and contemplate it for a while. The art gallery is open daily year-round. Hours: 10:00 a.m. Tuesday to Saturday and at 12:00 noon on Sunday and Monday. Admission is free. (1 hour)

★★★ **Kings Landing** • A re-created Loyalist village in a lovely setting on the Saint John River, Kings Landing is one of the province's major tourist draws (rivaled perhaps by the Acadian Historical Village outside Caraquet). There are some 70 buildings on the sprawling site, ranging from a sawmill and a country inn to a one-room schoolhouse to an assortment of furnished houses, each reflecting the occupant's wealth and status in village life in the 1800s. Costumed staff and volunteers work in and around the buildings and can answer just about any question you throw at them. On summer weekends, the site is crowded despite its size, so try to go on a week-day. Admission is $8 for adults and $20 for families. Hours: Daily from early June through to Thanksgiving Monday in October (Columbus Day in the U.S.), from 10:00 a.m. to 5:00 p.m. in June, September, and October, and 10:00 a.m. to 6:00 p.m. in July and August. Address: Exit 259 of the TransCanada, west of Fredricton. (506) 363-5805. (minimum 3 hours)

★★ **The Green and Waterloo Row** • Beginning behind the Beaverbrook Art Gallery, The Green is a tree-shaded area stretching east along the riverbank, parallel to Waterloo Row, where

Fredericton's toniest houses sit. Make that mansions—some of them
are breathtaking. With the river on one side and the mansions on the
other, The Green makes for an idyllic stroll. (1 hour)

✶✶ **Legislative Assembly Building** • This silver-domed Victorian
building on Queen Street between St. John and Church Streets has
been the seat of government in New Brunswick since 1882, the previous legislative building having burned down a couple of years earlier.
When the legislature is in session, visitors can sit in the public gallery
(appropriate attire only, and no applauding under any circumstances).
When it's not in session, you can actually go into the Assembly
Chamber. (½ hour)

✶ **Christ Church Cathedral** • An imposing example of decorated
Gothic architecture, Christ Church Cathedral was consecrated in 1853.
Free guided tours are available mid-June to Labor Day. The cathedral
stands between Queen, Brunswick, and Church Streets. (½ hour)

## FITNESS AND RECREATION

You can go horseback riding at the Royal Road Riding Stables,
which offers 2-hour trail rides with guides and refreshments and
welcomes all riders, first-time or otherwise; call (506) 450-3059. Saint
John River canoe excursions geared to novices are available at the
Bucket Club Activity Park, which also offers a 5-hour "Kool Kid's Fun
Camp" of supervised outdoor fun and games; phone (506) 451-9696.
Two thematic canoe tours of the river—one historical, the other ecological—are available from the Small Craft Aquatic Centre at (506)
458-5513. Joggers should head for The Green on the riverbank in
downtown Fredericton.

## FOOD

You'll find assorted fast-food and family restaurants in the central
district, or if you want upscale, try the **Maverick Room Steak
House** in the Lord Beaverbrook Hotel at (506) 455-3371. The **City
Motel** at 1216 Regent Street serves up delicious boiled lobster, fish
chowders and other seafood, along with a children's menu (506-450-
9900). The **J, M, &T Deli** at 66 Regent Street specializes in Montreal
smoked mean, Montreal bagels, fresh muffins, and home-made
desserts. **The Barn** is a family restaurant at 540 Queen Street.

## LODGING

The **Lord Beaverbrook Hotel** at 659 Queen Street is probably the most famous hotel in town, and among the ritziest. Room rates, lower than in comparable hotels in bigger cities, range from $89 to $119. Call (506) 455-3371 or (800) 561-7666. The **Sheraton Inn Fredericton**, at 225 Woodstock Road on the riverfront, is another luxury establishment that opened in 1992. Its rates run from $65 to $112 depending on the season; it also offers specials such as a family package featuring two nights' accommodation and passes to Kings Landing for a family of four for $229. Call (506) 457-7000 or (800) 325-3535. Also new is the **Best Western Mactaquac Inn**, which interestingly was developed by the native community of the Kingsclear Reserve at Mactaquac, 12 kilometers west of Fredericton off the TransCanada at exit 274. The resort is just across from the 18-hole Mactaquac Golf Course. Rates range from $79 to $135, depending on the room and season. Cottages are also available for $150 and up. Call (506) 363-5111 or (800) 561-5111.

For lower rates and a Victorian atmosphere, try a B&B; there are several in and around Fredericton. The **Carriage House** is a lovely old Victorian mansion, more the size of an inn than a private home, with some exquisitely furnished rooms. It's very centrally located and offers rooms for between $55 and $75. Write to Frank and Joan Gorham, 230 University Ave., Fredericton, N.B., Canada, E3B 4H7, or phone (506) 452-9924 locally or (800) 267-6068. There are complete B&B listings in the Fredericton Visitor Guide and in a brochure put out by the New Brunswick Bed & Breakfast Association Guide, both available from either the Fredericton or New Brunswick tourist information centers.

**City Motel** charges from $52 to $70 for a double room at 1216 Regent Street off the TransCanada (506) 450-9900. A motel strip along the TransCanada skirts the south end of the city.

## CAMPING

The closest campgrounds to the city include those in **Mactaquac Provincial Park** at (506) 363-3011 and **Hartt Island Campground**, 10 kilometers west of the Princess Margaret Bridge, at (506) 450-6057. Both charge $17 and up for serviced sites.

## HELPFUL HINTS

For information on New Brunswick, write to Economic Development and Tourism, P.O. Box 12345, Fredericton, N.B., Canada E3B 5C3, or phone (800) 561-0123. They can supply several publications, including a pre-trip activity planner, an accommodation and campground guide, and an outdoor-adventure booklet.

For information on Fredericton, write to the Fredericton Tourism Department, City Hall, P.O. Box 130, Fredericton, N.B., Canada E3B 4Y7, or phone (506) 452-9500.

In person, you can drop in to tourist information centers in Campbellton, Bathurst, or Chatham, as well as in Fredericton.

For travelers going the B&B route, a handy book called *Bed & Breakfast—The Great Atlantic Adventure*, by Peter Gates and Elizabeth Stark, describes B&Bs in all four Atlantic provinces. It costs $9.50 plus $2 for postage and handling and can be ordered from Atlantic Adventure, 645 Manawagonish Road, Saint John, N.B., Canada E2M 3W4.

There are all manner of annual events and festivals throughout New Brunswick. Most take place in the peak summer months. Fredericton, for example, turns into a party town each year on Canada Day, July 1. It also hosts the annual Harvest Jazz and Blues Festival, around mid-September. For detailed information and dates, consult the New Brunswick Travel Guide. Finally, note that New Brunswick, like Prince Edward Island and Nova Scotia, is one hour ahead of Quebec and Ontario Time.

## SIDE TRIPS FROM FREDERICTON

To get to the Acadian Peninsula, head north from Fredericton on Highway 8, which eventually turns into Highway 11 and skirts the shoreline of the Acadian coast. The **Aquarium and Marine Centre** on 2nd Avenue in Shippagan houses a collection of 125 species of aquatic life and a marine museum, as well as a restaurant and outdoor patio. Call (506) 336-3013 for more information. The **Popes Museum and Art Gallery** in Grande-Anse, a museum unique in North America, is devoted to portraits of all the Popes, plus a showcase dedicated to the current Pope and a model of St. Peter's Basilica in Rome. It's at 184 Acadie Street in Grande-Anse, near the **Acadian Historical Village**. Call (506) 732-3003 for information. The Acadian Historical Village, a re-created settlement just outside Caraquet on

# FREDERICTON

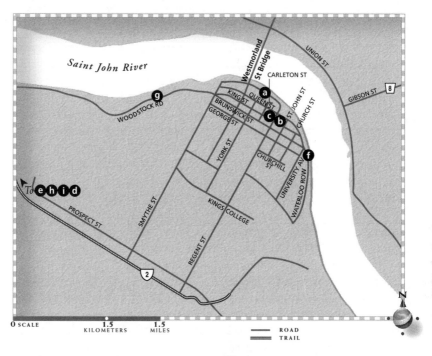

## Food

**ⓐ** The Barn

**ⓑ** Lobster Hut (City Motel)

**ⓒ** J, M, & T Deli

**ⓓ** Maverick Room Steak House (Lord Beaverbrook Hotel)

## Lodging

**ⓔ** Best Western Mactaquac Inn

**ⓕ** Carriage House

**ⓑ** City Motel

**ⓓ** Lord Beaverbrook Hotel

**ⓖ** Sheraton Inn Fredericton

## Camping

**ⓗ** Hartt Island Campground

**ⓘ** Mactaquac Provincial Park

Highway 330, tells the story of the Acadians in this part of the world by depicting their lives from 1780 to the early 1900s. The Acadians who came to northern New Brunswick were the victims of the colonial struggle between Britain and France over L'Acadie, made up of Nova Scotia and southern New Brunswick. When Britain deported some 75 percent of L'Acadie's French residents in 1755, many fled to northern New Brunswick. The Acadian Historical Village features costumed "residents" and special events and is one of the most popular tourist attractions in the province.

**Kouchibouguac National Park**, New Brunswick's largest park, has coastal beaches, sand dunes, swimming, camping, hiking, canoeing, and bicycling. From Fredericton, take Highway 10 heading east, and then Highway 116. From June 25 to September 6, the cost to get into Kouchibouguac is $5 per day per vehicle, or $10 for four days. The park is open Monday to Thursday from 10:00 a.m. to 6:00 p.m. and from 8:00 a.m. to 8:00 p.m. on Friday, Saturday, and Sunday. For information, call (506) 876-2443.

**MacDonald Farm Historic Park**, 20 kilometers (12 miles) northeast of Newcastle, is a recreation of a nineteenth-century working farm, complete with a stone manor house, outbuildings, orchards, and dock on the Miramichi River, which arches inland from Miramichi Bay on the Atlantic coast and is known for its salmon fishing. The farm, where costumed tour guides take visitors on interpretive tours, is at Bartibog Bridge on Route 11 off Highway 8. Phone: (506) 773-5761.

**Newcastle's** major claim to fame is that Lord Beaverbrook was raised here. The town square in Newcastle features a monument to Lord Beaverbrook that contains his ashes and various gifts from his lordship. His boyhood home, the Old Manse Library, is open to the public.

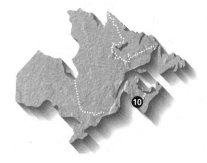

# 10
# THE FUNDY SHORE

The Bay of Fundy is one of the top natural destinations in Canada. Its coast, along the southern New Brunswick shore, is a panorama of serene inlets, rugged cliffs, picturesque Victorian villages, and home to the fabled Fundy tides, the highest in the world. At the western end of the bay, Franklin D. Roosevelt spent childhood summers on his beloved Campobello Island, one of the Fundy islands, in a humble "cottage" with 34 rooms. Another of the islands, Grand Manan, is like a piece of paradise for nature-lovers.

With a population of 125,000, Saint John is New Brunswick's largest city. It was the first city in Canada to be incorporated and is known as the Loyalist City because it was incorporated by Loyalists who arrived from the United States during the American Revolution. The city, particularly the downtown area with its lovely old buildings, is steeped in history, and the waterfront area has been beautifully restored in recent years. Saint John is also the New Brunswick terminal for the ferry to Digby, Nova Scotia, so there are plentiful facilities for visitors. ◩

# THE FUNDY SHORE

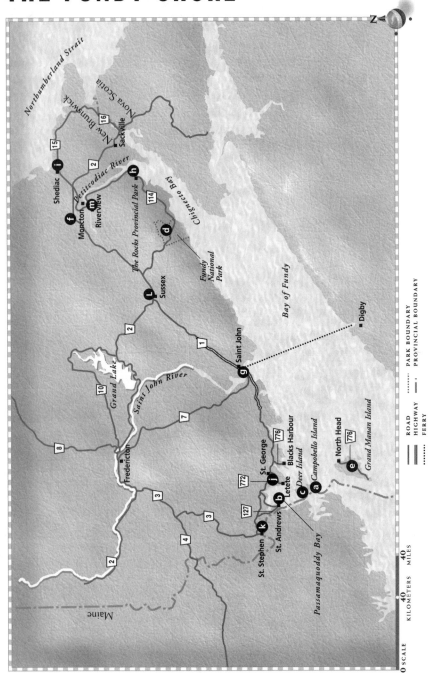

# Sightseeing Highlights

**ⓐ** Campobello Island

**ⓑ** Covenhoven

**ⓒ** Deer Island

**ⓓ** Fundy National Park

**ⓔ** Grand Manan Island

**ⓕ** Magnetic Hill

**ⓖ** Market Square

**ⓖ** The Old City Market

**ⓖ** Reversing Falls

**ⓗ** The Rocks Provincial Park

**ⓘ** Shediac

**ⓑ** St. Andrews

**ⓙ** St. George

**ⓚ** St. Stephen

**ⓛ** Sussex Covered Bridges

**ⓜ** Tidal Bore

*Note: Items with the same letter are in the same town or area.*

## A PERFECT DAY ON THE FUNDY SHORE

The coastal drive, to be sure, is scenic. But it's not so much the coast that draws me as the islands—specifically, Grand Manan Island. On Grand Manan, chances are that every time you look out over the water you'll spot whales of one variety or another, not to mention seals and porpoises. The island is etched with trails that lead through bird-filled forests and across the tops of soaring cliffs. Best of all, this scenic natural oasis is not yet overrun with tourists; you generally have the feeling you've got most of the place to yourself.

## SIGHTSEEING HIGHLIGHTS

★★★ **Campobello Island** • From Deer Island, a small private car ferry makes regular 45-minute crossings to Campobello. Confirm departure times at local information centers, since weather conditions can affect the ferry's operations. Note also that the ferry runs from late June until mid-September. Campobello contains a 2,800-acre international park, a joint Canada-U.S. venture that is supposed to symbolize the friendship between the two countries. The centerpiece of Roosevelt-Campobello International Park is U.S. President Franklin D. Roosevelt's summer "cottage," a red mansion with a green roof and 34 rooms, where Roosevelt spent most of the summers of his youth; he also came to Campobello three times during his presidency (1933 to 1945). The house is surrounded by attractive gardens, and there are several walking trails on the island, plus lighthouses, a golf course, and a stretch of pebbly beach. The park is open from 10:00 a.m. to 6:00 p.m. from late May until early October. Phone: (506) 752-2922. (3 hours)

★★★ **Fundy National Park** • This 207-square-kilometer park on the shores of the Bay of Fundy is a sanctuary of sloping cliffs, tide-washed beaches, clear streams, and hiking and nature trails. Driving through it takes from 1 to 3 hours, depending on how often you stop. During the summer, two information centers are open, and in the off-season information panels at Wolfe Lake and at the park administration building provide basic orientation. In summer there is also an interpretive program in which bilingual guides take you walking on the bottom of the sea at low tide or on nature walks. Entrance to the park is $5 per car. Phone: (506) 887-2000. (3 hours)

★★★ **Magnetic Hill** • What happens at Magnetic Hill, the little dirt road outside Moncton that "defies gravity" by pulling your car backward up what seems to be an uphill slope, is difficult to describe. You drive into Magnetic Hill Park, a tourist trap if there ever was one, complete with a mini-train, a "wharf village" of restaurants and stores, a water-slide park, and so on. Ignore all that; for one thing, it costs $53.25 for a family pass to the water park, and all you want to see is Magnetic Hill itself. Staff members direct you to the top of a gentle slope, although if there's a lineup of cars—and this is a hugely popular attraction, make no mistake—it'll take a while to get there. When you get to the front of the line, you're instructed to drive slowly down the slope and swing over to the left side of the road when you get to the bottom, where there's a kind of dip in the road. Then you put the car in neutral and sure enough, the car starts coasting backwards up the slope. It's all an optical illusion, I reckon, but don't tell anyone. The actual experience lasts about 45 seconds. Magnetic Hill Park is just off the TransCanada northwest of Moncton and well marked on the highway. Admission is $2 per car if you're only trying out the hill. Hours: Open from mid-May to mid-October, from 8:00 a.m. to 9:00 p.m. from late June to early September and slightly shorter hours in the other months. Phone: (506) 384-0303 or 853-3516. (15 minutes, if there's no lineup)

★★★ **The Rocks Provincial Park** • Sculpted by the mighty Fundy tides, the curious rock formations called the Flower Pot Rocks are known as the world's largest flower pots because that's sort of what they look like when the tide is out. Some are 15 meters (50 feet) tall. You can see them at any time, but only at low tide can you go down and explore the rock columns and caves. When the tide is in, the Flower Pot Rocks become ordinary islands. Schedules for low tides are posted. Address: Off Route 114 at Hopewell Cape. Phone: (506) 734-3429. (1 hour)

★★ **Market Square** • Market Square, part of the extensive restoration of Saint John's riverfront, is lined with boutiques, restaurants, and outdoor cafés. There's a harborfront boardwalk to stroll and plenty of atmosphere to absorb. Market Slip, where the Loyalists landed in 1783, adjoins Market Square. A tourist information center is in a nineteenth-century red schoolhouse next door to Market Slip. Pick up a pamphlet that describes the Loyalist Trail, a walking tour of central Saint John

that includes the Loyalist Burial Ground, the nineteenth-century empo-
rium known as Barbour's General Store (also on Market Square), the
Old Loyalist House with its authentic period furniture and eight fire-
places, and other Loyalist-related sites in the downtown area. (2 hours)

★★ **The Old City Market** • Open every day except Sunday, this Saint
John market is reputedly the oldest in Canada and offers a mind-
boggling array of seafood, vegetables, antiques, and myriad other
goods. The block-long building, constructed in 1876, was one of the
few public buildings to survive an 1877 fire that razed more than half
the city. Its interior was modeled after the inverted hull of a ship.
Address: 47 Charlotte Street, kitty-corner to King Square. (1 hour)

★★ **St. Andrews** • One of the oldest towns in the province, St.
Andrews-by-the-Sea (actually, it's by Passamaquoddy Bay, a small inlet
near the mouth of the Bay of Fundy) was founded in 1783 by United
Empire Loyalists. This is where you'll find Canada's first pre-fab
houses: many of the Loyalists dismantled their homes in Castine,
Maine; brought them over in barges; and reassembled them in St.
Andrews. Over half the town's buildings are more than 100 years old.
Walking-tour brochures are available at the St. Andrews Tourist
Bureau, where Highway 1 crosses Highway 127. There is also a
tourist information outlet on Harriet Street in town. The center of
town, crowded with restaurants and shops, runs for 4 blocks along
Water Street, anchored by the Market Wharf and the town square at
the end of King Street. For decades wealthy New Englanders flocked
to St. Andrews in the summer, many of them to stay at the famous
turret-topped Algonquin Hotel that broods over the town from a
nearby hill. (1 hour)

★★ **Tidal Bore** • Along with Magnetic Hill, Moncton's other natural
phenomenon is the tidal bore of the Petitcodiac River, which occurs
when the rising waters in the Bay of Fundy cause the water in the river
to roll back upstream in one wave. When the tides come in, twice a
day, one hundred billion tons of sea water rush up the shores of the
bay. At the bay's eastern extremity, the tide has been measured at 14.8
meters, or 48.4 feet. That's the height of a 4-story building, and the
reason why the Bay of Fundy tides are said to be the highest in the
world. In Moncton it used to be a real spectacle, but a causeway that
was built across the Petitcodiac River blocked the bore and nowadays
the river-wide wave is usually only a few inches high at most. Some

people, in fact, call it the Total Bore. Or, as American humorist
Erma Bombeck wrote after seeing what she had thought would be a
wonderful natural phenomenon: "A trickle of brown water, barely visible, slowly edged its way up the river toward us with all the excitement
of a stopped-up toilet." (15 minutes)

✯ **Covenhoven** • This house, located on Minister's Island near St.
Andrews, was built for a legendary Canadian railway baron, William
Cornelius Van Horne at the turn of the century. It's open to visitors—
but only at low tide, when a convenient gravel bar connects the island
to the mainland. Van Horne was the man who completed the Canadian
Pacific Railway out west. He reportedly once said that he liked his
houses "fat and bulgy like myself," and the 50-room Covenhoven is
indeed large and solid. When the Van Horne family summered on the
estate, there was a 33-person staff to look after them, including eight
gardeners. After Van Horne died in 1915, Covenhoven was used by the
family for another 20 years and then passed through a series of owners
before the New Brunswick government took it over and designated it a
historical site. Somewhere in there, most of the original furnishings
disappeared and the house is, alas, largely empty. The island is accessible from the end of Bar Road, where a notice advises visitors when it is
safe to make the crossing. Phone: (506) 529-5081. (1 hour)

✯ **Deer Island** • Catch the free government-operated ferry from
Letete to Deer Island, home to what are billed as the world's three
largest lobster pounds, in Northern Harbour on the island's west shore.
Old Sow, one of the world's largest whirlpools, can be seen off Deer
Island. (1 hour)

✯ **Reversing Falls** • If you get the timing right in Saint John, you can
see the Reversing Falls in action. Twice daily, the tides of the Bay of
Fundy reach such heights that they actually force the Saint John River
to flow upriver in a raging torrent of foam and whirlpools, creating this
unique phenomenon. Stop in at the Reversing Falls Information
Center at the western end of Falls Bridge on Highway 100 in Saint
John West, where there is also a lookout over the falls. (15 minutes)

✯ **St. George** • This fishing village is tattooed with granite outcrops
that make for some dramatic scenes. Magaguadavic Falls ranks among
the most picturesque. In summer, salmon on their way upriver to
spawn struggle up the man-made fish ladder that was built so they

could circumnavigate the falls. For some reason, St. George is also reputed to have the best drinking water in all of Canada. (½ hour)

✫ **St. Stephen** • St. Stephen is home to the Ganong chocolate factory, where Arthur Ganong invented the chocolate bar in 1906 by wrapping blocks of chocolate in paper as snacks for fishing trips. The factory is on Chocolate Drive (what else) on the outskirts of town. Tours are available only during the annual Chocolate Fest, usually in early August. The Chocolatier shop on Milltown Boulevard has historic candy-making equipment, chocolate-dipping demonstrations, and the world's tallest jelly-bean display. St. Stephen is also a major entry point for visitors from the United States. (1 hour)

✫ **Shediac** • The temperate waters of Shediac Bay are said to be the warmest salt waters north of the Carolinas; in summer, the water temperatures reach 24°–28°C (75°–85°F). Combined with the 3-kilometer (2-mile) sandy beach in nearby Parlee Beach Provincial Park, this makes Shediac a favorite summer tourist resort. Shediac, which calls itself "The Lobster Capital of the World," also hosts a lobster festival, usually during the second week of July, that's worth visiting. (1 hour)

✫ **Sussex Covered Bridges** • There are 17 covered bridges, many on bucolic country roads, in Sussex and the surrounding Kings County. Stop in at the Kings County Tourist Center in Sussex, or call (506) 433-3764, for a locator map for the bridges. During the third week of August Sussex hosts Country Living Days, a week of family-oriented events like horse and livestock shows, auctions, woodsmen's competitions, a parade, and a farmer's market. (1 hour)

## FITNESS AND RECREATION

You can go sea-kayaking out of St. Andrews; Seascape Kayak Tours offers tours to the Fundy Isles for beginners and experienced paddlers alike (506-529-4866). Cyclists can travel the whole Fundy Shore on two wheels. Hikers can explore the stretch of coast between St. Martin's and Fundy National Park; for their efforts, they'll be rewarded with stony beaches, clear cold brooks, forested promontories, and pristine shores.

## FOOD

The restaurants in Saint John's Market Square area range from fast-food to elegant. **Grannan's Seafood Restaurant and Oyster Bar** (506-634-1555) offers the catch of the day, oysters, or seafood platters at prices ranging from $11 to $25. The **Food Hall at Market Square** offers an assortment of fast-foods. **Mexicali Rosa's** at 88 Prince William Street (506-652-5252) specializes in "Cali-Mex" food and is moderately priced. **Incredible Edibles** at 42 Princess Street (506-633-7554) offers rich cheesecake and other desserts as well as salads, pasta dishes, and sandwiches. The cost is moderate—usually less than $15 for a meal.

## LODGING

Saint John has a good selection of bed and breakfasts. Try **Five Chimneys Bed and Breakfast**, midway between the Digby ferry slip and the city center. Billed as a four-star property, rates for a double run around $55. The address is 238 Charlotte Street West, Saint John, N.B. E2M 1Y3, (506) 635-1888.

The luxurious **Saint John Hilton** at One Market Square is right in the middle of things. Rates run $115 to $160 a night. Call 693-8484 locally or (800) 561-8282. A beautiful old Victorian house, the **Parkerhouse Inn**, is on Sydney Street a block from King Square. Rates begin at $65, including breakfast and parking. Call (506) 652-5054 or write to 71 Sydney Street, Saint John, N.B. E2L 2L5.

There are motels along Manawagonish Road and another strip of them along Rothesay Avenue, which crosses the TransCanada, otherwise known as Highway 100.

## CAMPING

A huge campground, **Rockwood Park**, lies just north of the downtown Saint John area. It has small lakes, attractive sites and a view of the city. It's close to the center of things, just north of Rothesay Avenue, and is open from May through October. The rate for tenters is $13, for fully serviced sites $18. Write to Rockwood Park, Horticultural Association, P.O. Box 535, Saint John, N.B., E2L 3Z8, or phone (506) 652-4050.

# SAINT JOHN

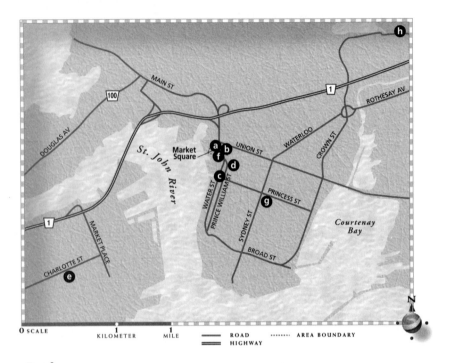

## Food

**a** Food Hall at Market Square

**b** Grannan's Seafood Restaurant and Oyster Bar

**c** Incredible Edibles

**d** Mexicali Rosa's

## Lodging

**e** Five Chimneys Bed and Breakfast

**f** Saint John Hilton

**g** Parkerhouse Inn

## Camping

**h** Rockwood Park

## FESTIVALS

Saint John hosts two fine festivals each summer, plus a third smaller but particularly entertaining one. The Loyalist Days Festival, usually the third week of July, features re-enactments of the landing of the United Empire Loyalists in 1783, complete with period costumes, plus parades, street casinos, horse-racing, and an antique fair. Festival by the Sea, a cultural festival normally held the second week of August, brings together up to 300 Canadian and international performers who provide some 125 performances in a 10-day period, with a special children's festival during the final 2 days. For sheer fun, usually over the first weekend of August, the 4-day Buskers on the Boardwalk festival features magic, mime, and music on the harborfront boardwalk at Market Square, plus fireworks.

## HELPFUL HINTS

In Saint John, the grand old Imperial Theater re-opened in 1994 after extensive renovations. To find out what's on, ask at the Market Square tourist information center.

For more information on Saint John, contact the Saint John Visitor & Convention Bureau, Box 1971, Saint John, N.B., Canada E2L 4L1, or phone the bureau at (506) 658-2990.

For more information on Moncton, refer to the New Brunswick Travel Guide or contact Moncton Convention and Visitor Services, City Hall, 774 Main Street, Moncton, N.B., Canada E1C 1E8, (506) 384-0303.

# *Scenic Route:* Grand Manan Island

The largest of the three Fundy Isles, Grand Manan is at once tranquil and exotically beautiful, with a mix of forests, towering cliffs, and long beaches. You can whale-watch, bird-watch, or just bake on the beach. In spring and summer, huge numbers of birds nest on the island's cliffs. Awed when he visited in the 1800s, John James Audubon did many of his sketches at Grand Manan. Indeed, the island is a wonderful place to sketch, paint, or take photos. The Hole-in-the-Wall, a massive shoreline rock formation that has a huge hole right through its middle, may be the most photographed scene on the island; it's in the North Head area, along a trail that begins near the Marathon Hotel.

The island requires at least a full day to explore properly. (Just to get there and back by ferry takes nearly 4 hours.) With Deer Island and Campobello, Grand Manan is the largest of the so-called West Isles Archipelago. To visit Grand Manan, turn south off Highway 1 about 5 kilometers (3 miles) east of St. George, onto Highway 785. It leads to Blacks Harbour, where car ferries to Grand Manan can be found. The ferries run year-round, three times a day from Labor Day until late June and six times a day from late June to Labor Day. Round-trip rates are $8.20 for adults and $4.10 for children 5 to 13, plus $24.60 per vehicle. Call Coastal Transport in Saint John at (506) 636-3922 for more information. The crossing to North Head on Grand Manan takes between 90 minutes and 2 hours.

With **scenic walking trails** all over the island, a full day on Grand Manan passes quickly. There are several small communities on Grand Manan, and it's possible to stay overnight, bearing in mind that it is wise to book ahead, since there aren't many accommodations.

North Head offers a couple of interesting places to stay. **The Compass Rose**, a heritage inn, is actually two old houses with antique-furnished rooms looking out towards the sea. Breakfast, lunch, afternoon tea, and dinner are all available in the dining room. The rooms are priced around $45 single and $55 double, including breakfast. Smoking isn't allowed, but pets are. Write to Compass Rose, North Head, Grand Manan, N.B. E0G 2M0, Canada, or phone (506) 662-8570 or (506) 446-5906 off-season.

The century-old **Marathon Inn** in North Head is relatively luxurious, complete with a heated swimming pool. Rates run from $49 to $89. Write to Marathon Inn, North Head, Grand Manan, N.B. E0G 2M0, Canada, or phone (506) 662-8144.

The **Fundy Folly Bed & Breakfast** offers no-smoking rooms plus breakfast for $45 double; write to them at Box 197, North Head, Grand Manan, N.B. E0G 2M0, Canada, or phone (506) 662-3731.

There are also inns or B&Bs in Seal Cove, including **Rosalie's Guest House** at $40 double (506-662-3344), and **McLaughlin's Wharf Inn**, a non-smoking establishment, for $60 (506-662-8760).

The only campground on Grand Manan, in **Anchorage Provincial Park**, is wheelchair accessible. It has 50 sites, with a little over half having partial service and the rest for tenters.

## GRAND MANAN ISLAND

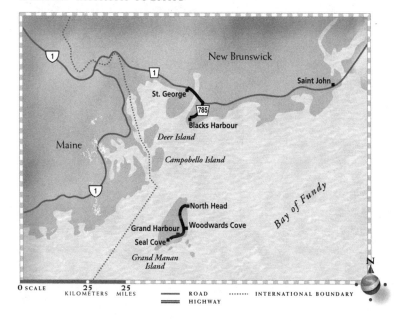

Write Anchorage Provincial Park, Grand Manan, N.B. E0G 3B0, Canada, or phone (506) 662-3215.

When it's time to eat, go for seafood, since fishing is the major occupation in this region. Restaurants on Grand Manan tend to be casual, including the **Griff-Inn** in North Head and the **Water's Edge** in Seal Cove, which serves homemade Italian dishes as well as seafood dinners. ◼

# 11
# PRINCE EDWARD ISLAND

Prince Edward Island is a tranquil place, with gently rolling hills and soft pink beaches that are among the best in Canada. Granted, it gets crowded in summer, when visitors swell the population of 130,400 fivefold; even so, long stretches of beach are deserted.

Situated in the Gulf of St. Lawrence, and separated from Nova Scotia and New Brunswick by the shallow Northumberland Strait, the crescent-shaped island is a mere 224 kilometers (135 miles) long and 60 kilometers (36 miles) wide at its widest point. Island life is based chiefly on the treasures of the sea and on farming the fertile red soil, notably potatoes, as well as on tourism. Canadians in other provinces generally refer to Prince Edward Island as "P.E.I.," while residents call it simply "the Island" and refer to nonresidents as being "from away." The Island has other names that reflect its history and character: the "Garden of the Gulf," the "Million-acre Farm," the "Cradle of Confederation," or, less lyrically, "Spud Island."

Part of P.E.I.'s unique character probably stems from its physical separation from the rest of the country. But this is going to change; a 14-kilometer (8½-mile) bridge is currently under construction and will replace the federally subsidized Borden-Cape Tormentine ferry service. Even after the bridge opens, the ferry linking the eastern end of P.E.I. with Nova Scotia will remain in service. ◪

# PRINCE EDWARD ISLAND

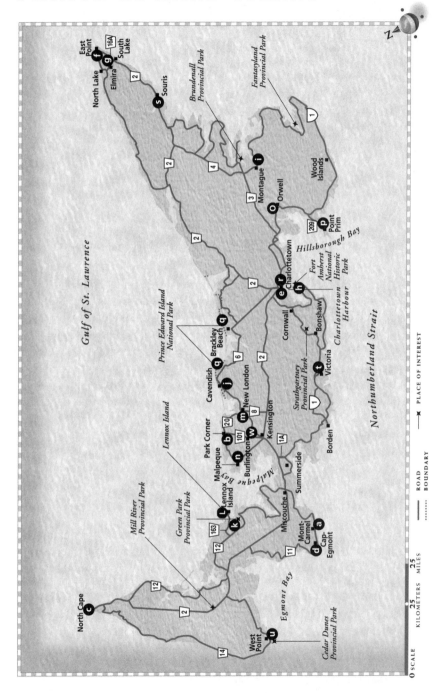

Gulf of St. Lawrence

East Point
South Lake
North Lake
Elmira
Souris
Brudenall Provincial Park
Fantasyland Provincial Park
Montague
Orwell
Wood Islands
Point Prim
Hillsborough Bay
Charlottetown
Fort Amberst National Historic Park
Cornwall
Bonshaw
Charlottetown Harbour
Prince Edward Island National Park
Brackley Beach
Cavendish
New London
Kensington
Strathgartney Provincial Park
Victoria
Lennox Island
Park Corner
Malpeque
Burlington
Borden
Northumberland Strait
Summerside
Miscouche
Mont-Carmel
Cap-Egmont
Mill River Provincial Park
Green Park Provincial Park
Lennox Island
Egmont Bay
North Cape
West Point
Cedar Dunes Provincial Park

SCALE
0    25    25
KILOMETERS    MILES

—— ROAD
········ BOUNDARY
✶ PLACE OF INTEREST

# SIGHTSEEING HIGHLIGHTS

**ⓐ** Acadian Pioneer Village

**ⓑ** Anne of Green Gables Museum at Silver Bush

**ⓒ** Atlantic Wind Test Site

**ⓓ** The Bottle Houses

**ⓔ** Confederation Centre Art Gallery and Museum

**ⓕ** East Point

**ⓖ** Elmira Railway Museum

**ⓗ** Fort Amherst/Port-La-Joye

**ⓘ** Garden of the Gulf Museum

**ⓙ** Green Gables House

**ⓚ** Green Park Provincial Park

**ⓛ** Lennox Island Micmac Nation

**ⓜ** Lucy Maud Montgomery Birthplace

**ⓝ** Malpeque Gardens

**ⓞ** Orwell Corner Historic Village

**ⓟ** Point Prim Lighthouse

**ⓠ** Prince Edward Island National Park

**ⓡ** Province House

**ⓢ** Souris

**ⓣ** Victoria

**ⓤ** West Point Lighthouse

**ⓦ** Woodleigh

## A PERFECT DAY ON PRINCE EDWARD ISLAND

I like to start off in Prince Edward Island National Park, where I can easily while away some lazy hours on the beach. Then I meander along Ladyslipper Drive, my favorite scenic route in the province because it hugs the shore pretty closely. Heading back to Charlottetown, I like to stop in the pretty little village of Victoria and browse through the quaint shops. Then it's off to find an all-you-can-eat lobster supper, put on by church and community groups across the island. Heaven!

## SOME P.E.I. HISTORY

French explorer Jacques Cartier described the Island in 1534 as "the fairest land that may possibly be seen," and indeed, its beauty helped provide Lucy Maud Montgomery with inspiration for her perennial bestseller, *Anne of Green Gables*. The coastline is indented with tidal inlets, steep sandstone bluffs, and long sandy beaches. But the most startling aspect of the island's topography is its rust-red soil, caused by heavy concentrations of iron oxide.

Some 8,000 to 10,000 years ago, ancestors of the Micmac Indians were the first humans to live in P.E.I., spending summers along the shore and feasting on the abundant shellfish. Eventually they stayed year-round, naming the island Abegweit, or "cradle in the waves." The first Europeans to arrive were the French, who began to settle the island in the 1720s. But after 1758, when Louisbourg (the capital of the French colony of Île Royal, or what is now Cape Breton Island) fell to the British, the Island was settled mainly by English, Scottish, and Irish immigrants. Today its population remains overwhelmingly British in origin; in fact it is arguably the most Celtic place in North America.

In 1864 representatives of Canada (Ontario and Quebec), Nova Scotia, New Brunswick, and P.E.I. met in Charlottetown to discuss federal union of the British North American colonies. It was the first of a series of meetings that led eventually to the Confederation of Canada. Charlottetown still calls itself the "Birthplace of Canada," even though when other colonies joined in the new federation in 1867, P.E.I. did not do so until 1873.

## ANNE OF GREEN GABLES

P.E.I.'s major claim to international fame, of course, is *Anne of Green Gables*, the novel by Lucy Maud Montgomery. Rescued from an orphanage, Anne wins the hearts of Matthew and Marilla Cuthbert and the community of Avonlea. But how could she not? She is articulate, plucky, sensitive, caring, and fiery, all at once. First published in 1908, the novel eventually won worldwide acclaim, and now some 1 million visitors descend each year on Green Gables House, the re-creation of the Cuthbert home in Cavendish, P.E.I. (see Sightseeing Highlights, below).

## GETTING TO PRINCE EDWARD ISLAND

Car ferries run from Cape Tormentine, New Brunswick, to Borden on Prince Edward Island. You don't pay to get onto the Island, you only pay when leaving it. Nor do you need to reserve a spot. In fact Marine Atlantic, which operates the ferry, won't take reservations. In peak season ferries leave every hour from 6:30 a.m. until 1:00 a.m. For a complete schedule of Marine Atlantic's various ferry routes, drop into a tourist information center or contact Marine Atlantic at its head office in North Sydney, N.S., at (902) 794-5700 from Canada or (800) 341-7981 from the U.S. The crossing takes about 45 minutes.

There is a tourist information center in Borden as soon as you get off the ferry, so if you don't already have the Visitors Guide put out by the provincial tourism board, stop in and pick one up. Then head for Charlottetown, the provincial capital, which I recommend as a base for your stay on the Island. Charlottetown is 56 kilometers (33 miles) from Borden on the TransCanada (Highway 1). It also has direct access to two of the island's three scenic drives and is only 60 kilometers (36 miles) from Wood Islands, where ferries cross to Nova Scotia.

## GETTING AROUND PRINCE EDWARD ISLAND

You can't go wrong as a visitor to P.E.I., which is geared towards looking after tourists. The *Prince Edward Island Visitors Guide*, a 200-page publication updated annually by the provincial tourist board, conveniently divides the island into three scenic drives: Lady Slipper Drive, around the western end of the island; Blue Heron Drive, around the central part; and Kings Byway Drive, around the eastern end. The routes are clearly marked both in the *Visitors Guide* and on the roads themselves. Blue Heron Drive is 190 kilometers (120 miles) long, Lady Slipper Drive 288 kilometers (180 miles), and Kings Byway 375 kilometers (234 miles). If you do go wrong, the worst thing that can happen is you go off down some side road and find red sandstone cliffs over a deserted beach or emerald hills rolling gently away towards the sea. P.E.I is so small that the sea is visible from most anywhere on the island, "if only in a tiny blue gap between distant hills," Lucy Maud Montgomery wrote, "or a turquoise gleam through the dark boughs of spruce fringing an estuary."

You needn't stick to the routes exactly. There are all manner of shortcuts if you want to skip some of the sights. For example, instead of following Lady Slipper Drive all the way around the western end of the island, you could travel up Highway 2 and make occasional forays to the coast. Have on hand a copy of the map of the province that comes with the *Visitors Guide*.

The Blue Heron Drive route is clearly marked with blue road signs featuring the silhouette of a heron. It follows a circular route around the center of P.E.I. Lady Slipper Drive is marked with red roadsigns depicting the lady slipper, P.E.I.'s provincial flower. The route winds around the contorted coastline of the western end of the island, providing views of red sandstone cliffs, pearly white beaches on the north shore, and red-sand beaches on the south shore. Part of Lady Slipper Drive also skirts Malpeque Bay, famous for its oyster beds. Kings Byway Drive is depicted by a crown and winds around the placid eastern end of Prince Edward Island, dotted with quiet fishing villages and tidy farming communities.

## SIGHTSEEING HIGHLIGHTS

✩✩✩ **Prince Edward Island National Park** • This park of lovely beaches, sand dunes, and sandstone cliffs runs in a narrow strip along 40 kilometers (24 miles) of the Island's north shore, facing the Gulf of St. Lawrence. Unfortunately, the incursion of tourists has done its share of damage here, and parts of the beach are closed to the public in summer to protect the Piping Plover, a small shorebird that has been declared an endangered species. Drive the Gulf Shore Parkway, which skirts the dunes, and stop to take one of the boardwalks and paths that lead to the water's edge (the boardwalks were built to protect the dunes from foot traffic). There is a park interpretive center at the Cavendish Visitor Centre at the western extremity of the park. Admission to the park is $6 per day per vehicle, $18 for a four-day pass or $30 for the season. Phone: (902) 963-2391 or 672-6350 in winter. (3 hours)

✩✩ **Acadian Pioneer Village (Mont-Carmel)** • This re-creation of the 1820s Acadian settlement of Mont-Carmel comes complete with

church, school, blacksmith shop, store, and houses. They're all log
structures; even the church's altar is made from logs. Open mid-June to
mid-September; $3.50 for adults and $2 for children. Address: Route
11 south of Miscouche, on Lady Slipper Drive south. Phone: (800)
567-3228. (2 hours)

★★ **Confederation Centre Art Gallery and Museum** • Housed in
the Confederation Centre of the Arts adjacent to Province House in
Charlottetown, the gallery's extensive permanent collection of works by
Canadian artists makes it one of Canada's major art galleries.
Admission is $3 for adults, $5 for families. Hours: From June to
September, 10:00 a.m. to 8:00 p.m. Phone: (902) 628-1864. (2 hours)

★★ **Green Gables House (Cavendish)** • If you loved *Anne of Green
Gables*, you naturally must visit Green Gables House, where author
Montgomery's cousins lived and on which she based her heroine's
house. It is now a museum that re-creates the house as described in the
novel. There is also an exhibit about the author and her works (there
were, in all, eight books about Anne). On the grounds outside, visitors
can explore the Haunted Wood, Lover's Lane, and other familiar set-
tings from the novel, not to mention the graves of Montgomery and
her husband. Expect to encounter hordes of visitors, including busloads
of Japanese tourists; they adore the novel and visit P.E.I. in great numbers to see Green Gables. The house is at the western end of Prince
Edward Island National Park. Open daily from mid-May to November
1. Admission is $2.50 for adults, $1.25 for kids, and $6 for families.
Phone: (902) 672-6350. (1 hour)

★★ **Province House (Charlottetown)** • This was the site of the historic 1864 Charlottetown Conference. Today it is a national historic
site; the Confederation Chamber where the meeting was held has been
restored to appear as it did in the 1800s. The building also houses the
provincial legislature. Entrance is free and regular guided tours are
available. Hours: Open weekdays year-round and daily from June
through August. Address: The corner of Great George and Richmond
Streets, right downtown. Phone: (902) 566-7626. (½ hour)

★★ **Victoria** • One of the few planned villages on the island, Victoria
has a neat, symmetrical layout. Nestled between hills and overlooking a
harbor, it's pleasantly quaint. The operating lighthouse has a museum
that relates Victoria's history, but mostly Victoria is just a nice place to

stroll around. Stop in at Island Chocolates if you're a chocoholic, and at The Studio Gallery for a sampling of photographs, batiks, etchings, and watercolors by local artists. (1 hour)

✸ **Anne of Green Gables Museum at Silver Bush (Park Corner)** • This was the home of Montgomery's uncle; she often visited it and her wedding was held in the drawing room. Now it contains an exhibit that includes the first editions of some of her books. Route 20. Open daily from June through October; $2.50 for adults, 75 cents for children under 16. Phone: (902) 886-2884 or 436-7329. (½ hour)

✸ **Atlantic Wind Test Site (North Cape)** • At the tip of the western end of the island is a series of wind turbines operated by the national wind test lab, which evaluates wind generators. At the visitors' center you can view a video and guides will answer questions. At the north end of Route 12, open daily in July and August. Admission is $2 for adults and $1 for seniors and students; children under 10 get in for free. Phone: (902) 882-2746. (½ hour)

✸ **The Bottle Houses (Cap-Egmont)** • These are so bizarre you must see them: a chapel, a house, and a tavern all made entirely of bottles cemented together. They are the work of the late Edouard Arsenault, a retired fisherman who began the project in the mid-1970s and used more than 25,000 bottles by the time he was through. You can go right inside each structure. Open daily from mid-June to late September, $3.25 for adults, $1 for children 6 to 16. Address: Lady Slipper Drive south, Route 11. Phone: (902) 854-2987. (½ hour)

✸ **East Point** • At the easternmost tip of the island, the East Point lighthouse is one of only three staffed lighthouses out of the island's 60-plus lighthouses. The others are at Souris and Wood Islands. Climb to the top and you'll have a view of the "meeting of the tides," where the waters of the Gulf of St. Lawrence and the Northumberland Strait meet and swirl together. Open June through early October; $2.50 for adults, $2 for seniors, $1 for children, and $4 for families. Phone: (902) 357-2106. (1 hour)

✸ **Elmira Railway Museum** • Once a real railway station, it's now a railway museum housing photos and information about the railway system of the nineteenth and early twentieth centuries. A must for railway buffs. Open mid-June to Labor Day; $2.50 for adults, $1.50 for kids.

Elmira is on Route 16A between North Lake and South Lake near the eastern extremity of the island. Phone: (902) 357-2481. (1½ hour)

✯ **Fort Amherst/Port-La-Joye** • Port-La-Joye (roughly, Joyous Port), the first French settlement on the island, was renamed Fort Amherst after it fell to the British in 1758. Only the earthworks of the original fort overlooking Charlottetown Harbour remain. It's a National Historic Site so there is an interpretive center that tells you all about it. Phone: (902) 675-2220. (½ hour)

✯ **Garden of the Gulf Museum (Montague)** • Some of the relics in this museum date back several centuries, such as a 1698 Bible. More recent artifacts include letters written by Lucy Maud Montgomery. Open mid-June to late September daily except Sunday; $2 for adults, free for children under 15. Address: Route 4 on the eastern coast of the island. Phone: (902) 838-2467. (1 hour)

✯ **Green Park Provincial Park** • A shipbuilding museum in the park traces the history of shipbuilding, the major industry on the island in the last century. Also worth seeing is Yeo House, the gabled Victorian home of James Yeo, wealthy owner of the shipyard that once occupied Green Park. Open June 15 to Labor Day; $2.50 for adults, free for children under 12. Address: Route 12 on Lady Slipper Drive north. Phone: (902) 831-2370 for the park and (902) 831-2206 for the museum. (½ hour)

✯ **Lennox Island Micmac Nation** • The Micmac families now living on the Lennox Island reserve are descendants of P.E.I.'s first human inhabitants. At the southern tip of the Island is a small museum with native artifacts and paintings, plus an arts-and-crafts shop nearby with silver, beaded jewelry, pottery, and carvings. From Route 12, take Route 163 to the island. Phone: (902) 831-2653. (½ hour)

✯ **Lucy Maud Montgomery Birthplace (New London)** • The author was born in 1874 in this house, which now contains period furniture and Montgomery memorabilia. It's at the intersection of Routes 6 and 8. Open June 1 to early October. Admission is $1 for adults and 50 cents for kids. Phone: (902) 963-2231. (½ hour)

✯ **Malpeque Gardens** • The gardens feature annuals and perennials, as well as the Anne of Green Gables Gardens with a miniature model of Green Gables surrounded by flower beds shaped to look like Anne's

flowered hat and other items from the novel. Open daily from mid-June
to mid-October; $4 for adults, $2 for children under 14. Address: Route
20 north of Kensington. Phone: (902) 836-5418. (1 hour)

✵✵ **Orwell Corner Historic Village** • A restored 1800s crossroads
farming village, Orwell Corner is now a historic site featuring farms, a
school, a church, and various other buildings. One of the most interesting structures is a farmhouse that also serves as a store and post
office and has a dressmaker's shop upstairs. All the buildings have been
restored and all are on their original sites. Open mid-May to mid-
October; $3 for adults, free for children under 12. Address: Off the
TransCanada 30 kilometers east of Charlottetown; just follow the
signs. Phone: (902) 651-2013. (2 hours)

✵ **Point Prim Lighthouse** • Built in 1845, the oldest lighthouse on
the island is still in use. It's also billed as the only round brick structure
in Canada. The lantern house at the peak provides a view over
Northumberland Strait. Open mid-June to Labor Day; free admission.
Address: Point Prim at the end of Route 209, 10 kilometers (6 miles)
south of the TransCanada between Orwell and Wood Islands. Phone:
(902) 659-2672. (½ hour)

✵ **Souris** • Souris, oddly enough, means "mice" in English. This fishing port and ferry terminal may have been so named after it was overrun with plagues of field mice in the 1800s. Souris is the terminal for
ferries to and from Quebec's Magdalen Islands (more correctly, Îles-de-
la-Madeleine), an archipelago of windswept but charming islands in the
middle of the Gulf of St. Lawrence that are closer to P.E.I. and Nova
Scotia than to Quebec. Aside from the ferry service to and from Souris,
the Magdalens are accessible only by ferry from Carleton on the Gaspé
Peninsula or by plane from Montreal, Halifax, Gaspé, or Quebec City.
If you have the time, the islands are well worth roaming around, with
their long sand dunes, cliffs, lagoons, bright wooden houses, and hos-
pitable inhabitants. (For more information on the Magdalens, contact
Quebec's tourist information line at 800-363-7777.) (½ hour)

✵ **West Point Lighthouse (Cedar Dunes Provincial Park)** • This
black-and-white-striped structure, now a museum, was built in 1875
and offers a fine view across the park's red dunes to Northumberland
Strait. Route 14 in the park. Open daily from mid-May to mid-

September; $2 for adults, $1.25 for children, $1.65 for seniors, $6 for families. Phone: (902) 859-3605. (½ hour)

☆ **Woodleigh (Burlington)** • Woodleigh is a collection of large-scale models of historic British buildings and castles, painstakingly hand-constructed by the late (and presumably eccentric) Lt. Col. E. W. Johnston. You'll find the Tower of London, and Dunvegan Castle, among other famous structures, plus a Shakespeare section with replicas of his mother's home and Anne Hathaway's cottage in Stratford-upon-Avon. Some replicas are large enough to walk into and are furnished with authentic items imported from Britain. Open daily from late May to mid-October; $7.35 for adults, $6.75 for seniors, $4.10 for children from 6 to 12. Address: Route 101 north of Kensington. Phone: (902) 836-5418. (2 hours)

## FITNESS AND RECREATION

Prince Edward Island seems custom-made for cyclists. It's not flat exactly, but the slopes are gentle. And it rarely gets really hot, what with all those ocean breezes. You needn't stick to the roads, either—miles of abandoned rail lines have been converted into a network of trails for hikers and cyclists. For information on cycling day tours, call **Sport PEI** at (902) 368-4110. Hikers won't find anything really challenging, but the national park has marked trails ranging from 1 to 8 kilometers. Four provincial parks—**Green Park**, **Mill River**, **Strathgartney**, and **Brudenell**—also have marked trails. The island is dotted with golf courses; call **Golf Prince Edward Island** at (902) 368-4130 or the tourist information line for details.

## FOOD

Surrounded by waters abundant with lobsters, mackerel, scallops, mussels, oysters, and clams, the entire island is clearly a seafood lover's paradise. (This is not to say you can't eat other types of meals; even the seafood restaurants tend to offer steak as well). Partake of a lobster supper if you can. These all-you-can-eat feasts of lobster, fresh vegetables, and homemade breads are offered by many local church and community groups. You'll see ads for them all over the place.

In Charlottetown, dining options range from the aforementioned seafood to Chinese and pub-style dining. **Smitty's Family Restaurant**

# CHARLOTTETOWN

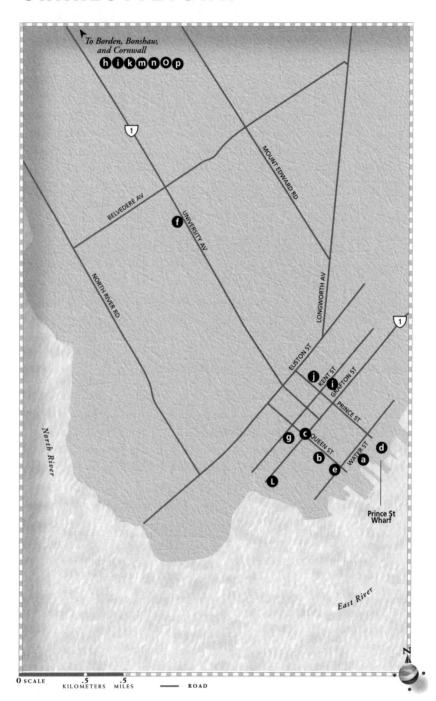

To Borden, Bonshaw, and Cornwall

North River

East River

MOUNT EDWARD RD

BELVEDERE AV

UNIVERSITY AV

NORTH RIVER RD

LONGWORTH AV

EUSTON ST

KENT ST

GRAFTON ST

PRINCE ST

QUEEN ST

WATER ST

Prince St Wharf

0 SCALE · .5 · .5
KILOMETERS · MILES · ROAD

N

# Food

**ⓐ** Anchor & Oar House

**ⓑ** Canton Cafe

**ⓒ** Courtyard Restaurant

**ⓓ** Lobsterman's Landing

**ⓔ** The Merchantman Pub

**ⓕ** Smitty's Family Restaurant

# Lodging

**ⓖ** The Charlottetown

**ⓗ** Chez Nous Bed & Breakfast

**ⓘ** Dalvay-By-The-Sea Country Inn

**ⓙ** The Duchess of Kent Inn

**ⓚ** Dunrovin Lodge Cottages and Farms

**ⓛ** Heritage Harbour House

**ⓜ** Shaw's Hotel

**ⓝ** Strathgartney Country Inn

**ⓞ** Windsong Farm

# Camping

**ⓟ** Strathgartney Provincial Park

at 449 University Avenue offers a wide range of fare plus children's and seniors' menus (902-892-5752). For Chinese, there's the **Canton Cafe** at 73 Queen Street (902-892-2527). The specialty at **Lobsterman's Landing** on the Prince Street Wharf is self-evident (902-368-2888). **The Merchantman Pub** on the corner of Queen and Water Streets is a good bet for a light meal (902-892-9150), while the **Anchor & Oar House** on the boardwalk beside the Prince Edward Hotel serves up seafood and hamburgers from mid-May to mid-October (902-566-2222). Culture vultures might want to try the **Courtyard Restaurant** in the Confederation Center of the Arts, which features a varied menu for adults, a special menu for children, and a view of the Sculpture Court (902-628-6107).

## LODGING

P.E.I. has numerous country inns, B&Bs, farm vacation homes, and seaside cottages. Many are open only in season, meaning generally May to October. Following are some suggestions in Charlottetown or within about 20 minutes of it, on or close to the Blue Heron route.

**Dunrovin Lodge Cottages and Farms**, with a large lawn, a barn kids can play in, and a horse they can ride, is especially suitable for families. It overlooks the village of Victoria, about a third of the way to Charlottetown from Borden on the TransCanada. Pets are welcome. Room rates begin at $37; call Mrs. Kay (MacQuarrie) Wood at (902) 658-2375. In Bonshaw, about 10 kilometers further east on the TransCanada, the **Strathgartney Country Inn** is a 100-year-old homestead set amid 30 acres of countryside and gardens. Rates at this smoke-free establishment range from $69 to $125; call (902) 675-4711. In Cornwall, 10 minutes east of Charlottetown, **Chez Nous Bed & Breakfast**, a rambling country house set among birch and maple trees, has four spacious guest rooms and a solarium where breakfast is served. Rates are $55 to $70; call Sandi and Paul Gallant at (902) 566-2779.

In Charlottetown, **The Duchess of Kent Inn** is an 1875 designated heritage home that's now a three-star bed and breakfast inn, with eight guest rooms and period furniture throughout. Rates are $48 to $60; no smoking. Call (902) 566-5826. **Heritage Harbour House**, another historic property, is in a quiet area downtown. Rates start at $55; no smoking. Call (902) 892-6633. If you want real luxury in Charlottetown, stay at **The Charlottetown**, a grandly elegant hotel built by the Canadian National Railway in 1930–31.

It's accessible by wheelchair with assistance. Pets are permitted. Rates range from $101 to $141; call (800) 565-7633.

In Brackley Beach on the north shore, 20 kilometers (12 miles) northwest of Charlottetown on Highway 15, **Windsong Farm** is a pre-Victorian farmhouse nestled in the countryside with antique-furnished guest rooms. Rates are $55 to $65 and no smoking is allowed; call Jean and John Huck at (902) 672-2874. Or try **Shaw's Hotel**, a white-shingled, red-roofed 1860 building that claims to be Canada's oldest continuously family-operated inn. Pets are welcome. Rates for rooms run from $170 to $190; call (902) 672-2022.

Finally, **Dalvay-By-The-Sea Country Inn** is renowned for its dining room, but the rest of the inn is attractive too. None of the 26 guest rooms in the gingerbready Victorian mansion has a telephone, radio, or TV, and the main activity is relaxing. It's wheelchair accessible with assistance. Pets are permitted. The inn is near the eastern boundary of Prince Edward Island National Park, which runs along the central north shore. From Charlottetown, about 20 minutes away, take Highway 2 east for 10 kilometers (6 miles) and turn left on Highway 6. From Highway 6, turn off into the park. Rates range from $150 to $270; call (902) 672-2048.

You might also want to consider staying on a farm. Island farm families have opened their homes to guests for many years. They're all working farms and most have housekeeping units or cottages on their land. *Farm Vacations*, a pamphlet from the Prince Edward Island Farm Vacation Association, lists more than 24 such establishments around the island; call the provincial tourist information line for a copy. Individual farm homes are also listed in the province's visitors guide.

No matter what kind of accommodation you choose, reservations are advised, especially in July and August.

## CAMPING

There are campgrounds and trailer parks throughout the province; 13 are in provincial parks and three in Prince Edward Island National Park, while some three dozen are privately run. One of the most convenient ones for this itinerary is in **Strathgartney Provincial Park**, 20 kilometers (12 miles) southwest of Charlottetown on the TransCanada, with rates of $14 and $17 and grounds that include a nature trail and playground. The campground is wheelchair accessible with assistance. Phone: (902) 675-3599.

Campgrounds in provincial parks accept reservations through any of the province's tourist information centers scattered around the island, or write to Provincial Parks, Box 2000, Charlottetown, P.E.I., Canada C1A 7N8. National park campgrounds do not accept reservations, but visitor information centers can supply information about vacancies. In the case of privately operated campgrounds, call direct.

## SHOPPING

In addition to the usual goods, more than 80 craft outlets throughout the island offer everything from pottery and woodworking to hand-painted silk. There are also antique shops aplenty.

There is a 10-percent provincial sales tax on most purchases, including accommodations (except campgrounds) and restaurant meals. Clothing and shoes are exempt to a limit of $100 apiece.

## THEATER

Many visitors consider the musical *Anne of Green Gables* a must. In summer it's performed nightly at the **Confederation Centre of the Arts** as part of the annual Charlottetown Festival. Call (902) 566-1267 or (800) 565-0278 from New Brunswick, Nova Scotia, and P.E.I.

## HELPFUL HINTS

P.E.I.'s tourism industry is geared in many ways toward families with young kids, and you'll find all manner of amusement parks. Just for starters, there is Santa's Woods, a Christmas theme park; Fantasyland Provincial Park, featuring statues of storybook characters and a fort-shaped playhouse; and P.E.I. Fairyland, where visitors can take a mile-long ride on a miniature train.

For the visitors guide, contact Prince Edward Island Tourism, Visitor Services, P.O. Box 940, Charlottetown, P.E.I., C1A 7M5, or phone (800) 463-4PEI. The Tour the Island Visitor Information Centre in Oak Tree Place on University Avenue in Charlottetown is open year-round. Seven other provincial tourist information centers operate seasonally, in Borden, Portage, Summerside, Cavendish, Wood Islands, Montague, and Souris. Privately operated tourist information centers are also scattered around the island.

Finally, Charlottetown Visitor Information Center is at Queen and Kent Streets downtown; the phone number is (902) 566-5548.

# 12
# HALIFAX

Halifax, capital of Nova Scotia, is a seafaring city of 115,000 on the south-central coast. The event that most people connect with it is the famous Halifax Explosion of December 6, 1917. On that wartime morning, the French munitions ship *Mont Blanc* barely bumped the Belgian relief ship *Imo* in the Halifax harbor and exploded with the most powerful man-made blast in history before the atom bomb. The ship's anchor flew almost 3 kilometers (2 miles). The blast shattered windows as far away as Truro, some 100 kilometers (60 miles) to the northeast, and was heard on Prince Edward Island. It also emptied the harbor beneath the *Mont Blanc*'s keel, creating a tidal wave that roared up city streets. When the horror was over, more than 1,600 people were dead and 9,000 injured. One-fifth of the seaport, which had a population of 50,000 at the time, was devastated.

Today, Halifax is the largest city in Atlantic Canada and sits on one of the largest harbors in the world. The central part of the city occupies a fat peninsula of land girded by Bedford Basin to the north, a long, slender inlet called the Northwest Arm to the southwest, and Halifax Harbor and the Atlantic to the south. Across the Narrows, which link Bedford Basin and Halifax Harbor, lies the city of Dartmouth. Commuter ferries cross regularly between the two cities.

Halifax is also the cultural center of Nova Scotia, offering all manner of music, art, and theater. It further boasts that it has the highest ratio of educational facilities per capita of any city in North America, and because it is a university town, there are numerous second-hand bookstores and a lively nightlife. In 1995 another crowd-pleaser opened in town: a casino.

# HALIFAX

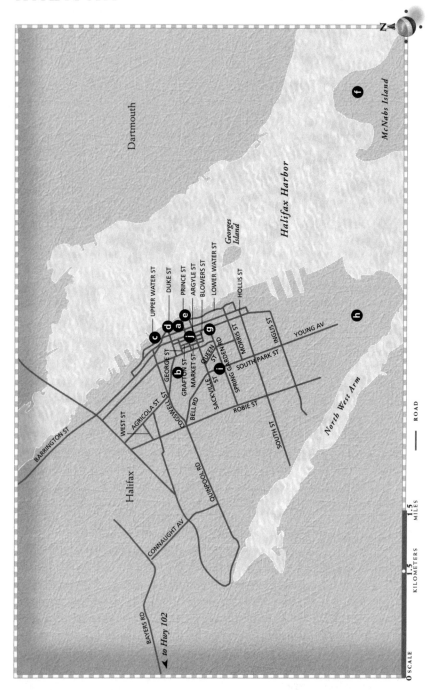

Dartmouth

McNabs Island

**f**

Halifax Harbor

Georges Island

UPPER WATER ST
DUKE ST
PRINCE ST
ARGYLE ST
BLOWERS ST
LOWER WATER ST
HOLLIS ST

**c**
**d**
**a**
**e**
**j**
**g**

GEORGE ST
MARKET ST
QUEEN RD
MORRIS ST
INGLIS ST
YOUNG AV

**b**
GRAFTON ST
SACKVILLE ST
SPRING GARDEN RD
SOUTH PARK ST

**i**

**h**

AGRICOLA ST
WEST ST
BARRINGTON ST
TOBIN ST
BELL RD
ROBIE ST
SOUTH ST

North West Arm

Halifax

QUINPOOL RD

CONNAUGHT AV

BAYERS RD

▶ to Hwy 102

0 SCALE

1.5
KILOMETERS

1.5
MILES

——— ROAD

## Sightseeing Highlights

**ⓐ** Art Gallery of Nova Scotia

**ⓑ** Halifax Casino

**ⓒ** The Halifax Citadel

**ⓓ** Historic Properties

**ⓔ** The Maritime Museum of the Atlantic

**ⓕ** McNabs Island

**ⓖ** The Old Burying Ground

**ⓗ** Point Pleasant Park

**ⓘ** Public Gardens

**ⓙ** St. Paul's Anglican Church

## A PERFECT DAY IN HALIFAX

The glorious Halifax Public Gardens are perfect for a morning stroll, followed by a wander along Spring Garden Road to check out the trendy shops. After lunch at one of the waterfront restaurants, I'd wander through Historic Properties and finish up at the Maritime Museum of the Atlantic, which I find fascinating. Then it would be dinner, either at the Granite Brewery to get in the mood for the pub crawl later, or a splurge on seafood at The Five Fishermen.

## NOVA SCOTIA

Nova Scotia, an elongated peninsula that hangs beneath New Brunswick, has a vaguely lobster-like shape on a map. Inland, there are fertile river valleys, glaciated rock formations, and, on Cape Breton Island at the northeastern end of the province, highlands that are eerily reminiscent of Scotland. Nova Scotia is only 560 kilometers (340 miles) long and never more than 130 kilometers (78 miles) wide, but its serrated coastline runs for 7,400 kilometers (4,600 miles) past harbors, inlets, bays, long beaches, and rugged cliffs. Its physical beauty has made tourism into a major industry; in fact after a few days in Nova Scotia, a traveling companion remarked that the province is really one big tourist trap. But he didn't mean it in a negative way; it had taken him a while even to realize it. While the province is markedly geared towards tourism, it manages for the most part to be tasteful about it.

Colonial Nova Scotia changed hands several times as the British and French fought over it. At one point in the mid-1700s, the British expelled 6,000 French-speaking Acadians from Nova Scotia; the "Cajuns" in modern-day Louisiana are descended from some of those deportees. Some Acadians eventually returned to Nova Scotia, and French is still spoken in parts of the province, notably on the north-west coast.

The French were finally defeated after building the magnificent Fortress of Louisbourg on Cape Breton Island. The British later ordered the fortress destroyed, but it is now slowly being reconstructed and is open to visitors.

Nova Scotia drew settlers mainly from Britain, although an influx of German Protestants led to the founding of German-flavored Lunenberg, famous for both its shipbuilding and its annual Octoberfest. Thousands of New Englanders and, later, Loyalists also came to Nova Scotia from south of the border. The indigenous people, the Micmacs, were decimated by European diseases and territorial clashes and now number about 10,000. The major industries are fishing, agriculture, mining (mainly coal) and forestry. And, of course, tourism.

## GETTING AROUND HALIFAX

Walking is the way to go in Halifax. The major sights are all in a fairly compact area in the center of the city. Begin at the Citadel and work your way down toward the waterfront. If you get lost in central Halifax and can't see a street name, walk to the nearest corner and look down: the names of streets are carved into the sidewalk at each corner.

On the other hand, parking isn't the problem in Halifax that it is in some other Canadian cities. If you want to drive, there is parking both at the Citadel and at Historic Properties.

There is a provincial tourist information center in the Red Store Building in Historic Properties, while Tourism Halifax runs a year-round information center in City Hall at the corner of Barrington and Duke Streets and a seasonal information center in the Public Gardens at the top of Sackville Street.

## SIGHTSEEING HIGHLIGHTS

✩✩✩ **The Halifax Citadel** • This star-shaped fortress provides not just a history lesson but a dramatic view of the city and harbor below. Halifax was for years the bastion of British imperial control in North America. The present fortress, constructed between 1828 and 1856, is actually the fourth citadel on this site. The previous fortifications date back to 1749, the year Halifax was founded. The citadel was never attacked. When the British garrison finally departed in 1906, the site was handed over to the Canadian militia. It was manned by Canadian forces during both world wars and, during World War Two, served as a temporary barracks for troops heading overseas. It was declared a national historic park in 1956.

In summer, soldiers in nineteenth-century uniforms drill on the parade grounds, and there's usually a bagpiper on hand. The firing of the noon gun is worth seeing. (On my last visit, the gun misfired, much to the crowd's amusement. Disconcerted soldiers assured spectators that it almost never happens.) There are sentries, vaulted barracks, and a musketry gallery. For the best view of the city and the Old Town Clock, go up on the ramparts. The Old Town Clock, almost as much a Halifax landmark as the Citadel, was completed in 1803 and served as the garrison clock. It's so big it blocks part of the view of the city. Guided tours of the Citadel leave every half-hour between 9:30 a.m. and 5:00 p.m. from near the entrance. Admission is $5 for adults, $2.50 for children 6 to 16, $3.75 for seniors, and free for children under 5. Hours: 9:00 a.m. to 5:00 p.m., May 15 to November 30. Phone: (902) 426-5080. (2 hours)

✩✩✩ **Historic Properties** • This is a picturesque waterfront complex of boutiques, restaurants, and pubs in ten restored wood-and-stone buildings that date back to the early 1800s and are said to be Canada's oldest waterfront buildings. With a waterside boardwalk and outdoor cafés, it's a nice area just to stroll, even if you're not in a shopping mood. This is also where harbor cruises depart from. Take one; you get to see much more of the cityscape, including Point Pleasant Park at the southern end of the city and McNabs Island in the harbor. Evening cruises are available as well. Prices for a 2-hour cruise on the Harbor Queen are $15 for adults, $14 for seniors, $12 for youths 13 to 18, and $9.50 for kids from 5 to 12 years old. The family rate is $29.50, while a dinner cruise costs $29.50 per person. If you haven't time for a 2-hour cruise, take the ferry across to Dartmouth and back; the ferry terminal is just south of

Historic Properties, and the 7-minute round-trip provides a good view
of the skyline and some of the harbor for $2. Historic Properties is off
Upper Water Street at the base of Duke Street. (2 hours)

★★★ **The Maritime Museum of the Atlantic** • If for nothing else,
stop in here to see an exhibit called Halifax Wrecked: The Story of the
Halifax Explosion. It takes up only one small corner of the museum
and it is fascinating, perhaps because the story of the explosion is so
compelling. The display includes photographs, artifacts (such as a
comb and pencil belonging to school kids), and a 17-minute video
about the disastrous event. Elsewhere in the museum is a collection of
quite extraordinary ship models plus some real life-size boats, ranging
from Queen Victoria's royal barge and a beautiful *Bluenose*-class sloop
to a couple of dories (small boats used aboard fishing schooners
because they were easily hoisted and lowered and could carry two men,
their gear, and the catch). Upstairs, a display called The Age of Steam
has models of everything from Arctic patrol vessels and Great Lakes
freighters to magnificent Cunard liners. (Company founder Samuel
Cunard was born in Halifax.) Berthed at the dock outside the museum
is the C.S.S. *Acadia*, a onetime hydrographic survey vessel that is now a
museum ship. Admission is $3 for adults, 50 cents for kids 5 to 16, and
$6.50 for families. Hours: 9:30 a.m. to 5:30 p.m. Monday to Saturday
(to 8:00 p.m. on Tuesday); 1:00 to 5:30 p.m. Sunday, from June to mid-
October; slightly different hours the rest of the year. Address: 1675
Lower Water Street between Prince and Sackville Streets.
Phone: (902) 424-7490. (2 hours)

★★★ **Public Gardens** • The peaceful and picturesque Public Gardens
lie just to the southwest of Citadel Hill at the corner of Spring Garden
Road and South Park Street. Formal Victorian gardens, lush with
roses, hibiscus, dracaenas, and other varieties, are laid out around a
lovely Victorian bandstand where there are musical performances on
Sunday afternoons. The gardens are open from spring to late fall, and
admission is free. (1 hour)

★★ **Art Gallery of Nova Scotia** • The permanent collection includes
mainly Nova Scotian artists but gives some space to Canadian, British,
and European works as well. There is also an extensive folk-art section
on the mezzanine level. Temporary exhibits change every 6 to 12
weeks. Admission is free but donations are welcome. Hours: 10:00 a.m.
to 5:00 p.m. Tuesday to Saturday, 10:00 a.m. to 9:00 p.m. Thursday,

12:00 noon to 5:30 p.m. Sunday, closed Monday. Address: 1741 Hollis Street, between George and Prince Streets, not far from Historic Properties. Phone: (902) 424-7542. (1½ hours)

★★ **McNabs Island** • There are nearly 20 kilometers (about 12 miles) of bicycle trails leading to beaches, past old forts, and through wilderness on historic McNabs Island, just inside the entrance to Halifax Harbor. In fact there are no vehicles on the island, nor services of any kind, so pack a picnic lunch. McNabs is famous for its Hangman's Beach, so named because 100 years ago the British used to punish errant soldiers by tarring them and hanging them, leaving them swinging above the beach as a warning to sailors coming in and out of town. The ruins of Fort McNab are another historical highlight. A ferry for the island departs at 9:00 a.m. daily from Murphy's On The Water on the Halifax waterfront.

★★ **St. Paul's Anglican Church** • Constructed in 1750, St. Paul's is the oldest standing building in Halifax as well as the oldest Protestant church in Canada. Its greatest claim to fame is the third window on the right on the upper level after you enter the church. You'll notice immediately there seems to be a silhouette of a man's profile etched on the pane. Local lore has it that a piece of flying debris crashed through this window during the Halifax Explosion and left a hole whose outline duplicates the profile of the parson of the day, who was killed in the explosion. To get to St. Paul's, walk down Prince or George Street to Argyle Street. Address: the Grand Parade between Barrington and Argyle Streets. The Grand Parade, a one-time parade ground in the middle of the city, has ample green space and often hosts live entertainment in summer. (15 minutes)

★ **Halifax Casino** • The first casino to open in Atlantic Canada is in the Sheraton Hotel. It has hundreds of slots, blackjack tables, and roulette wheels. A bigger casino is expected to open in Halifax in 1998. Address: 1919 Upper Water Street. (5 minutes to hours at a time, depending on your tastes)

★ **The Old Burying Ground** • The oldest burial ground in Halifax, located on Barrington Street and the corner of Spring Garden Road, has gravestones dating as far back as 1754. It was declared a national historic site in 1991 and is being gradually restored as an outdoor museum and park. (15 minutes)

☆ **Point Pleasant Park** • The other major green oasis in Halifax is Point Pleasant Park at the southern tip of the city. With an unimpeded view of the Atlantic Ocean and miles of paths, it's a perfect place for a picnic, a walk, or a swim off Black Rock beach. No cars are permitted inside the park, but there is ample parking at both eastern and western entrances. (2 hours)

## FITNESS AND RECREATION

McNab's Island and Point Pleasant Park are good for cycling, jogging, walking, or swimming. A couple of places in Dartmouth rent kayaks and offer kayak tours; call Mayak Ventures at (902) 463-9639 or Regal Tours at (902) 468-8183. There are several diving clubs in Halifax-Dartmouth. In fact some 3,000 shipwrecks have occurred along Nova Scotia's rocky shores over the centuries, so the entire province offers interesting opportunities for scuba diving. Passport to Diving, a booklet listing dive sites, clubs, and air stations around the province, is put out by the Nova Scotia Underwater Council; call (902) 425-5450. For information on other outdoor sporting activities, call Sport Nova Scotia in Halifax at (902) 425-5450.

## FOOD

The Privateer's Warehouse is a three-restaurant complex in Historic Properties; the higher you go, the higher the prices. The Lower Deck is a pub on the ground floor, with long communal tables and inexpensive, fresh seafood; call (902) 425-1501. The Middle Deck offers ocean views and local food; call (902) 425-1500. Bradley's, on the upper deck, serves dishes such as smoked salmon tartar appetizer and other culinary delights, all at upscale prices; call (902) 422-1289.

Other noteworthy seafood places (and seafood is naturally the way to go in Halifax) include **The Five Fishermen**, housed in a 175-year-old building at 1740 Argyle Street at the corner of George Street (902-422-4421), and **Salty's**, a two-level place at the end of the Historic Properties Pier with pub-style dining downstairs and seafood aplenty upstairs (902-423-6818).

But Halifax has other types of restaurants too. The **Granite Brewery** serves bitters, stout, and other beers along with pub-style food in a warm atmosphere at 1222 Barrington Street. There's a vegetarian restaurant, **Satisfaction Feast**, at 1581 Grafton Street (902-

422-3540). **The Green Bean Coffeehouse** serves excellent coffee and food at 5220 Blowers Street. A large complex of interconnected restaurant-bars at 1740 Argyle Street at the corner of George Street includes **The Atrium**, **My Apartment**, and **Cheers**. If you can't immediately decide what kind of food or decor you want, wander through the place until something strikes your fancy.

## LODGING

Staying in one of Halifax's attractive old inns is a good bet for their prices, their atmosphere, and their central locations. The **Waverley Inn** is a charming antique-furnished Victorian establishment at 1266 Barrington Street, with double rooms running from $60 to $90, including breakfast; call (902) 423-9346. The **King Edward Inn** at 5780 West Street is another Victorian-style inn with room rates ranging from $59 to $83; call (902) 422-3266. The **Queen Street Inn** at 1266 Queen Street is in an old stone house near downtown, with rates running around $50 for a double. No smoking, no pets, and no children allowed; call (902) 422-9828.

At the upscale end of things, the **Halifax Sheraton** is right in the heart of the action on Upper Water Street next to the Historic Properties area. Double rooms begin around $165; phone (902) 421-1700 or (800) 325-3535. The **Delta Barrington** is less pricey but also right next to Historic Properties and it offers no-smoking rooms. Room rates begin around $90; call (902) 429-7410 or (800) 268-1133 from Canada, or (800) 877-1133 from the U.S. The **Château Halifax** at 1990 Barrington Street offers doubles for $125 to $160; call (902) 425-6700 or (800) 441-1414. At the **Prince George Hotel**, 1725 Market Street, double rooms begin around $160; call (902) 425-1986 or (800) 565-1567.

The 300-page visitors guide published by the Nova Scotia Department of Tourism and Culture contains pages and pages of accommodations listings, conveniently broken down by location. There is also a handy brochure from the Metropolitan Area Tourism Association called *Guide to Bed and Breakfast and Country Inns of Metropolitan Halifax-Dartmouth*, listing more than 30 B&Bs and inns.

The province's tourist information line doubles as a booking service called Check In. You can reserve hotels, motels, inns, bed and breakfasts, resorts, campgrounds, and car rentals simply by calling the number, but have a particular place or two in mind before phoning to make a reservation. From Canada, the phone number is (800) 565-0000; from the U.S., (800) 341-6096; and in Halifax, (902) 425-5781.

# HALIFAX

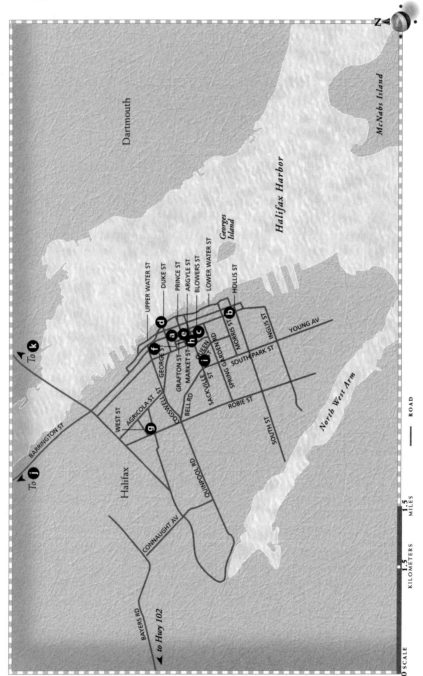

# Food

**ⓐ** The Atrium

**ⓑ** Cheers

**ⓒ** The Five Fishermen

**ⓓ** Granite Brewery

**ⓔ** The Green Bean Coffeehouse

**ⓕ** My Apartment

**ⓖ** The Privateer's Warehouse

**ⓗ** Salty's

**ⓘ** Satisfaction Feast

# Lodging

**ⓙ** Chateau Halifax

**ⓚ** Delta Barrington

**ⓛ** Halifax Sheraton

**ⓜ** King Edward Inn

**ⓝ** Prince George Hotel

**ⓞ** Queen Street Inn

**ⓟ** Waverley Inn

# Camping

**ⓠ** Laurie Provincial Park

**ⓡ** Shubie Park

**ⓢ** Woodhaven Park

**ⓣ** Colonial Camping

# CAMPING

Nova Scotia has an abundance of campgrounds in its two national parks (Kejimkujik in the center of southwestern Nova Scotia and Cape Breton Highlands National Park), in some provincial parks, and in more than 100 privately run operations.

There are four campgrounds within easy driving distance of Halifax-Dartmouth. **Laurie Provincial Park** is a wooded campground on Route 2 at Grand Lake. Rates begin at $9; call (902) 861-1623. **Shubie Park** is on Route 318 in Dartmouth and offers swimming, fishing, nature trails, a play area, and a tennis court. Rates begin at $14; call (902) 435-8328. **Woodhaven Park** is a wooded campground on Hammonds Plains Road. Rates are $15 and up; call (902) 835-2271. **Colonial Camping** in Upper Sackville is on a river and offers swimming, boating, a playground, boat rental, and mini-golf. Rates begin at $11.50; call (902) 865-4342.

# NIGHTLIFE

This is a port city, so consider a pub crawl. Pick up a copy of a *Halifax Pub Guide* from the tourist office in the Old Red Store and start crawling. The aforementioned Privateer's Warehouse in Historic Properties is popular for drinking as well as eating, since two of its three levels offer live music in the evenings. A guitarist or jazz group plays from 10:00 p.m. to midnight, Monday through Saturday, at the Middle Deck (902-425-1500). Things are more boisterous one floor below, at the Lower Deck (902-425-1501), where a singer leads the crowd in maritime folk songs from 9:00 p.m. on.

Culture vultures also have ample choice, with professional concerts and drama offered by the Neptune Theater, the Dalhousie University Arts Centre, and Symphony Nova Scotia. Check the *Chronicle-Herald* or the *Mail Star* for up-to-date listings.

# SHOPPING

Halifax's smartest shops are on the Granville Promenade, on Granville Street north of Duke Street. The promenade has been restored and is part of Historic Properties.

## FESTIVALS

N ova Scotia likes to call itself the Festival Province because it offers something like 350 festivals a year. In Halifax-Dartmouth, the most interesting summertime fests include the Summer Entertainment Series of outdoor concerts, running in Dartmouth throughout July; the Festival of Light fireworks extravaganza jointly hosted by both cities around mid-July; Yarmouth's Seafest, a seaside festival the third week of July; the annual Atlantic Jazz Festival in Halifax around the same time; and Halifax's International Buskerfest the second week of August. The Nova Scotia visitors guide contains long listings of what's afoot throughout the province.

## SIDE TRIP FROM HALIFAX

T he Marine Drive runs from Halifax along the length of the southeastern coast (the so-called eastern shore) and around the shore of Chedabucto Bay to Antigonish. This is a coastal drive all the way, zigzagging along bays, inlets, headlands, beaches, and coves, and is about 340 kilometers (200 miles) long. It is a particularly unspoiled part of the province, with no big tourist resorts or amusement parks to mar the landscape.

Noteworthy stops include the **Black Cultural Centre** in Westphal and the **Railway Museum** in Musquodoboit Harbour. A smokehouse at Tangier produces smoked salmon, mackerel, and eels. **Sherbrooke Village**, a restored riverside pioneer village that is part of the provincial museums system, is a short sidetrip from the Marine Drive.

## HELPFUL HINTS

T he provincial tourist information line, Check In, can make lodging and car rental reservations and supply all manner of information, chiefly in the bulky annual visitors guide titled *Nova Scotia—The Doers and Dreamers Complete Guide*. Another handy publication, at least for travelers who enjoy fine dining, is a booklet titled *Taste of Nova Scotia*. The numbers for Check-In are (800) 565-0000 from Canada and (800) 341-6096 from the United States. In Halifax, the local phone number is 425-5781. Tourism Halifax's phone number is (902) 421-8736.

# 13
# THE LIGHTHOUSE ROUTE

The Lighthouse Route runs along the south coast from Halifax to just before Yarmouth, at the western tip of the Nova Scotia, through such remarkably picturesque towns as Peggy's Cove, Mahone Bay, and Lunenburg. From Halifax, follow Highway 333 to Peggy's Cove. After that, just follow the road signs for the Lighthouse Route (silhouette of a lighthouse) to Yarmouth. Yarmouth is the province's largest seaport east of Halifax, and also the terminal for the ferry service from Bar Harbour and Portland, Maine. Downtown, many nineteenth-century buildings have been preserved. The Yarmouth County Museum at 22 Collins Street displays model ships and paintings and is home to one of the largest collections of this kind in Canada.

The average driving speed on the Lighthouse Route is about 70 kilometers an hour (42 mph), so you'll pretty much have to take your time. But you'll find you want to linger often along the way anyway. ◼

# THE LIGHTHOUSE ROUTE

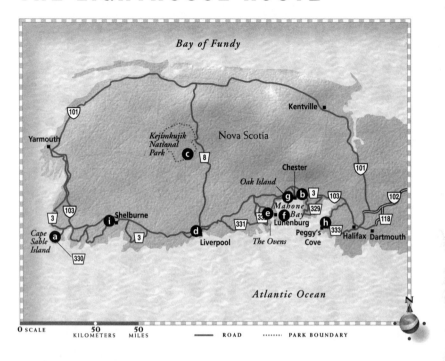

## Sightseeing Hightlights

- **a** Cape Sable Island
- **b** Chester
- **c** Kejimkujik National Park
- **d** Liverpool
- **e** Lunenburg
- **f** Mahone Bay
- **g** Oak Island
- **h** Peggy's Cove
- **i** Shelburne

## A PERFECT DAY ON THE LIGHTHOUSE ROUTE

I like to get to Peggy's Cove as early in the day as possible, to beat the crowds. But after that there's no rush, and the rest of the day is devoted to meandering along this lovely route at whatever pace I choose. Oak Island is probably the only place along the coast that's not particularly scenic, but I find it fascinating because of its fabled buried treasure and the massive (but so far fruitless) efforts of various people to get at it. I like to stop in Lunenberg for lunch at the Compass Rose Inn. Cape Sable Island, known to sailors as one of the graveyards of the Atlantic, is another place where I like to linger, contemplating the awesome destructive power of the sea.

## SIGHTSEEING HIGHLIGHTS

✬✬✬ **Lunenburg** • Lunenburg is the famous shipbuilding center where both the original *Bluenose*—the schooner depicted on the Canadian dime—and the replica *Bluenose II* were built. The town was honored in 1995 when the United Nations designated its Old Town portion a World Heritage site. The U.N. selection committee called Lunenburg "an outstanding example of planned European colonial settlement in North America in terms both of its conception and its remarkable level of conservation."

This exceedingly picturesque town boasts some beautiful old restored buildings. Pick up a walking-tour pamphlet from the local tourist information center, which is housed in a lighthouse replica in Blockhouse Hill, a public park that provides a panoramic view of the town and harbor. One of the annual festivals in Lunenburg arises out of the town's German heritage: Octoberfest, with activities for all ages, takes place in early October. Other events worth checking out are the Lunenburg Fold Harbor Festival, usually the second weekend of August, and, a couple of weeks later, the Nova Scotia Fisheries Exhibition and Fishermen's Reunion.

Lunenburg was long one of Canada's great fishing ports. Stop in at the Fisheries Museum of the Atlantic, consisting of two floating vessels moored at the quay as well as museum buildings. The most interesting ship is the restored *Theresa E. Connor*, the last Canadian schooner to fish Newfoundland's Grand Banks. The other ship is the *Cape Sable*, a steel-hulled trawler. The adjacent museum buildings house an aquarium, a display of Bluenose mementos, a theater, and a gift shop. Entrance is $3 for adults, 50 cents for children, and $5.50 for families. (2 hours)

★★★ **Oak Island** • Oak Island, 5 minutes outside Mahone Bay, has a fascinating history. Legend has it that Captain Kidd's treasure is buried in a pit on Oak Island, but the head of the Triton consortium that has so far invested $3 million in exploration on Oak Island thinks it may hold Sir Francis Drake's booty from plundered French and Spanish ships. For decades, serious treasure hunters have been trying to figure out how to solve the mystery of the so-called Money Pit. It contains an elaborate system of shafts and tunnels that were apparently designed to cave in or flood with sea water when disturbed. So far, nobody has succeeded in this great treasure hunt, though searchers have spent millions trying to get to the bottom of it all and at least six people have died trying. In summer, you can tour the island by bus and view a video about the continuing exploration. The cost is $3.50 for adults and $2 for children. (1 hour)

★★★ **Mahone Bay** • Mahone Bay is famous for its three churches (Anglican, Lutheran, and United), which stand in a row at the head of the town's harbor. Perhaps less well-known but equally interesting is the nearby heritage cemetery; take the time to stroll through it. Mahone Bay, which calls itself "one of the prettiest towns in Canada," is a fine place in which to stroll, shop, and eat. The Teazer, named after a ghost ship, is popular for souvenir shopping. And stop in at Suttles & Seawinds, located in a giant pink house on Main Street. It sells clothes and quilts, and is worth a visit just to see the inside of the house. For pewter goods, try Amos Pewterers, also on Main Street. (1 hour)

★★★ **Peggy's Cove** • Peggy's Cove is a tiny fishing village, renowned for its picturesque setting and rustic buildings, about a half-hour's drive southwest of Halifax. It's such a well-known attraction that it's always crowded. The only way to see it properly without elbow-to-elbow crowds is to get there first thing in the morning. And I mean early—get in and out before 9:00 a.m., when the tour buses start arriving. This is a beautiful spot and well worth a visit if you can do it that way. Park in the parking lot at the edge of the village and walk down the slope. Peggy's Cove sits in a calm little inlet, and when you get into the center of the village you'll understand why it's one of the most photographed parts of Nova Scotia. Take a few shots; they'll come out looking like picture-perfect postcards, because that's exactly how Peggy's Cove looks. Then continue along the road toward the lighthouse, which sits on a point and doubles as a post office during tourist season. The coastline here is made up of huge, gently rounded granite boulders with surf splashing against them. It's a powerfully stark scene; take some time to walk over the rocks and sit a while contemplating the sea. But wear sneakers and be careful! Every once in a while, when the weather is stormy, someone on the rocks at Peggy's Cove is swept out to sea. So beware the weather. Of all the souvenir shops in Peggy's Cove, the one worth searching out is Beales Bailiwick, which offers wares from pewter and oilcloth coats to pretty pottery, mohair sweaters, and high-quality sweatshirts and T-shirts. (2 hours)

✷✷ **Cape Sable Island** • Cape Sable Island, Nova Scotia's most southerly point, is linked by a 1,200-meter causeway (3,925 feet) to Barrington Passage, a tiny village on the mainland south of Clark's Harbour. The island's other claim to fame is that over the years, hundreds of ships have run afoul of the submerged shoals here; the cape has long been known to sailors as one of the graveyards of the Atlantic. In the tiny community of Centreville on Cape Sable Island, the Archelaus Smith Museum exhibits items salvaged from vessels shipwrecked in the area. Admission is free. (1 hour)

✷✷ **Chester** • An old resort town where lots of wealthy Americans used to spend their summers, Chester has some lovely old mansions, including the Sword and Anchor Inn, built in the early 1800s. The town has long attracted sailors and yachters, and the busiest week of the year is Chester Race Week, the second week of August. It's Atlantic Canada's largest sailing regatta, and everybody goes. (1 hour)

✷ **Kejimkujik National Park** • One of Nova Scotia's two national parks lies inland, about 55 kilometers (33 miles) north of Liverpool on Route 8. Kejimkujik is a wooded, gently rolling wilderness area dotted with lakes, rivers, and hiking trails. There is also a family campground. Canoeing is a particularly popular activity; rentals are available. In summer, park naturalists give lectures and lead guided walks and canoe trips. For information, call (902) 682-2772. (3 hours)

✷ **Liverpool** • Liverpool is designated as the Port of Privateers in honor of the period 1750 to 1812, when it was perfectly legal to scour the seas looking for victims. Local merchants would launch fleets of fighting ships that pirated goods from vessels sailing from the North Atlantic to the Caribbean. One merchant, Simeon Perkins, even hired militiamen to guard the town against other marauders. Nowadays if you go through Liverpool on a tour bus, you may find yourself "hijacked" by musket-toting militiamen, just to give you a taste of what life in Liverpool was once like. There's at least one required stop in town: the **Simeon Perkins House**, built in 1766. Located at 105 Main Street, it's now a provincial museum. In addition to eighteenth-century furniture, the house contains a copy of Perkins' diaries, which he kept painstakingly for 40 years, providing succeeding generations with a vivid record of daily life in a colonial town. For some reason, he was particularly detailed about any illness in the family. Admission is free.

Then take a stroll along some of Liverpool's tree-lined streets, where fine old houses dating from the Loyalist influx still stand. The local tourist information center is located in Centennial Park. Liverpool's major annual festival is Privateer Days, held around the weekend of the July 1 Canada Day holiday. (1 hour)

✩ **Shelburne** • For a time after it was first settled by Loyalists in 1783, Shelburne was the third-largest town in North America. Eventually many Loyalists moved on, but the town's tourist literature encourages visitors to trace their roots because so many colonists funneled through Shelburne. You never know. Many of the town's houses date from Loyalist times, including the Ross-Thompson House, built in 1784 and now a provincial museum. Part of the museum is a restored Loyalist store displaying period merchandise. Settlers George and Robert Ross originally opened the store in the 1780s and sold salt, tobacco, molasses, and dry goods to the other settlers. Admission is free. There is a tourist information center on Dock Street in Shelburne, and the Shelburne County Genealogical Society is also on Dock Street. Near Shelburne, The Islands Provincial Park, connected to the mainland by a causeway, offers picnic tables and a campground. Shelburne hosts a big lobster festival every year in early June. (1 hour)

## FITNESS AND RECREATION

Kejimkujik National Park offers numerous hiking trails as well as canoeing and other outdoorsy activities. For information on hiking trails, contact Parks Canada in Halifax at (902) 426-3436.

## FOOD

In Mahone Bay, try the **Innlet Cafe**, which has fresh seafood, salads, and sandwiches plus a view of the three churches from its location in the Kedy's Landing complex at the head of the Bay. The **Mug and**

**Anchor Pub** has imported draught and hearty food; it's located in the Mader's Wharf Mall at 643 Main Street in Mahone Bay. The **Tingle Bridge Tea House**, 3 kilometers (2 miles) outside Mahone Bay on Highway 3 towards Lunenburg, offers a huge range of teas plus a lunch menu and afternoon-tea-type goodies like pies and cheese cake. **The Galley**, 3 kilometers (2 miles) west of Chester on Route 3, specializes in seafood and has a children's menu. In Shelburne, **The Curiosity Shoppe**, in addition to being a souvenir shop, has a dining room that serves home cooked food. One stop in Shelburne offers two different restaurants — **Bruce's Wharf** and **McGowan's**, at 1 Dock Street. Bruce's Wharf is a pub downstairs and McGowan's is a restaurant upstairs. In Liverpool, **Lane's Privateer Inn** at 27 Bristol Avenue boasts no less than 3 dining rooms.

## LODGING

There are delightful heritage inns and B&Bs in towns all along the Lighthouse Trail. In Lunenburg, the exquisite old **Lunenburg Inn** at 26 Dufferin Street offers rates between $60 and $90 (902-634-3963). The **Compass Rose Inn**, another heritage property in Lunenburg, is at 15 King Street and its rooms run from $55 to $70 (800-565-8509). In Shelburne, the **Loyalist Inn** at 160 Water Street runs about $50 for a double room, plus a dining room (902-875-2343 or 875-3537. Another one-time Loyalist home is the **Hopkins House Bed and Breakfast** at 120 Main Street in Liverpool, with rates running around $50 a room (902-354-5484). In Mahone Bay, the **Edgewater Bed and Breakfast** at 44 Mader's Cove Road serves guests breakfast on the deck overlooking the water. A double room costs $55 (902-624-9382). **The Sou'Wester Inn** at 788 Main Street, once a Victorian shipbuilder's home, is another Mahone Bay bed and breakfast with a verandah overlooking the bay. Rates begin at $65 for a double (902-624-9269). In Chester, try the **Captain's House Inn** at 129 Central Street, with rates of about $75 for a double (902-275-3501). At 78 Queen Street in Chester, the **Mecklenburgh Inn** heritage property has rooms for about $60 (902-275-4638).

## CAMPING

The **Lunenburg Board of Trade Campground** is adjacent to the tourist information center on Blockhouse Hill Road. Rates begin at $12 (902-634-8100 or 634-3656). Twelve kilometers (8 miles) south-

# THE LIGHTHOUSE ROUTE

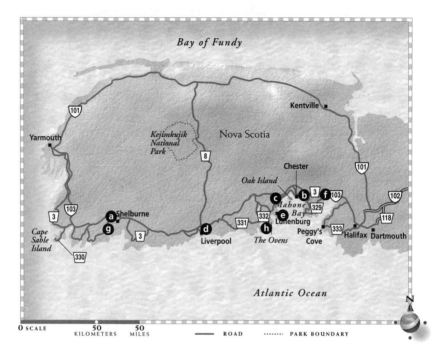

## Food

**a** Bruce's Wharf and McGowan's
(Shelburne)

**a** The Curiosity Shoppe
(Shelburne)

**b** The Galley (Chester)

**c** Innlet Cafe (Mahone Bay)

**d** Lane's Privateer Inn
(Liverpool)

**c** Mug and Anchor Pub
(Mahone Bay)

**c** Tingle Bridge Tea House
(Mahone Bay)

## Lodging

**b** Captain's House Inn (Chester)

**e** Compass Rose Inn
(Lunenburg)

**c** Edgewater Bed and Breakfast
(Mahone Bay)

**d** Hopkins House Bed and
Breakfast (Liverpool)

**a** Loyalist Inn (Shelburne)

**e** Lunenburg Inn (Lunenburg)

**b** Mecklenburgh Inn (Chester)

**c** Sou'Wester Inn (Mahone Bay)

## Camping

**f** Graves Island Park

**g** The Islands Provincial Park

**e** Lunenburg Board of Trade
Campground

**h** Ovens Natural Park Family
Campground

*Note: Items with the same letter are in the same town or area.*

west of Lunenburg on Route 332, the **Ovens Natural Park Family Campground** is right by the ocean and has a licensed restaurant. Rates start at $14 (902-766-4621 or 677-2694). Five kilometers (3 miles) west of Shelburne on Route 3, there is a campground in **The Islands Provincial Park**, with sites starting at $9 (902-875-4303). **Graves Island Park**, another provincial park, is 3 kilometers (2 miles) east of Chester and has rates beginning at $12 (902-275-4425).

## HELPFUL HINTS

S everal major Acadian festivals take place in Yarmouth, notably the Seafest, a week of activities in July. There's a big tourist-information center at the ferry docks in Yarmouth, at 228 Main Street, offering both local and province-wide information. It's open from May through October.

# 14
# THE EVANGELINE TRAIL

The Evangeline Trail leads from Yarmouth, along the part of the Bay of Fundy coast known as the Acadian Shore, through Annapolis Royal and the Annapolis Valley. Annapolis Royal is a lovely little place that retains its unspoiled small-town atmosphere and beauty despite being such a popular tourist destination.

Blessed with more sunny days and milder weather than most other parts of the Maritime provinces, the fertile Annapolis Valley is dotted with small, peaceful villages and apple orchards. This is apple-growing country. In May and June, the apple trees turn a marvelous pink with blossoms; an annual 5-day Apple Blossom Festival is held throughout the valley at the height of the blossoms in late May. The Annapolis Valley is flanked by ridges known locally as the North and South Mountains, with the North Mountain running along the Bay of Fundy shore. The Evangeline Trail runs through the center of this bucolic valley, passing through tranquil villages that boast some glorious old Victorian houses. On a sunny day, being here is like drifting through a little piece of heaven on earth.

Evangeline was a young Acadian woman separated from her betrothed, Gabriel, when the Acadians were deported from Nova Scotia. The lovers reunited only at the end of their lives, as Gabriel lay dying. American poet Henry Wadsworth Longfellow heard the story and immortalized it in his haunting poem, *Evangeline: A Tale of Acadie.* ◣

# THE EVANGELINE TRAIL

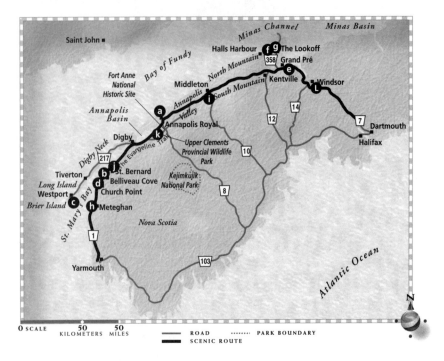

## Sightseeing Highlights

**a** Annapolis Royal Historic Gardens

**a** Annapolis Royal Tidal Power Generating Station

**a** Annapolis Royal Walking Tour

**b** Belliveau Cove

**c** Brier Island

**d** Church Point (Point de l'Église)

**a** Fort Anne National Historic Site

**e** Grand Pré

**f** Hall's Harbour

**g** The Lookoff

**h** Meteghan

**i** Middleton

**j** St-Bernard

**k** Upper Clements Family Vacation Park

**k** Upper Clements Wildlife Park

**l** Windsor

*Note: Items with the same letter are located in the same town or area.*

# ANNAPOLIS ROYAL

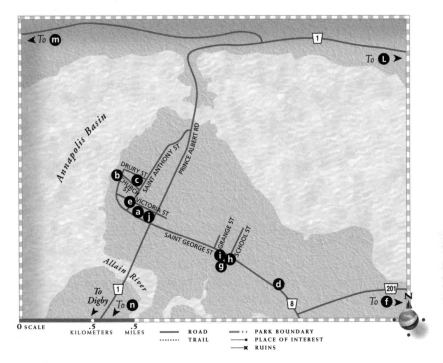

## Food

**a** Garrison House Inn

**b** Newman's Restaurant

**c** Ye Old Town Pub

## Lodging

**d** Amulree

**e** Bread & Roses

**f** English Oaks B&B

**a** Garrison House Inn

**g** Hillsdale House

**h** King George House Bed & Breakfast

**i** Queen Anne Inn

**j** Turret Bed & Breakfast

## Camping

**L** Dunromin Campsite and Trailer Cout

**m** Fundy Trail Campground

**n** House of Roth

*Note: Items with the same letter are located in the same town or area.*

## A PERFECT DAY ON THE EVANGELINE TRAIL

The Giant's Causeway on Brier Island is utterly compelling to me, and the drive along Digby Neck that takes you there is particularly pleasant. Afterwards, on the way to Annapolis Royal, I would make sure to stop at the Upper Clements Wildlife Park to view native animals in a more-or-less natural setting. Annapolis Royal is another favorite of mine, particularly the peaceful Royal Historic Gardens and the waterfront promenade overlooking the river. Then I'd continue to Hall's Harbour, a tiny, picturesque fishing village north of Kentville, before heading to the Lookoff for its remarkable view of the Annapolis Valley.

## A BIT OF HISTORY

When French explorers Samuel de Champlain and Sieur de Monts first came across the Annapolis River basin in 1604, they named the area Port-Royal. Within a couple of years, a small band of French farmers had settled there, making it the oldest European settlement in Canada. Port-Royal changed hands several times as the French and British battled over Nova Scotia. It was eventually renamed Annapolis in honor of Queen Anne, and it served as the capital of Nova Scotia for a time before Halifax was founded. Later, after the Acadians were expelled, the area was resettled by New Englanders and Loyalists, and the two names merged to become Annapolis Royal. St. George Street, parallel to the waterfront downtown, claims to be the oldest town street in Canada, lined with restored buildings housing small historical museums, shops, and restaurants.

## SIGHTSEEING HIGHLIGHTS

✯✯✯ **Brier Island** • Brier Island is home to tall, strange rock pillars that extend from the shore hundreds of meters into the sea like ragged rows of marching columns. The site is called the Giant's Causeway. Ask for directions in Westport, the only community on the island. Brier Island is at the tip of a thin peninsula called Digby Neck and the Island that stretches west from Digby. To get to it, take Route 217 from Digby, catch a ferry from East Ferry to Tiverton on Long Island and, at the far end of Long Island, catch another ferry from Freeport across to Westport. Ferries run regularly. Brier Island, about 65 kilometers (40 miles) from Digby, is also known for whale- and bird-watching.

In Tiverton, ask at the tourist bureau for directions to the Balancing Rock, a strange coastal rock formation that looks like it's about to keel over into the water. Getting to the Balancing Rock used to involve a hardy hike through patches of skunk cabbage and over a ridge, but recently a 1-kilometer trail was completed that, with steps, boardwalks, and a path, makes it somewhat easier. (2 hours)

★★★ **Hall's Harbour** • This lovely little fishing village slopes steeply down to the shore, where the tides rise and fall to an astounding extent. When we were there, the tide was out, and fishing boats were grounded far below wharf level. Stranded fish flopped about in the small pools of water left behind. You can also go for a walk on a gravel beach bordered by 25-meter (80-foot) cliffs. (½ hour)

★★★ **The Lookoff** • The Lookoff, about 20 minutes from the Evangeline Trail, is well worth the side trip for its panoramic view over the Minas Basin and the patchwork fields of the Annapolis Valley. (½ hour)

★★ **Annapolis Royal Historic Gardens** • The grounds boast pretty theme gardens and winding pathways in a setting that slopes gently down to the Allains River. The gardens, located at the traffic lights on Route 8 (Saint George Street), are open daily from May to October. Admission is $3.50 for adults, $3 for seniors and children, and $9.75 for families. Phone: (902) 532-7018. (1½ hours)

★★ **Upper Clements Wildlife Park** • This province-run wildlife park features lynx, cougar, porcupines, foxes, and other native Nova Scotian animals in large enclosures along a forested trail in a natural setting. You can choose between two trails through the park; one is 1 kilometer (½ mile) long, the other 6 kilometers (4 miles). Both are wheelchair accessible. Admission is free. (1 hour)

★★ **Windsor** • This is a good place to view the tidal bore, the tumbling wave that moves upriver with the advancing tide from the Bay of Fundy. It can vary from a few inches to several feet in height and is most dramatic as it enters certain rivers that empty into the bay. Along this shore, the bore is most pronounced in the Meander River near Windsor. Ask at the Windsor Tourist Bureau for tidal times and directions. Stop in at Shand House, a magnificently gingerbready late-Victorian home that is now a provincial museum furnished with

just about everything ever acquired by the Shand family, down to tro-
phies won by Clifford Shand in high-wheeled bicycle races. Windsor
calls itself the Giant Pumpkin Capital of the World. How big are
these gargantuans? The annual pumpkin festival at Thanksgiving has
produced pumpkins and squash in excess of 275 kilos (600 pounds).
Windsor is known as the eastern gateway to the Annapolis Valley.
(2 hours)

★ **Annapolis Royal Tidal Power Generating Station** • This is the
only saltwater generated power plant on the North American continent. An interpretation center demonstrates how the plant generates
hydroelectric power from the Bay of Fundy tides. The station is
located at the Annapolis River Causeway. Admission is free. Phone:
(902) 532-5454. (½ hour)

★ **Annapolis Royal Walking Tour** • Pick up a walking tour pamphlet from the local tourist information bureau in the railway station
at the base of Victoria Street. Running parallel to St. George Street
behind King's Theater, a waterfront promenade overlooks the
Annapolis River and the village of Granville Ferry, where the falling
Fundy tides leave vessels berthed at the wharf, high and dry.
(1½ hours)

★ **Belliveau Cove** • Stop here to see what the tide is doing.
Belliveau Cove has a well-protected harbor, and the tides of St.
Mary's Bay, a Bay of Fundy inlet, are extremely high. (15 minutes)

★ **Church Point (Pointe de l'Église)** • Church Point boasts St.
Mary's Church, one of the largest wooden churches in North
America, built between 1903 and 1905. The spire reaches 56 meters
(183 feet) into the air and is weighted down inside with tons of rock
to act as ballast in the strong winds that come in off St. Mary's Bay.
Guided tours are available in summer. (½ hour)

★ **Fort Anne National Historic Site** • Here you'll find earthwork
fortifications built by the French in the 1600s, as well as a reconstructed British Field Officers' Quarters dating from 1797, with displays recounting the struggle between the French and English in the
area. One outstanding exhibit is the Heritage Tapestry, which depicts
400 years of history and was stitched by volunteers. There is a nomi-

nal admission charge. Hours: Daily from 9:00 a.m. to 6:00 p.m.
Phone: (902) 532-2397. (1 hour)

✯ **Grand Pré** • Grand Pré National Historic Park marks the site of
the expulsion of the Acadians. The park contains formal gardens, a
commemorative church, and a statue of Evangeline. A growing number of artisans are settling in Grand Pré, so it's a good place to
browse for arts and crafts. Grand Pré is also the center of Nova
Scotia's wine industry; the Grand Pré Winery offers tours, tastings,
and a wine and gift boutique. (2 hours)

✯ **Meteghan** • Just before the village of Meteghan, stop in at
Smugglers Cove Provincial Park, which offers a lovely vista of St.
Mary's Bay. Meteghan, a small but busy port, is where a mystery man
known only as Jerome is buried. He apparently materialized on the
beach at Sandy Cove, across the bay from Meteghan, in 1854. He was
dressed in clean clothes and had a supply of water and biscuits, but
his legs had been amputated above the knees. He was unable to speak
and never revealed his origins. He was named Jerome by local residents, who cared for him until his death 58 years later. (½ hour)

✯ **Middleton** • Known as the "Heart of the Valley," Middleton hosts
a Heart of the Valley Festival in mid-July, complete with parades and
fireworks. Middleton is also home to the Annapolis Valley Macdonald
Museum (902-825-6116), which features a collection of antique
clocks and watches, a natural history exhibit, an art gallery, and
because it used to be a school, a re-creation of a turn-of-the-century
classroom. Admission is $1 per person or $3 for a family.

✯ **St-Bernard** • There is another big church here, an enormous
gothic granite building that dominates the village and seats 1,000
people. Guided tours are available. (½ hour)

✯ **Upper Clements Family Vacation Park** • Families might want
to stop in at this theme park just outside Annapolis Royal on Route 1.
It combines re-creations of Nova Scotia's heritage and history with
amusement-park rides. It's open from mid-May to mid-October—
daily in July and August, and on weekends only the rest of the time.
Entrance to the park is free, but you pay for each ride and attraction
once inside. From Atlantic Canada, phone (800) 565-PARK. (2 hours)

## FITNESS AND RECREATION

The Mickey Hill Pocket Wilderness, featuring graveled trails with boardwalks in rough areas and steep staircases through rocks, lies 10 kilometers (6 miles) south of Annapolis Royal on Route 8. Further down Route 8 is Kejimkujik National Park, offering canoeing, hiking and assorted other activities (see Lighthouse Route chapter).

The Annapolis Valley is ideal for cycling because it's so flat. There are several resources on cycling around the province. A 50-page booklet, *Bicycle Tours in Nova Scotia*, contains descriptions and maps of 20 popular routes around the province; write to the Touring Chairman, Bicycle Nova Scotia, Box 3010 South, Halifax, N.S. B3J 3G6. *The Nova Scotia Bicycle Book* is a 310-page primer on routes, repair facilities, attractions, and other related information; write to Gary Conrod, Atlantic Canada Cycling, Box 1555, Station M, Halifax, N.S. B3J 2Y3, or phone (902) 423-2453.

## FOOD

In Annapolis Royal, **Ye Old Town Pub**, at 9 Church Street, serves fish and chips, clam and chips, and 16-ounce burgers for lunch and dinner (902-532-2244). For more upscale dining, try the **Garrison House Inn** at 350 Saint George Street (902-532-5750) or **Newman's Restaurant** at 218 Saint George Street (902-532-5502).

## LODGING

Several exquisite old Victorian inns in Annapolis Royal offer rooms in the $50 to $85 range. The **Queen Anne Inn** is just up the road from the Annapolis Royal Historic Gardens at 494 Upper Saint George Street; phone (902) 532-7850 (no smoking). The **Garrison House Inn** at 350 Saint George Street also boasts a wonderful restaurant; call (902) 532-5750. The **Bread & Roses** at 82 Victoria Street is a restored Victorian brick mansion; call (902) 532-5727 (no smoking and no children under 12). Located on a large estate with a duck sanctuary, the **Hillsdale House** at 519 Saint George Street is a registered heritage property furnished with antiques and is known for its artwork. Children are welcome. Call (902) 532-2345.

A number of B&Bs in the area have rates beginning around $40 for a double room. Try **English Oaks B&B**, a modern house on lovely riverside property just outside town; call (902) 532-2066. The **King**

**George House Bed & Breakfast** at 548 Upper Saint George Street is a registered heritage property with antique furnishings and a library; call (902) 532-5286 (no smoking). The **Turret Bed & Breakfast**, yet another registered historic property, is at 372 Saint George Street; call (902) 532-5770 (no smoking). Or try **Amulree**, a comfortable old home at 703 Saint George Street; (902) 532-7206.

Digby, 38 kilometers (23 miles) west of Annapolis Royal, has plentiful hotels, motels, and B&Bs because it's the terminal for the ferry to Saint John, N.B.

## CAMPING

There are several campgrounds near Annapolis Royal. **Dunromin Campsite and Trailer Court**, a wooded and open campground with a grocery store, laundromat, boating, a swimming area, and a play area, is minutes west of town on Route 1. Rates begin at $12.50. Call (902) 532-2808. **House of Roth** in Clementsport, another campground offering both wooded and open sites plus a pool, hiking trails, and play areas, is 13 kilometers (8 miles) west of Annapolis Royal. Rates begin at $10; call (902) 638-8053. **Fundy Trail Campground** is on the Bay of Fundy, 19 kilometers (12 miles) north of Route 1, and has a recreation hall, laundromat, canteen, pool, and walking trails as well as wilderness sites on a freshwater brook. It's near a theme park and features family days. Rates begin at $11. Call (902) 532-7711.

## HELPFUL HINT

The Evangeline Trail follows Route 1, which snakes through the heart of the Annapolis Valley. If you want a change of scenery, there are numerous side roads leading to fishing villages along the Minas Channel shoreline. In fact the shoreline is never more than 15 kilometers (9 miles) due north.

# 15
# CAPE BRETON ISLAND

The Cabot Trail on Nova Scotia's Cape Breton Island, one of Canada's most famous scenic routes, offers up astounding natural beauty that can literally take your breath away. It follows the Gulf of St. Lawrence shoreline around the magnificent Cape Breton Highlands National Park and along the Atlantic coast. The scenery is rapturously beautiful, all cliffs and crashing waves and remarkable vistas. Fortunately, the route is dotted with lookouts where you can pull off the road to absorb the panorama without causing an accident.

The route, which runs in a loop, is about 300 kilometers (180 miles) long in all, with the park accounting for roughly 100 kilometers (60 miles) of the drive. It can be done in a day or a week, depending on how much you dawdle. It doesn't particularly matter which direction you travel in. The bigger of two park information centers is at the western entrance outside Cheticamp, inviting clockwise travel.

I recommend Baddeck as a base for your time on Cape Breton Island. It's centrally located and, as the gateway to the Cabot Trail, offers many tourist facilities. ◼

# CAPE BRETON ISLAND

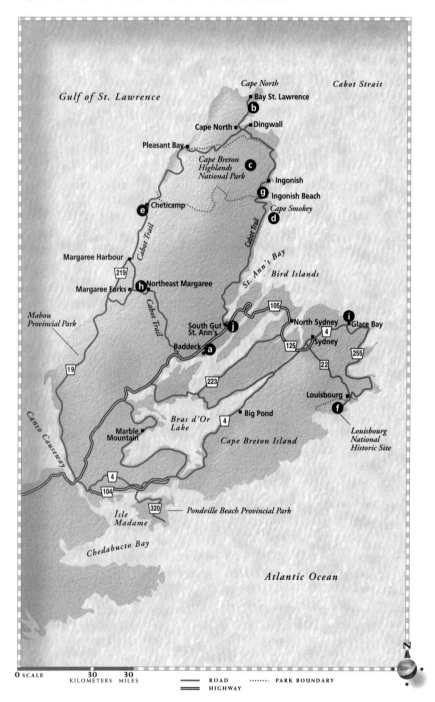

Cape North

Cabot Strait

Gulf of St. Lawrence

■ Bay St. Lawrence
**b**

Cape North ■ ■ Dingwall

Pleasant Bay ■

*Cape Breton
Highlands
National Park* **c**

■ Ingonish
**g** ■ Ingonish Beach

*Cape Smokey*
**d**

**e** ■ Cheticamp

Margaree Harbour ■

219

■ Northeast Margaree **h**

Margaree Forks ■

*Maboú
Provincial Park*

*Cabot Trail*

*Cabot Trail*

*St. Ann's Bay*

*Bird Islands*

105

South Gut
St. Ann's **j**

■ North Sydney **i** ■ Glace Bay

4

125 ■ Sydney

Baddeck ■ **a**

255

223

22

19

Louisbourg ■

**f**

*Canso Causeway*

*Bras d'Or
Lake*

4 ■ Big Pond

Marble ■
Mountain

*Cape Breton Island*

*Louisbourg
National
Historic Site*

4

104

320 — *Pondville Beach Provincial Park*

*Isle
Madame*

*Chedabucto Bay*

*Atlantic Ocean*

N

0 SCALE    30    30
KILOMETERS  MILES        ▬▬ ROAD   ········ PARK BOUNDARY
                         ▬▬ HIGHWAY

## Sightseeing Highlights

**ⓐ** Alexander Graham Bell National Historic Park

**ⓑ** Cabot Landing

**ⓒ** Cape Breton Highlands National Park

**ⓓ** Cape Smokey

**ⓔ** Cheticamp

**ⓕ** Fortress of Louisbourg

**ⓖ** Ingonish Beach

**ⓗ** Margaree Valley

**ⓘ** Miners' Museum (Glace Bay)

**ⓙ** South Gut St. Ann's

## A PERFECT DAY ON THE CABOT TRAIL

When the weather is sunny and sparkling, there's nowhere more spectacular than Cape Breton Highlands National Park. I like to stop at virtually every lookout, which makes the drive take hours and hours, but it's worth it. I pack a picnic and stop at Beulach Ban Falls in the Aspy River Valley, along the part of the route that drops down into deep-walled canyons in the heart of the park.

## SIGHTSEEING HIGHLIGHTS

★★★ **Cape Breton Highlands National Park** • Here's where you'll get the most scenic vistas—sandy beaches and plunging cliffs along the coast and dizzying canyons when the road swings eastward across the top of the peninsula. There are 28 hiking trails in the park, ranging from 20-minute strolls to challenging treks. At French Lake, for instance, you can take a walk along the Bog Trail, a short, wheelchair-accessible path into the heart of bog life. Elsewhere, you can visit Mary Ann Falls, one of the prettiest and most accessible waterfalls in the park. Signs along the route indicate lookouts and nature trails. In summer, the Cabot Trail is like a hilly ocean of green dropping steeply to the water below; in autumn, when the leaves change, it's truly incredible, and some people swear it's the best time of all to visit.

You never know what you'll find around the next corner; at one lookout not far north of Cheticamp, for example, there is a moving inscription dedicated to all the Canadians who have died overseas in the service of their country "who will never know the beauty of this place or the changing of the seasons."

Wildlife is abundant, including deer, bobcat, mink, moose, eagles, and dozens of bird species. Admission to the park is $5 per vehicle. The information center at Cheticamp (or the one at Ingonish at the park's eastern entrance if that's the way you're traveling) has everything you need to know about the park. Both information centers are open from 8:00 a.m. to 9:00 p.m. from late June to Labor Day and from 9:00 a.m. to 5:00 p.m. from mid-May to late June and from Labor Day to late October. In winter, information is available only by phone. Call (902) 285-2691 or (902) 285-2270. (3 hours and up)

★★★ **Fortress of Louisbourg** • This is definitely among the best re-created historic village in Canada. The Louisbourg fortress was the center of French power in the region and covered 20 hectares (50 acres), surrounded by a wall almost 3 kilometers (2 miles) long. The French took more than 20 years to build Louisbourg, but when an army of New Englanders backed by the British Royal Navy attacked the following year, the Louisbourg garrison was unprepared and its defenses weak, and it fell after a 49-day siege. Three years later, in 1748, Louisbourg was handed back to France only to be recaptured by the British in 1758. The fall of Louisbourg, along with the fall of Quebec City, marked the end of French colonial power in North America. A few years later the British prime minister ordered the demolition of all fortifications at Louisbourg.

Nowadays, the Fortress of Louisbourg National Historic Site is the largest historical reconstruction project in Canada. One-quarter of the town has been reconstructed, including many buildings and some of the fortifications. You can visit all manner of period buildings, from homes to soldiers' barracks to a noisy waterfront tavern. From June to early September, it's all brought to life by costumed guides, soldiers, merchants, sea captains, and other "residents" who re-create the community of the summer of 1744 and regale visitors with stories, dances, music, and the "latest" local gossip. The weather tends to be cool and damp even in summer, so bring a sweater and raincoat and wear comfortable walking shoes. Louisbourg lies 55 kilometers (35 miles) south of North Sydney on Route 22, at the south end of the Marconi Trail, another of the province's scenic routes.

Admission is $7.50 for adults, $6 for seniors, $4.25 for children, and $19.25 for families. For taped information, phone (902) 733-3100; for specific information, call (902) 733-2280. (full day)

⭐⭐ **Alexander Graham Bell National Historic Park** • Bell first visited the Baddeck area in 1885 and eventually returned to settle there. On a headland overlooking Baddeck Bay, he built a home that he named Beinn Breagh—"beautiful mountain" in Gaelic. He died there in 1922 and was buried on the summit of his beautiful mountain. The home is not open to the public; Bell's descendants still live there. But the Alexander Graham Bell National Historic Park houses a museum devoted to the life and work of the Scottish-born genius. Besides inventing the telephone, he conducted aviation research leading to the first-ever flight in the British Empire when, in 1909, his *Silver Dart* flew over Baddeck Bay. The museum displays the *Silver Dart* and other such Bell inventions as a huge HD-4 hydrodrome (a forerunner of hydrofoil boats), a vacuum jacket (an early version of the iron lung), and, of course, early telephone equipment. Hours: 9:00 a.m. to 9:00 p.m. from July 1 to Sept. 30, 9:00 a.m. to 5:00 p.m. the rest of the year. Nominal admission fee. Phone: (902) 295-2069.

⭐ **Cabot Landing** • The Cabot's Landing Provincial Picnic Park near Cape North features a monument to explorer John Cabot, who is presumed to have made landfall here in 1497. The Cabot Trail is named after him. The park is near Cape North. (1 hour)

⭐ **Cape Smokey** • At 366 meters (1,200 feet) high, you can't miss this massive headland just south of Ingonish. Cape Smokey Provincial Park provides a magnificent lookout over the ocean and coastline. Drive carefully and slowly; there are a lot of hairpin turns coming down off Cape Smokey. (½ hour)

⭐ **Cheticamp** • This Acadian fishing village at the western entrance to Cape Breton Highlands National Park was originally settled by Acadians who were expelled from the mainland in 1755. Its streets are lined with shops and restaurants with French signs. Stop in at *Les Trois Pignons* (The Three Gables), a museum and cultural center where one of the galleries houses hooked rugs, something Acadian artisans have elevated to an art form. The Cape Breton Highlands National Park information center, which is wheelchair accessible, is just north of Cheticamp. (1 hour)

✯ **Ingonish Beach** • This is the eastern entrance to Cape Breton Highlands National Park. It is also the site of Keltic Lodge, a lovely old resort set atop cliffs overlooking the ocean. Call (902) 285-2880 or (800) 565-0444, if you're interested in staying there. (½ hour)

✯ **Margaree Valley** • Formed by the Margaree River and its many branches, this pastoral valley is renowned for salmon fishing. Northeast Margaree, one of several villages in the valley (the others are Margaree Centre, Margaree Forks, Margaree Valley, East Margaree, and Margaree Harbour) has a salmon museum describing the river's features and displaying fishing gear. In Margaree Harbour, a restored schooner, the *Marion Elizabeth*, built by the same Lunenburg company that built the *Bluenose*, is now a floating museum and restaurant. Margaree Harbour also offers several souvenir shops. If you're lacking tourist information, there is a tourist bureau in Margaree Forks. (1 hour)

✯ **Miners' Museum** • At the Miners Museum in Glace Bay, you can tour a real coal mine with a retired miner as your guide. The site tells the story of coal mining in this area and contains typical miners' houses, a company store, and a restaurant. Admission is $3.75 for adults and $1.75 for children, plus a fee for the mine tour. Phone: (902) 849-4522. (1 hour)

✯ **South Gut St. Ann's** • This is the site of the Gaelic College of Celtic Arts and Crafts, the only Gaelic educational institution in North America. In summer it offers courses ranging from bagpipe playing to tartan weaving to Gaelic language courses. The college's Great Hall of the Clans depicts Scottish history and culture. The town was originally settled by a group of Highland Scots whose ship had blown off course. The town is the site of an annual week-long festival of Celtic culture, the Gaelic Mod, usually held during the first week of August. (½ hour)

## FITNESS AND RECREATION

Cape Breton Islands National Park is laced with 27 walking and hiking trails, and you can't do better for the scenery. Some are short strolls, some are long and strenuous, and some are wheelchair accessible. Stop in at the Cheticamp visitor information center to pick up some pamphlets or to buy a copy of *Walking in the Highlands*, on sale in the large nature bookstore at the information center. Or, if you're getting organized ahead of time, contact Parks Canada in Halifax at (902) 426-3436.

## FOOD

B addeck has a full range of eateries to choose from. One of the best restaurants in the area is the **Bell Buoy** on the lower end of Chebucto Street; call (902) 295-2581 for reservations. **Baddeck Lobster Suppers** is, needless to say, for seafood lovers; call (902) 295-3307. The **Highwheeler Cafe** is a combined cafe, deli, and bakery right downtown. Also downtown, **Wong's Family Restaurant** serves up Chinese food. Near the entrance to the Cabot Trail, the **Red Barn Restaurant** offers a full menu specializing in seafood.

## LODGING

A s the official start and end of the Cabot Trail circuit, Baddeck has plentiful tourist facilities. Accommodations run the gamut from motels to stately resorts. Rates tend to be rather high except at the B&Bs because this area draws so many visitors.

**Duffus House Inn** is a country inn overlooking Bras d'Or Lake with room rates running from $60 to $85. It's a non-smoking property and no pets are allowed; phone (902) 295-2172. Another non-smoking country inn, **MacNeil House**, is particularly upscale, offering one- or two-bedroom suites, each with a Jacuzzi, fireplace, and kitchen, beginning at $125 a night; call (902) 295-2340. The **Inverary Inn Resort** at Exit 8 on Route 205 is a large resort offering rooms from about $70 to $175. No pets are allowed; call (800) 565-5660.

At the budget end of things, local B&Bs offer rooms for around $40. Try The **Bay Tourist Home Bed & Breakfast** at Exit 10 off the TransCanada (no smoking or pets, 902-295-2046) or **An Seanne Mhanse**, in the same area (no smoking, 902-295-2538).

Cape Breton also runs a bed and breakfast program whose members offer common rates ($40 for a double at last notice). All members are listed in a brochure titled *Cape Breton Bed & Breakfast Program*; you can get it from the provincial tourist information people or by contacting the Cape Breton Tourism Distribution Center, 20 Keltic Drive. P.O. Box 1448, Sydney, N.S., Canada B1P 6R7, or phoning (800) 565-9464.

Book ahead for accommodations in Baddeck. Contact the establishment directly or call the provincial Check In line (800-565-0000

# BADDECK

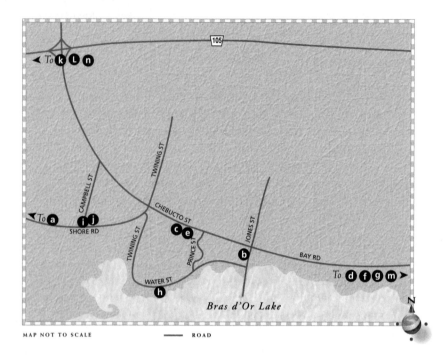

## Food

- **ⓐ** Baddeck Lobster Suppers
- **ⓑ** Bell Buoy
- **ⓒ** Highwheeler Cafe
- **ⓓ** Red Barn Restaurant
- **ⓔ** Wong's Family Restaurant

## Lodging

- **ⓕ** An Seanne Mhanse
- **ⓖ** Bay Tourist Home Bed & Breakfast
- **ⓗ** Duffus House Inn
- **ⓘ** Inverary Inn Resort
- **ⓙ** MacNeil House

## Camping

- **ⓚ** Baddeck Cabot Trail KOA Campground
- **ⓛ** Bras d'Or Lakes Campground
- **ⓜ** Cape Breton Highland National Park
- **ⓝ** Silver Spruce Resort

from Canada or 800-341-6096 from the United States). Also there are motels, hotels, cottages, inns, and B&Bs in various towns along the Cabot Trail.

## CAMPING

There are three campgrounds in the immediate Baddeck area, all offering plentiful facilities. **Baddeck Cabot Trail KOA Campground**, on a river 8 kilometers (5 miles) west of town off the TransCanada, offers rates of $14 and up; call (902) 295-2288. **Bras d'Or Lakes Campground** is on the lake, 5 kilometers (3 miles) west of Baddeck off the TransCanada, with rates starting at $15; call (902) 295-2329 or 295-3392. And **Silver Spruce Resort** is 8 kilometers (5 miles) west of town off the TransCanada, with a minimum rate of $15; call (902) 295-2417.

If you want to stay in Cape Breton Highlands National Park, it boasts no less than eight campgrounds.

## HELPFUL HINTS

There are a variety of whale- and bird-watching cruises available from different places along the Cabot Trail. For instance, whale-watching cruises are offered from Cheticamp, Pleasant Bay, Bay St. Lawrence (north of Cape North), and Dingwall (between Cape North and Ingonish on the eastern coast). Tours to Bird Islands are available from South Gut St. Ann's. Bird Islands, two small islands off St. Ann's Bay, are the nesting site of thousands of seabirds, including Atlantic puffins, cormorants, gulls, and razor bills.

## SIDE TRIPS ON CAPE BRETON ISLAND

The 107-kilometer (65-mile) Ceilidh Trail scenic route leads north along Route 19 from the Canso Causeway to Margaree Harbour on the Cabot Trail, running along the coast most of the way. All over Cape Breton Island and the rest of Nova Scotia, but particularly along this route, you'll see the phrase "Ciad Mile Failte." It's Gaelic for "A Hundred Thousand Welcomes" to this region originally settled by Scottish highlanders. There are beaches, cliff-top views, sheep on the hillsides, and landscapes eerily reminiscent of Scotland. Stop in at Mabou Provincial Park, which offers a panoramic view of the Mabou Valley.

The scenic Fleur-de-lis Trail leads south from the Canso Causeway along the southern rim of Bras d'Or Lake all the way to Louisbourg. It's Acadian country mainly. Pondville Beach Provincial Park boasts a sandy beach that's a kilometer long (more than half a mile), plus picnic tables and a lagoon. At Marble Mountain, a museum tells the story of the marble quarrying industry in the late 1800s and early 1900s. The village also has a marble-chip beach. Île Madame, an island to the south accessible by causeway, has a strong Acadian heritage and several shoreline picnic areas. In July, Big Pond, a tiny village on Bras d'Or Lake, is the site of a major Cape Breton folk concert. Big Pond is also the home town of famous Cape Breton singer Rita MacNeil; Rita's Tea House in town displays her awards and records.

# 16
## ST. JOHN'S

St. John's, Newfoundland's capital city, lies on the east coast of the Avalon Peninsula. I've never really seen St. John's. I've been there, I've spent time there, but I haven't viewed the city from afar as I approached it, because it was always blanketed in fog. It became a running joke: here comes the fog, we must be getting near St. John's. Wandering around St. John's in such weather can be an agreeable if faintly eerie experience. This doesn't happen all the time, but when it does, it can last for days. Part of what makes Newfoundlanders so hardy is the weather in their area of the world. They talk a lot about it.

One of the oldest settlements in North America, St. John's is built on high hills surrounding the harbor. The downtown core is more or less on level land but as soon as you venture further afield you're climbing steep hills lined with colorful wooden row houses. The hills, the harbor, and the houses are what make this historic port city so picturesque. St. John's, which has a population of 172,000, is home to most of the province's social, educational, and religious institutions.

It's eminently possible to explore the entire Avalon peninsula in day trips from St. John's, so I recommend you base yourself in the city for the duration of your visit to the area. ◼

# ST. JOHN'S

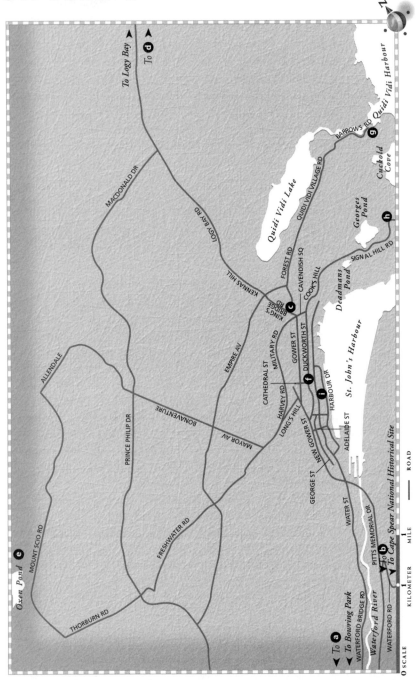

Quidi Vidi Harbour

To Logy Bay

To **d**

BARROWS RD

Quidi Vidi Lake

QUIDI VIDI VILLAGE RD

MACDONALD DR

LOGY BAY RD

**g**

Cuckold Cove

Georges Pond

**h**

SIGNAL HILL RD

FOREST RD

CAVENDISH SQ

KENNA'S HILL

COOK'S HILL

KING'S BRIDGE RD

**c**

Deadmans Pond

St. John's Harbour

ALLENDALE

EMPIRE AV

GOWER ST

DUCKWORTH ST

MILITARY RD

CATHEDRAL ST

**f**

HARVEY RD

**i**

HARBOUR DR

PRINCE PHILIP DR

BONAVENTURE

MAYOR AV

LONG'S HILL

ADELAIDE ST

MOUNT SCIO RD

Oxen Pond

**e**

NEW GOWER ST

GEORGE ST

WATER ST

FRESHWATER RD

PITTS MEMORIAL DR

To **b**

To Cape Spear National Historical Site

THORBURN RD

WATERFORD BRIDGE RD

Waterford River

WATERFORD RD

To **a**

To Bowring Park

0 SCALE

1 KILOMETER

1 MILE

— ROAD

## Sightseeing Highlights

**ⓐ** Bowring Park

**ⓑ** Cape Spear National Historic Site

**ⓒ** Commissariat House

**ⓓ** Logy Bay

**ⓔ** Memorial University Botanical Gardens

**ⓕ** Newfoundland Museum

**ⓖ** Quidi Vidi Battery

**ⓗ** Signal Hill

**ⓘ** St. John's Waterfront

## A PERFECT DAY IN ST. JOHN'S

If it's not foggy, I like to start with Signal Hill because of its wonderful view of the city and harbor. Then I like to wander the waterfront and maybe do some browsing in the Murray Premises, a restored mercantile complex on Water Street bordering the harbor. For lunch I'd head for one of the wonderful fish-and-chips places on Freshwater Road. Then I'd head out to Cape Spear National Historic Site. The most easterly point in North America is also home to Newfoundland's oldest lighthouse and offers a closeup view of the forbidding North Atlantic. Back in the city, I'd go for a walk through the Memorial University Botanical Gardens and then head down to George Street for dinner and some live music long into the night.

## AN INTRODUCTION TO NEWFOUNDLAND

Newfoundland sits at the easternmost edge of Canada and is known as The Rock; you'll understand why once you see it. It doesn't attract the huge numbers of tourists the other three Atlantic provinces do, which is both fortunate and unfortunate: fortunate because it remains largely unspoiled; unfortunate because Newfoundland is the poorest province in Canada and could use the revenue. Travelers who are interested in things other than amusement parks and beaches should make a real effort to visit this province. It is

different from the rest of Canada—different from anywhere else in
North America, in fact. The landscape ranges from forests to barrens,
the rugged coast is steep and rocky and wild, and the people are warm
and wry. "When you live in this province," one St. John's native said to
me, "all you've got going for you is your sense of humor."

There are actually two parts to the province—Newfoundland, a
vast island, and Labrador, on the mainland to the northwest, separated
from the island of Newfoundland by the Strait of Belle Isle. Labrador,
the much larger of the two but by far less populated, lies north of the
province of Quebec. It is remote and undeveloped except for small
ports along the coast and a few towns inland, and is home to the
largest caribou herd in the world. Officially, the province is called
Newfoundland and Labrador, but everyone calls it Newfoundland
unless referring specifically to Labrador.

The indigenous people, the Beothuks, are extinct and almost nothing is known about their society or history. In the tenth century, the
Norse established a temporary settlement at L'Anse aux Meadows on
the Great Northern Peninsula on Newfoundland's west coast. Explorer
John Cabot, sailing for England, is believed to have made landfall somewhere on Newfoundland's coast in 1497 (the province is planning a
major celebration to mark the 500th anniversary in 1997). By the sixteenth century, fishermen from a variety of European countries were
working the prolific waters around Newfoundland and Labrador. To
this day the vast majority of Newfoundlanders are descended from
English and Irish fishermen who settled Newfoundland's shores. A
government with full colonial status was established in 1855, and
Newfoundland remained a British colony until 1949, when it finally
joined Canada more than 80 years after Confederation.

Newfoundlanders lived a hardscrabble existence in a remote area,
and perhaps nothing better illustrates their psychological and physical
separateness than the long years of resisting confederation. Even when
Newfoundland finally became Canada's youngest province, it was only
after a hard-fought referendum passed by a narrow margin.

Major industries include forestry, oil (an offshore megaproject
called Hibernia is scheduled to begin producing oil in 1997), and the
fisheries. The richest fishing grounds in the world lie off the coast of
Newfoundland and Labrador—except that lately the supply has dwin-
dled disastrously. In 1992, the federal government imposed a mora-
torium on Newfoundland's northern cod fishing because supplies were
so drastically depleted. Cod is an important part of the Newfoundland
fishery, accounting for 40 percent of all fish landed in 1991.

Fortunately for visitors, the whales remain. Seventeen species of whales frequent the waters of Newfoundland and Labrador, and the best time to see them is summer, when they're migrating northward. The most common species are the humpback, minke, and fin whales, with less-frequent sightings of white-sided dolphins, harbor porpoises, belugas, sperm whales, and common dolphins. You can often spot whales from shore, but the best hope of seeing them is out on the ocean.

If you're there in late spring or early summer, the other large bodies you may see floating in the waters off Newfoundland are icebergs. Some years they drift southward as late as August, other years there are no more after early June. Some years there are hardly any, other years there are thousands.

The names of some communities and geographical features attest to Newfoundlanders' sense of humor—Backside Pond, Blow Me Down, Chase Me Further Pond. Newfoundland's natural beauty notwithstanding, the best thing about the province is its people. Spend as much time as possible getting to know them. You probably won't have to go out of your way to make friends; in Newfoundland, everybody says "hello" and usually much more.

A word about the Newfie accent. It takes some getting used to. It's a mixture of English and Irish dialects that have mingled into a quite distinct language. But don't worry. You'll be able to understand most of it right away and virtually all of it after a couple of days, when you get accustomed to some of the expressions. "B'y," for instance, means "boy," while "away" means the mainland, as in "When I lived away I noticed the beer labels were different."

Don't expect hot weather in Newfoundland, even in July and August. It happens occasionally, but so do rain and fog and cool temperatures, so travel with appropriate clothing.

When you set foot on Newfoundland soil, set your watch ahead 30 minutes. Newfoundland's time zone is half an hour ahead of the Atlantic Time Zone and 90 minutes ahead of the Eastern Time Zone. When it's 5:00 p.m. in Montreal and 6:00 p.m. in Halifax, it's 6:30 p.m. in Newfoundland.

# GETTING TO NEWFOUNDLAND: THE NEWFOUNDLAND FERRY

From North Sydney, N.S., separate ferries go to Argentia (pronounced ar-jen-cha, more or less) on Newfoundland's Avalon Peninsula on the east coast, and to Port aux Basques (pronounced port-o-BASK) on the west coast. The Avalon Peninsula incorporates St. John's and a varied landscape of rocky shore and windswept tundra. The west coast is the site of Gros Morne National Park, one of Atlantic Canada's most scenic areas. Exploring both coasts is the ideal plan, and travelers with plenty of time should by all means do so. You could take the ferry to Port aux Basques, travel through Gros Morne and beyond, then drive across to the east coast, explore St. John's and the Avalon Peninsula, and return to North Sydney via the ferry from Argentia. It would probably take a minimum of a week; it's a 900-kilometer (540-mile) drive across the province from Port aux Basques to St. John's.

The ferry schedule can vary slightly from summer to summer. In 1995, the ferry to Argentia ran twice a week between mid-June and the end of September, departing at 7:00 a.m. on Tuesday and Friday from mid-June to September 10, and at 4:00 p.m. on Tuesday and Friday from September 11 to September 30. The crossing takes 14 hours. One-way rates in 1995 were $107 per car plus $49 per adult passenger, $24.50 for children 5 to 12, and $36.75 for seniors. Rates for cabins ranged from $95 to $125 extra.

The afternoon departure means you spend the night on the ferry and have to sit up if the cabins are all booked. The huge, modern, cruise-ship-like ferry has large lounges, a casino with slot machines, a cafeteria, a dining room, a playroom for kids, and lots of quite comfortable chairs scattered throughout the vessel.

The morning departure means you're on the ferry for an entire day and arrive in Newfoundland after dark. Be sure to reserve ahead for accommodations in the Argentia area (see next page).

In the opposite direction, in 1995 the ferry ran twice a week from Argentia to North Sydney between June and late September, departing at 9:00 a.m. on Wednesdays and Saturdays. It meant passengers arrived in North Sydney around 11:00 p.m. Again, remember to reserve lodgings in North Sydney.

The ferry from North Sydney to Port aux Basques runs between one to four times daily in peak season. In 1995, one-way rates were $55 per vehicle, plus $17.75 per adult, $9.50 for children 5 to 12, and $13.75 for seniors. The crossing takes about 5 hours.

It's important to call well ahead of time to find out the schedule, nail down your itinerary, reserve passage on the ferry, and, depending on the time of sailings, book accommodations at both ends of the ferry crossing. The ferries are operated by Marine Atlantic; call (902) 794-5700 from Canada (except Newfoundland and Labrador) or (800) 341-

7981 from the United States. From Newfoundland and Labrador, call (709) 772-7701 in St. John's or (709) 695-7081 in Port aux Basques. Or write to Marine Atlantic Reservations Bureau, P.O. Box 250, North Sydney, N.S., Canada B2A 3M3.

## LODGING IN NORTH SYDNEY

D epending on when the ferries are running, you may need to spend a night in North Sydney. The North Sydney–Sydney area is referred to by the provincial tourism people as "industrial Cape Breton" and there isn't much to see. But North Sydney, the terminal for ferries to and from Newfoundland, has ample roadside accommodations and eateries to cater to all the tourists passing through. **MacNeil's Motel** on the TransCanada, about 5 kilometers (3 miles) before you get to the ferry terminal, has room rates beginning around $45; call (902) 736-9106 or (902) 736-2692. The **Clansman Motel** on Peppitt Street has rates from $58 to $75 for a double; call (902) 794-7226. The **Heritage Home B&B** at 110 Queen St. offers doubles for $45 to $55; call (902) 794-7226. The pricier **North Star Inn** at 39 Forrest Street has rates beginning at $80; call (902) 794-8581.

## LODGING IN NEWFOUNDLAND

A s noted, you should reserve ahead for accommodations in Newfoundland if you're traveling on the day ferry to Argentia. Placentia (pronounced pla-sen-cha), the town nearest the Argentia ferry slip, has several hotels and motels. Those cited here all offer room rates around $60 for a double. **Ocean View Apartments** has rooms with cooking facilities and the rates include Continental breakfast; call (709) 227-5151. Similarly, the **Harold Hotel** on Main Street has 23 rooms and continental breakfast is included in the price; call (709) 227-2107. **Rosedale Manor** has four rooms and breakfast is included; call (709) 227-3613. The **Unicorn Guest Home** has three rooms; call (709) 227-5424. The **Coffey House** has two double and three single rooms, and its rates include a full home-cooked breakfast; call (709) 227-2262 or (709) 227-7303.

## GETTING TO AND AROUND ST. JOHN'S

T he most direct route from the ferry terminal at Argentia is via Route 100 north and then the TransCanada east. Total distance is

113 kilometers (70 miles), which will take perhaps 90 minutes to drive. Coming into St. John's, enter the northwest section of the city via Route 2, which leads to the downtown area on the waterfront. St. John's was destroyed by fire several times in the nineteenth century. The worst blaze, which raged for 24 hours in 1892 and razed more than half the town, has come to be known as The Great Fire. The town was rebuilt each time in a rather haphazard manner, so this city is anything but planned. Except for the heart of downtown, finding your way around can be confusing. Arm yourself with a good map and don't hesitate to ask for directions. It's very hilly, so wandering around turns out to be a form of exercise in itself. Outside the downtown core, the best way to get around is by car. Harbour Drive runs along the harborfront, with Water Street (reputedly one of the oldest streets on the continent) and Duckworth Street parallel to Harbour Drive. Signal Hill Road is off the eastern end of Duckworth Street. At its western end, Duckworth runs into New Gower Street.

The St. John's tourist information center is in an old restored railway car on the waterfront; you can't miss it. You can pick up all manner of information there, including pamphlets describing walking tours of four different areas of the city. You can also join the free "Nice to Meet You" program, whereby you're issued a credit-card-style card that provides for various discounts at shops, hotels, restaurants, and attractions around town.

## SIGHTSEEING HIGHLIGHTS

✱✱✱ **St. John's Waterfront** • To get a real sense of this historic port city, stroll along the waterfront. The harbor will doubtless be crowded with vessels from all over the world and with small fishing boats. The St. John's tourist information center is in an old railway car on the waterfront. Pick up some walking-tour pamphlets and wander Water Street and Duckworth Road, lined with restaurants, cafés, and stores. Stop in at the James J. O'Mara Pharmacy Museum, a heritage drugstore depicting a working pharmacy circa 1895, at 488 Water Street. George Street, between Water and New Gower, is the hub of the city's nightlife, lined with restaurants and bars; walk up Adelaide Street to see it. Then continue another block along Adelaide to New Gower. City Hall is across the road; Mile "0," the point where the TransCanada Highway begins, is located at City Hall. (2 hours)

✱✱✱ **Signal Hill** • Signal Hill, now a national historic park, is the best place to start a tour of St. John's because it affords a magnificent view over the city, the harbor, and the Atlantic (when not fogged in). A majestic rock guarding the narrow harbor entrance, Signal Hill lies around a curve of the shoreline east of the harborfront area. The access road, Signal Hill Road, runs off the end of Duckworth Street. The English and French fought several times for control of Signal Hill, and it was here that the last battle of the Seven Years' War was fought in North America, in 1762. In 1901, Guglielmo Marconi received the world's first transatlantic radio transmission on Signal Hill. It was the letter "S"; Marconi said it stood for Success. The Queen's Battery, fortifications dating from the Napoleonic Wars, and the imposing Cabot Tower, a monument built in 1897 to commemorate the 400th anniversary of the European arrival in Newfoundland, are also on Signal Hill. In July and August, the Signal Hill Tattoo performs twice a day from Wednesday through Saturday, at 3:00 p.m. and 7:00 p.m., weather permitting.

The interpretation center, about halfway up Signal Hill Road, has exhibits spanning 1,000 years of Newfoundland history from the Viking era to the province's entrance into the Confederation in 1949. Gibbet Hill, to the right of the interpretation center, has a rather ghoulish history. In the 1700s, anyone who broke the law was hanged there and left for a week as a deterrent to would-be criminals. From all over town, people could see the bodies swinging up on Gibbet Hill. After a week of dangling in chains, the bodies were stuffed into barrels, weighted, and dumped into Dead Man's Pond. Signal Hill National Historic Park is open year-round, from 8:30 a.m. to 8:00 p.m. from mid-June to Labor Day and 8:30 a.m. to 4:30 p.m. the rest of the year. Nominal admission. Phone: (709) 772-5367. (1½ hours)

★★ **Bowring Park** • If you're with children, make time for this large park. It boasts a replica of the famous *Peter Pan* statue in London's Kensington Gardens. The park was given to the city by the Bowrings, a wealthy business family. Legend has it that Sir Edward Bowring persuaded the sculptor of the original statue to make the replica in memory of his godchild, Betty Munn, who died in a disaster at sea in 1918. The park, which has picnic sites, a swimming pool, and a playground, is on Waterford Bridge Road in the west end of the city. Phone: (709) 576-8452. (1 hour)

★★ **Cape Spear National Historic Site** • This is the most easterly point of North America and lies roughly 10 kilometers (6 miles) from downtown St. John's. The oldest lighthouse in Newfoundland stands on a rocky cliff at Cape Spear. It was built in 1835, remained in use until 1955, and is now a museum. The scenery hereabouts is rugged and beautiful. To get to Cape Spear, head west on New Gower Street and take the first exit after crossing the Waterford River. Once there, you're closer to Ireland than you are to Manitoba. The site is wheelchair accessible and has a nominal admission fee. Phone: (709) 772-5367. (1 hour)

⭐⭐ **Memorial University Botanical Gardens** • These gardens cover 45 hectares of land at Oxen Pond in C. A. Pippy Park, the vast park north of downtown. Flower gardens include a rock garden, peat and woodland beds, a cottage garden, a perennial garden, and a heather bed. There is also a nature reserve with trails leading through a variety of habitats such as boreal forests and bog. Admission is free, but donations are welcome. Hours: Daily except Monday and Tuesday from 10:00 a.m. to 5:30 p.m. between May and November. There are guided tours every Sunday at 3:00 p.m. Phone: (709) 737-8590. (1 hour)

⭐⭐ **Quidi Vidi Battery** • Another dizzying view, this time of Quidi Vidi Village and Cuckold Cove. (Quidi Vidi is pronounced "kitty vitty.") The battery was built by French troops during their brief occupation of St. John's in 1762. It was later manned by British troops and has now been restored to its 1812 condition. Guides dressed in period uniforms are on hand to answer questions. The battery, a provincial historic site, is open daily in summer. Phone: (709) 729-0862 or 729-2977. (1 hour)

⭐ **Commissariat House** • This gracious, restored Georgian house was constructed between 1818 and 1821 and served as the home of the Assistant Commissary General. It is now a provincial historic site, furnished to the 1830 period, with costumed guides on hand. The house, on Kings Bridge Road, is open daily in summer from 10:00 a.m. to 6:00 p.m. Admission is free. Phone: (709) 729-0862 or (709) 729-6730. (½ hour)

⭐ **Logy Bay** • The Ocean Research Laboratory, operated by Memorial University at Logy Bay (5 kilometers—3 miles—east of the city), specializes in cold-ocean biology and oceanography. Guided tours are available in summer, from 10:00 a.m. to 5:00 p.m. Admission is $2.50 for adults and $1.50 for students and seniors. Address: Marine Lab Road at Logy Bay off Route 30. Phone: (709) 737-3706. (1 hour)

✳ **Newfoundland Museum** • This museum depicts 1,000 years of Newfoundland and Labrador history, beginning with the Vikings. Exhibits illustrate the lifestyles of native people, settlers, fishermen, and townspeople. Admission is free. Hours: 9:00 a.m. to 4:45 p.m. weekdays and 10:00 a.m. to 5:45 p.m. weekends. Address: Duckworth Street at Cathedral Street. The museum has a branch at Murray Premises, a restored nineteenth-century building on Water Street, that features maritime, military, and natural-history displays. For information on either branch, phone: (709) 729-0916. (1½ hours)

## FITNESS AND RECREATION

C.A. Pippy Park presents the best opportunity for hiking, walking, or jogging in the city, while Bowring Park has a swimming pool and tennis courts. Bicycle rentals are available from Avalon Bicycle Tours; call (709) 576-1951. Canoeing, kayaking, and sailboarding are popular activities on Quidi Vidi Lake.

## FOOD

For a small city, St. John's has quite a wide range of decent restaurants. Following are some suggestions, in no particular order. For lunch, try the **Classic Cafe** at 364 Duckworth or, for more elegant surroundings, the **Cabot Room** in the Hotel Newfoundland. For delicious fish and chips, try either **Ches's Fish and Chips** on Freshwater Road or **Leo's Fish and Chips,** also on Freshwater Road. The two have had a bit of a running feud for years and St. John's residents are divided on the merits of each place, but in fact both are excellent and serve huge orders of fish and chips for about $5. **Biarritz on the Square** at 188 Duckworth, another establishment that seats barely 30, specializes in both Cajun food and seafood; call (709) 726-3885. **Stone House**, located in one of St. John's oldest houses at 8 Kennas Hill, specializes in seafood, game, and traditional Newfoundland dishes; call (709) 753-2380. For pub fare, try **The Rose & Thistle** at 208 Water Street. The **Casa Grande** is a good Mexican restaurant at 108 Duckworth; call (709) 753-6108.

# ST. JOHN'S

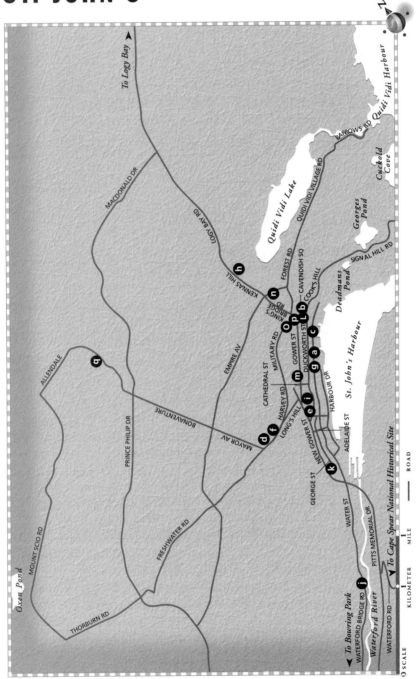

## Food

**ⓐ**  Biarritz on the Square

**ⓑ**  Cabot Room (Hotel Newfoundland)

**ⓒ**  Casa Grande

**ⓓ**  Ches's Fish and Chips

**ⓔ**  Classic Cafe

**ⓕ**  Leo's Fish and Chips

**ⓖ**  The Rose & Thistle

**ⓗ**  Stone House

## Lodging

**ⓘ**  Bonne Esperance Bed & Breakfast

**ⓙ**  Compton House

**ⓚ**  Delta St. John's Hotel

**ⓛ**  Fort William Bed & Breakfast

**ⓜ**  Gower House

**ⓝ**  Kincora Hospitality Home

**ⓞ**  Hotel Newfoundland

**ⓟ**  Prescott Inn Bed and Breakfast

**ⓠ**  The Roses Bed and Breakfast

## Camping

**ⓖ**  Pippy Park Trailer Park

*Note: Items with the same letter are located in the same place.*

## LODGING

O ne of the ritziest hotels in town is the landmark **Hotel Newfoundland** on Cavendish Square, with room rates starting at $150 for a double in high season; call (709) 726-4980 or (800) 268-9420 from Ontario and Quebec, (800) 268-9411 from elsewhere in Canada, and (800) 828-7447 from the U.S. The other establishment for big spenders is the **Delta St. John's Hotel**, which has a convention center connected to it and room rates ranging from $130 to $155. The **Delta** is at 120 New Gower Street; call (709)739-6404.

Historic city that it is, St. John's also has a good number of heritage-style inns and B&Bs. The **Prescott Inn Bed and Breakfast** at 17–19 Military Road and **The Roses Bed and Breakfast** at 9 Military Road are two of the nicest such establishments and happen to be owned by the same people. Room rates are around $70 at both places, which are just down the road from the Hotel Newfoundland. Call (709) 753-6063 for reservations at either. **Fort William Bed & Breakfast**, at 5 Gower Street across from the Hotel Newfoundland, offers double rooms for around $65, including breakfast; call (709) 726-3161. **Compton House** is a Victorian mansion on a landscaped estate at 26 Waterford Bridge Road, with room rates of between $70 and $100, including breakfast; call (709) 739-5789 (no smoking). Another Victorian-era home furnished with antiques, the **Kincora Hospitality Home**, at 36 King's Bridge Road, offers rooms beginning around $60; call (709) 576-7415 (no smoking). Other centrally located places offering double rooms for between $55 and $70 include the smoke-free **Gower House** at 180 Gower Street, (709) 754-0047 or (800) 563-3959, and **Bonne Esperance Bed & Breakfast** at 20 Gower Street, also nonsmoking, (709) 726-3835.

## CAMPING

T he best bet for camping is the fully serviced 156-site trailer park-campground in C. A. Pippy Park, an enormous green space fully within city limits. Contact the **Pippy Park Trailer Park** at (709) 737-3669 or (709) 737-3655. The 1,343-hectare park (just under 3,320 acres) also has a golf course, hiking trails, a fitness trail, playground, snack bar, convenience store, and other recreation facilities. Pets are welcome. Rates range from $5.50 to $15 a night.

## NIGHTLIFE

Newfoundlanders are great partyers, and St. John's is renowned for its lively nightlife and thriving live music scene, which encompasses everything from jazz and rock to toe-tapping jigs and reels. The center of it all is George Street, lined with pubs, dance bars, and restaurants; just wander until something strikes your fancy. In summer, outdoor concerts and other organized events take place on George Street.

## SHOPPING

Both Water and Duckworth streets are lined with shops and boutiques selling wool sweaters and scarves, woven goods, quilts, stoneware pottery, and handcrafted silver jewelry. Nature-lovers should stop in at Wild Things, 124 Water Street, offering nature art and photography plus wildlife T-shirts, locally handmade jewelry, and souvenirs, all featuring whales, puffins, eagles, and other Newfoundland wildlife.

The retail sales tax in Newfoundland is a whopping 12 percent; with the cascading GST, you're paying a total tax of somewhere around 20 percent. The good news is that visitors who purchase goods and take them out of the province within 30 days are entitled to a refund of the sales tax paid. To apply for the visitor's tax refund, you need to buy at least $100 worth of taxable goods with a total of $12 in provincial retail sales tax. You can pick up a refund application from provincial tourist information centers and mail it, along with original receipts, to the address on the form. Remember to apply first for the GST refund (see Practical Tips), since the federal government will return your original receipts to you but Newfoundland won't.

## FESTIVALS

A variety of festivals are held in St. John's each summer. On the weekend closest to June 24, the city hosts St. John's Days Celebrations, a 4-day festival commemorating its birthday. (John Cabot arrived here on June 24, 1497.) Events include a parade, a street dance, and indoor and outdoor concerts.

Another major annual event is the Newfoundland and Labrador Craft Development Association's Summer Craft Fair, a 3-day event in

early July. The St. John's Regatta, held the first Wednesday in August
on Quidi Vidi Lake, dates from the 1820s and is the oldest continuous
sporting event in North America. The regatta itself is actually a rowing
race. The attendant carnival is more fun.

## HELPFUL HINTS

Newfoundland's Department of Development publishes a thick
annual guide titled *Newfoundland and Labrador Travel Guide*. For
a free copy and any other information you might need, call (800) 563-
6353 or (709) 729-2830 in St. John's, or write: Department of Tourism
and Culture, Box 8730, St. John's, Nfld., Canada A1B 4K2.

As soon as you arrive in St. John's, make reservations for any
guided excursions you'd like to take later into the surrounding area,
such as whale-watching cruises. The *Newfoundland and Labrador Travel
Guide* has several pages of adventure-tour operators offering trips of
anywhere from a day to a week.

If money is no object, flightseeing tours of St. John's and the
Avalon region are available from Aviation Career Academy (709-576-
1891) and Universal Helicopters Newfoundland (709-576-4611).

# 17
# THE AVALON PENINSULA

The Avalon Peninsula, an H-shaped land mass that juts from the southeast corner of Newfoundland, presents a richly diverse landscape in a relatively small area. You'll come across windswept coastal villages, barren heathlands where caribou wander, and a noisy seabird sanctuary on three rocky islands offshore. Don't miss a cruise out to the sanctuary. Cape St. Mary's wondrous Bird Rock, where more than 20,000 birds nest, is a must-see, as is Salmonier Nature Park.

It's easy to explore the Avalon Peninsula when starting at St. John's. Begin on Route 10 and continue as it turns into Route 90, at the bottom of what Newfoundlanders call the Southern Shore. Follow the 90 to Salmonier Nature Park. Then backtrack to St. Catherine's and turn onto Route 91 and then Route 92 south, to get to the Cape St. Mary Ecological Reserve. From there, continue following the coast road, which leads past tiny villages nestled in "dokes"—long, wooded, river valleys that all seem to end in calm blue lagoons separated from the sea by stretches of sandy beach. The hilltops offer great opportunities for photography. Eventually you'll find yourself back on the TransCanada; head east back into St. John's. ◨

# AVALON PENINSULA

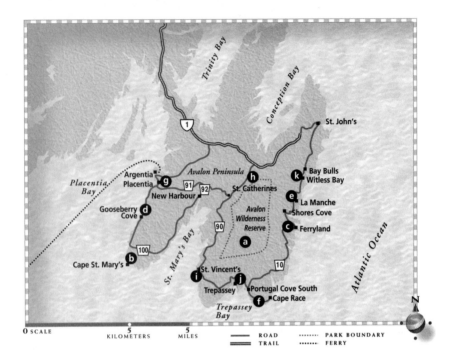

## Sightseeing Highlights

**a** Avalon Wilderness Reserve

**b** Cape St. Mary's Seabird Ecological Reserve

**c** Ferryland

**d** Gooseberry Cove

**e** La Manche Provincial Park

**f** Mistaken Point Ecological Reserve

**g** Placentia

**h** Salmonier Nature Park

**i** St. Vincent's

**j** Trepassey

**k** Witless Bay Ecological Reserve

## A PERFECT DAY ON THE AVALON PENINSULA

I'd plot a day where nature prevails, and for me that means, in particular, the Southern Shore. I'd start with a whale- and bird-watching cruise out to the Witless Bay Ecological Reserve. Continuing south, I'd have a picnic lunch in La Manche Provincial Park. After visiting the archaeological dig at Ferryland, I'd head across the tundra-like barrens, where I know I would see lots of caribou. The remarkable Cape St. Mary's seabird sanctuary would be next on the list, followed by a visit to the Salmonier Nature Park.

## SIGHTSEEING HIGHLIGHTS

★★★ **Cape St. Mary's Seabird Ecological Reserve** • The 12-kilometer (7-mile) dirt road that leads from Route 100 south to Cape St. Mary's is a bumpy drive pocked with mega-potholes; take it slowly. Park at the lighthouse and go into the sanctuary headquarters for information on the bird colony. Then follow the trail along the clifftops. It's an awesome sight when you get there—thousands upon thousands of huge, golden-headed gannets and other birds crowded onto near-vertical 150-meter (490-foot) cliffs, with waves crashing below. An estimated 53,000 birds blanket the cliffs at Cape St. Mary's in summertime, making it one of the best spots in the province for seeing a seabird colony up close. If you go all the way, it's a 30-minute walk to Bird Rock, but you can get a good view after about 10 minutes of walking. Dress warmly; the weather can be cold and foggy, and it's always very windy. There will probably be sheep wandering around the clifftops, so leave your dog in the car or keep it on a leash. Take binoculars, and keep an eye out for whales in the water below. There's a picnic table near the lighthouse, but it'll probably be too gusty to enjoy a meal. (1 hour)

★★★ **Salmonier Nature Park** • Salmonier Nature Park is really a zoo, but a zoo with a big difference. It's beautiful and peaceful, with a boardwalk winding through woodlands and past ponds and streams, and all the animals are there because they cannot be released back to nature for one reason or another. Each species resides in a large area that resembles its natural habitat as closely as possible. The beavers, for example, live in a vast pond. There are a snowy owl, a peregrine falcon, and a bald eagle, as well as lynx, moose, mink, arctic fox, caribou, and other species. Stop in at the visitors center to see the displays and then begin walking. The boardwalk not only protects the site, it also makes the park accessible for people in wheelchairs or with young kids in strollers. There are several shortcuts if you don't want to do the whole circuit. Wear comfortable shoes and remember to take binoculars and camera. Insect repellent will also probably come in handy if the weather is warm. Salmonier Nature Park is 12 kilometers (7 miles) south of the TransCanada on Route 90. Admission is free. Hours: 12:00 noon to 7:00 p.m. daily from early June until Labor Day; closed on Tuesdays and Wednesdays. Phone (709) 729-6974. (1½ hours)

★★★ **Witless Bay Ecological Reserve** • Even if you're not particularly a bird-, whale-, or nature-lover, I strongly recommend a cruise out to Gull Island, Green Island, and Great Island. Together they comprise the Witless Bay Ecological Reserve. You can book aboard Bird Island Charters or its partner company, Humpback Whale Tours, at (709) 753-4850 or (709) 334-2355; Bird Island Boat Tours at (709) 334-2002; or Gatherall's Boat Tours at (709) 334-2887. Whichever company you choose, you should have a terrific time. Not only do you get to see unbelievably dense colonies of Atlantic puffins, razorbills, murres, kittiwakes, and other species (the nesting season runs from mid-June to late July), you'll probably spot some whales, and you may even see some towering icebergs. Moreover, you'll be treated to some down-home Newfoundland-style hospitality on board, complete with music, songs, stories dancing, and nature lore. We booked with Bird Island Charters, operated by Loyola O'Brien, a gregarious charmer who could talk the birds down off the cliffs. His brother Joe operates Humpback Whale Tours and cruises the identical route. The seabird colonies demonstrate what the province means when it says it has one of the greatest concentrations of seabirds in the world. The cost for the 2½-hour cruise with either of the O'Briens is $25 per adult, $15 for kids 6 to 15, and $10 for children 2 to 5. Gatherall's Boat Tours, operated by the Gatherall family, offers similar cruises at similar rates, while Bird Island Boat Tours' 2-hour cruises, billed as the most economical way to see the birds and whales in Witless Bay, cost $20 for adults and $10 for kids. The cruises depart from Bay Bulls. Remember to dress warmly and bring your camera and binoculars. (3 hours)

★★ **Ferryland** • No, this is not an amusement park, but a village on a picturesque harbor rimmed with steep cliffs. It has a rather interesting history. In 1621, Sir George Calvert, who later became Lord Baltimore, established a colony here. After a few harsh winters and some battles with the French, he up and transferred his colony to Virginia. Later, another settlement also failed, whereupon some of the cod fishermen who had been ousted by the colonists returned. In the eighteenth century, during periods of Anglo-French and Anglo-American conflict, the fishing settlement was fortified. The 1700s also saw a large influx of Irish to what had been a predominately English settlement. The remains of seventeenth-century settlements around the inner harbor are now being excavated. The dig goes on each summer, and visitors can watch the excavations and visit an on-site archaeology lab. A visitor center has information about what's been found at the dig. Phone: (709) 432-2820. You can also visit the lighthouse, which affords a particularly good view of the harbor. It's near the church, off Route 10, and is open daily in summer. After Ferryland, the coastline gets wilder and the inland landscape increasingly tundra-like. When the road veers away from the sea, you'll feel as if you are driving across the moors—especially if it's misty, as it often is in these parts. (2 hours)

☆ **Avalon Wilderness Reserve** • If you're a real outdoor type, this is the place for you. But first you have to get a permit from the provincial Department of Environment and Lands. This vast, protected region lies in the middle of the peninsula; the single road into it is just before Shore's Cove as you're traveling south on Route 10. The reserve has rolling barrens, a panoramic viewpoint, and thousands of roaming caribou; nowhere else in North America does such a large population of caribou dwell so close to a city. The area attracts mainly hikers, canoeists, wilderness campers, photographers, and anglers. To reserve entry permits and find out more about the reserve, contact the Department of Environment and Lands, Parks Division, P.O. Box 8700, St. John's, Nfld., Canada A1B 4J6, phone (709) 729-2431. From May to September, you can also get Avalon permits at several other provincial parks, including Butter Pot or La Manche; the latter is adjacent to the reserve. (full day)

☆ **Gooseberry Cove** • About halfway between Cape St. Mary's and Placentia, Gooseberry Cove is a small provincial park with a long sandy beach and a lagoon surrounded by grassy banks. (½ hour)

☆ **La Manche Provincial Park** • La Manche, French for "sleeve," is named for the shape of the harbor at the abandoned coastal fishing village of La Manche. The village was destroyed one January day in 1966 when a severe winter storm hit, bringing an enormous tide that washed away boats, anchors, many buildings, and the suspension bridge that connected the two sides of the harbor. Miraculously, no lives were lost, but with the entire village economy wiped out, residents agreed to be resettled by the government. You can visit what remains of the village—not much beyond house foundations—by hiking a trail in the park. Another trail leads to a spectacular waterfall above La Manche Pond. More than 50 species of birds have been recorded in the park; you may also see moose, beavers, and wild mink. Route 10 skirts the edge of the park, which encompasses the scenic La Manche River Valley. There are picnic facilities if you want to bring lunch along. (1 hour)

✯ **Mistaken Point Ecological Reserve** • The world's richest find of Precambrian fossils—records of marine creatures that flourished some 500 million years ago—was made at Mistaken Point in 1968. The area was declared an ecological reserve to preserve the find, and it is one of the most important fossil sites in Canada. It's off Route 10, 16 kilometers (10 miles) southeast of Portugal Cove South. A little further along the same road, past Mistaken Point, is the Cape Race lighthouse. First operated in 1856, it was proclaimed a federal heritage structure in 1990. (½ hour)

✯ **Placentia** • Placentia was once a French fortification and is now a fishing community and service center for Placentia Bay. You can visit the old fortifications at Castle Hill National Historic Park above town. The visitors center houses an exhibit about what life was like in Plaisance, as Placentia was called by the French. The park provides a sweeping view over Placentia Bay. Admission is free. (½ hour)

✯ **St. Vincent's** • A long, sandy beach runs along the side of the highway as it passes through this town at the junction of Holyrood Bay and Holyrood Pond. It's not for swimming (Newfoundlanders can spend their entire lives never learning to swim because the Atlantic is so cold), but it is a good place to stop, stretch your legs, and breathe in the sea air. You might also see whales, who can come in very close to shore to feed at that particular spot because the ocean bottom drops sharply just off shore. (15 minutes)

✯ **Trepassey** • This town at the bottom of the southern shore drive has a history linked to aviation. The first plane to cross the Atlantic Ocean from west to east departed from here in 1919. Three U.S. Navy seaplanes attempted the trip; two were forced down at sea, but the third touched down in the Azores and then flew on to Portugal. In 1928 Amelia Earhart left from Trepassey on her first transatlantic flight—as a passenger. Reportedly, the thrill of that crossing convinced her to make aviation her career. The local museum has pictures of both the first transatlantic flight and Earhart. After Trepassey, you'll probably start seeing caribou herds, some quite close to the highway. (½ hour)

## FITNESS AND RECREATION

A number of provincial parks on the Avalon Peninsula offer hiking and walking trails. You can go horseback riding in Carbonear South; call Earles Riding Horses at (709) 596-7854. Newfoundland Diving Adventures gives guided tours of some of the shipwrecks off Bell Island; call (709) 895-3705. Ocean Adventures offers wrecks and reef walls in Bonavista Bay; call (709) 462-3211. The sailing is reportedly excellent off Holyrood at the southern end of Conception Bay. Avalon Wilderness Reserve is an ideal destination for hikers and canoeists. There's swimming at Cochran Pond Provincial Park, just 20 kilometers west of St. John's on the TransCanada. Butter Pot Provincial Park, 36 kilometers west of St. John's on the TransCanada, has an entertaining mini-golf course with a Newfoundland theme, complete with little replicas of Signal Hill, a ferry, and the Confederation Building. It's set amongst the trees, so take insect repellent. "Butter pot," by the way, is the term for a prominent rounded hill; this park is named after Butter Pot Hill, found within its boundaries.

## HELPFUL HINTS

Take along clothes for all climates. Any time you venture outside of St. John's, you're likely to experience firsthand the vagaries of Newfoundland weather, ranging from cold rain and fog to medium-warm sunshine in a single day.

I advise strongly against driving at night in the Newfoundland countryside. The roads are winding and badly marked, often with no outside lines and only faint center lines. Furthermore, sheep and moose may wander across the road and you won't see them in the dark until you're practically on top of them.

## SIDE TRIP: SAINT-PIERRE AND MIQUELON

O fficially, the French islands of St-Pierre and Miquelon have noth-
ing to do with Newfoundland, or for that matter with Canada.
I'm mentioning them here because they're only 25 kilometers (15
miles) off the south coast of Newfoundland in the Gulf of St.
Lawrence, and there is ferry service to them from a town called
Fortune. There are several crossings a day in summer; the trip lasts just
under an hour. Fortune is about 350 kilometers (210 miles) from St.
John's along the TransCanada and Route 210.

The tiny islands of St-Pierre, Miquelon, and Langlade, left over
from the days of New France, form a little French outpost where you
pay in French francs and chat with gendarmes. It's like visiting France
without having to cross the Atlantic. St-Pierre is where most of the
residents live, while Miquelon and Langlade, connected by a sandbar,
are home mainly to wild deer and large seal colonies, plus some 80
species of birds. In July and August, there is a ferry service from
St-Pierre to Miquelon several times a week. The island isthmus con-
necting Langlade and Miquelon reputedly conceals the remains of
hundreds of ships that went aground in storms over the past centuries.

The major industry on these islands has always been fishing. The
only other economic activity is tourism, which has been growing in
recent years. The climate is windy, damp, and generally harsh.

You can also fly to St-Pierre and Miquelon from Sydney or
Halifax in Nova Scotia, or from Montreal.

For more information, write to the St-Pierre & Miquelon Tourist
Office, B.P. 4274, 97500—St-Pierre & Miquelon, phone (508) 41-22-
22; or contact the French Government Tourist Office, 1981 McGill
College Ave., Suite 490, Montreal, Que., Canada H3A 2W9, phone
(514) 288-4264 or (514) 987-9761. There is also a French Government
Tourist Office in Toronto at (416) 593-6427, and in New York City at
(212) 757-1125.

# *Scenic Route:* Conception Bay

Conception Bay is accented with brooding cliffs and dotted with dozens of small outports where wooden houses cling to the hillsides. Some of Newfoundland's most striking coastal scenery is along this route. Wander at your own pace, taking time to absorb the atmosphere of life along the rugged Newfoundland shore. This is best done when the sun is shining, though fog and misty rain are common.

From St. John's, follow Route 60 past Topsail and on to Route 70 between Brigus and South River. Route 70 heads north along the western shore of Conception Bay, becoming Route 80 at Bay de Verde. Route 80 follows the eastern shore of Trinity Bay back to the TransCanada, at which point you can either take the TransCanada east back into St. John's or head west, and then north, along the western shore of Trinity Bay to the Bonavista Peninsula.

**Topsail** provides a good view of Conception Bay and three islands in the bay: Bell, Little Bell, and Kelly's. Until 1966, huge

## CONCEPTION BAY

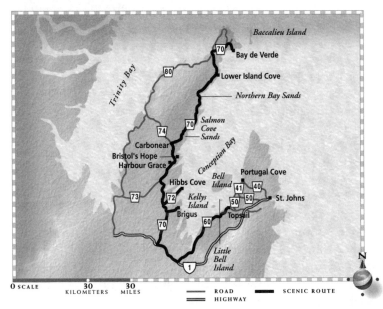

iron-ore deposits were mined at Bell Island, which was first settled 240 years ago as a fishing and farming community, and has had its ups and downs since. The town's history is displayed in a series of huge murals on local buildings; if you're interested, there's a ferry to Bell Island from Portugal Cove, located about 25 kilometers (15 miles) north of Topsail. Kelly's Island is named after a pirate who is said to have made his headquarters there some three centuries ago.

The view is lovely as you drive down into **Brigus**, a charming village on a long, thin inlet. Arctic explorer Robert Abram "Bob" Bartlett, who commanded ships in the polar expedition of Commodore Perry, was born here in 1875. His former home, Hawthorne Cottage, stills stands in Brigus and has been designated an historic site. The local museum, Ye Olde Stone Barn Museum, is housed in an 1820s dwelling that is a rare example of stone-house construction in a province where the vast majority of houses are made of wood.

**Hibbs Cove**, where the small, rock-ringed harbor is rimmed with square wooden houses, is so picturesque (yet so typical of Newfoundland outports) that artists and photographers are frequently drawn to it. The Port de Grave Fishermen's Museum here displays furniture and artifacts used by early settlers and fishermen.

Historic **Habor Grace** was settled in the early 1500s, and one of its earliest claims to fame is that it was headquarters to the infamous pirate Peter Easton. Beginning in 1919, it was the departure point for several early attempts to fly across the Atlantic. In 1931, Wiley Post began a round-the-world flight from Harbour Grace. And in 1932, famed aviatrix Amelia Earhart left Harbour Grace to fly to Northern Ireland, becoming the first woman to fly solo across the Atlantic. The community museum in Harbour Grace has an exhibit chronicling the town's role in the history of transatlantic flight. An extensive collection of fishing boat models, period furniture, old photographs, and other articles are also displayed. The museum is open daily in summer and admission is free. Habour Grace is also the site of the oldest stone church in the province—St. Paul's Anglican Church, built in 1835, on Cochrane Street.

There is a picnic area off the highway on a rise overlooking **Carbonear**. A seventeenth-century Irish princess, whose story is the stuff of fairy tales, is buried in a private garden in Carbonear. Her gravestone reads: "Sheila Na Geira, wife of Gilbert Pike and daughter of John Na Geira, King of County Down." During the reign of Elizabeth I, English pirate Gilbert Pike, a lieutenant of Peter Easton fell in love with Sheila Na Geira after he rescued her from the Dutch warship, where she was being held prisoner after being kidnapped from a ship in the English Channel. The princess wed (and reformed) Pike, and the couple decided to make a new life for themselves in the New World. They ended up in nearby Bristol's Hope. Shades of the Past Museum on High Road North in Carbonear tells the history of Conception Bay. One of the best times to visit Carbonear is during the Conception Bay Folk Festival in late July or early August.

Possible stop-off points along the road between Carbonear and Bay de Verde include two provincial parks with sandy beaches (Salmon Cove Sands Provincial Park and Northern Bay Sands Provincial Park) and the scenic Lower Island Cove area. The isolated fishing community of **Bay de Verde,** seated at the top of the peninsula separating Conception and Trinity Bays, was originally settled by "planters," colonists who were trying to avoid French raiders in the 1600s. In the early 1900s, two kegs of Spanish gold—believed to be pirate booty—were dredged up from a small cove here by local fishermen. Offshore is **Baccalieu Island**, a nesting site for puffins, gannets, gulls, and other birds. A short trail leads from Bears Cove above town to a scenic lookout. ◪

# 18
# WESTERN NEWFOUNDLAND

Newfoundland's west coast is a natural wonder, a panoply of cavernous fjords, dense forests, tufted heathlands, and ancient mountains that run from Port aux Basques in the south to L'Anse aux Meadows at the northern tip of the Great Northern Peninsula. The Viking Trail, a scenic route along the coast, links two UNESCO World Heritage sites—the magnificent Gros Morne National Park at its base and L'Anse aux Meadows at its tip, where Vikings settled some 1,000 years ago. With a geological history as old as the planet, the Great Northern Peninsula is endlessly fascinating.

You can get there by taking the ferry from North Sydney, Nova Scotia, to Port aux Basques or by driving across the province from St. John's. It's 570 kilometers (353 miles) from St. John's to Deer Lake, the start of the Viking Trail. The Viking Trail (Route 430) snakes all the way up the west coast to L'Anse aux Meadows. This is a long trip: 230 kilometers (144 miles) from Port aux Basques to Deer Lake and about 370 kilometers (230 miles) from there to L'Anse aux Meadows. You'll obviously need a minimum of 2 days, and you could probably easily spend 10 days exploring the peninsula.

The only other way to get to Newfoundland's west coast is to fly; there are small airports in Stephenville, Deer Lake, and St. Anthony. ◪

# WESTERN NEWFOUNDLAND

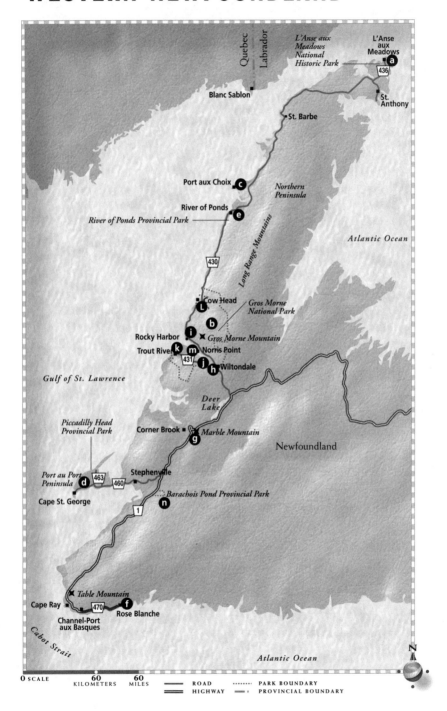

Quebec

Labrador

*L'Anse aux Meadows National Historic Park*

L'Anse aux Meadows

436

Blanc Sablon

St. Anthony

St. Barbe

Port aux Choix

*Northern Peninsula*

River of Ponds

*River of Ponds Provincial Park*

*Atlantic Ocean*

*Long Range Mountains*

430

Cow Head

*Gros Morne National Park*

Rocky Harbor

*Gros Morne Mountain*

Trout River

Norris Point

431

Wiltondale

*Gulf of St. Lawrence*

*Deer Lake*

*Piccadilly Head Provincial Park*

Corner Brook

*Marble Mountain*

*Newfoundland*

Port au Port Peninsula

463

460

Stephenville

Cape St. George

*Barachois Pond Provincial Park*

1

Cape Ray

*Table Mountain*

470

Rose Blanche

Channel-Port aux Basques

*Cabot Strait*

*Atlantic Ocean*

N

0 SCALE    60    60
KILOMETERS    MILES    ——— ROAD    ········ PARK BOUNDARY
═══ HIGHWAY    —·— PROVINCIAL BOUNDARY

## Sightseeing Highlights

**ⓐ** L'Anse aux Meadows

**ⓑ** Gros Morne National Park

**ⓒ** Port au Choix

**ⓓ** Port aux Port Peninsula

**ⓔ** River of Ponds Provincial Park

**ⓕ** Rose Blanche

**ⓖ** Table Mountain

**ⓗ** Wiltondale Pioneer Village

## Lodging

**ⓘ** Bay Side Housekeeping Units

**ⓙ** Crocker's Cabins

**ⓘ** Evergreen Bed and Breakfast

**ⓚ** The Feeder Bed and Breakfast

**ⓛ** Shallow Bay Motel and Cabins

**ⓜ** Terry's Bed and Breakfast

## Camping

**ⓝ** Barachois Pond Provincial Park

**ⓑ** Gros Morne National Park—5 campgrounds

*Note: Items with the same letter are in the same town or area.*

## A PERFECT DAY IN WESTERN NEWFOUNDLAND

Gros Morne National Park is the indisputable highlight in this part of the world. There are several things I like to do in the park. One is to take a cruise along Western Brook Pond, an immense 16-kilometer (10-mile) lake surrounded by towering cliffs, a setting that invariably reminds me of Norway. Another is to stop in Trout River for the magnificent views of the coast and then to head from there to the Tablelands, a plateau that has some of the oldest and oddest rocks in the world. If it's sunny, I'll stop by St. Paul's Inlet to see if there are any harbor seals sunning themselves on the rocks there. The hike along the James Callaghan Trail to the peak of Gros Morne Mountain is arduous, but the view at the end is positively exhilarating. My favorite picnic spot is South East Hill near Neddy Harbour. One of the highest points of road elevation in the province, it provides a panoramic view of the East Lomond Valley and the Long Range Mountains.

## SIGHTSEEING HIGHLIGHTS

★★★ **Gros Morne National Park** • Gros Morne, which was declared a UNESCO World Heritage Site in 1988, may be the single most compelling reason to see the west coast of Newfoundland. Located northwest of Deer Lake, it has an outstanding and remarkably varied landscape. Barren rock ridges, tundra-like plateaus, densely forested foothills, glacier-carved fjords, boggy coastal plains, grasslands, lakes, huge sand dunes, and picturesque villages are all found within the 2,000-square-kilometer park. Scientists theorize that billions of years ago, the floor of the ocean ruptured, sending lava and chunks of ocean bed up onto the edge of North America. Rocks from deep inside the earth also ended up along the edge of the continent; they are now to be found on the Tablelands, a plateau in the southwest corner of the park. Other areas of the park were carved out by succeeding ice ages—towering canyons, deep lakes, serpentine gorges, bogs, and lowlands. There are marvelous opportunities for spotting wildlife, including caribou, arctic hares, black bears, lynx, moose, and offshore, seals and whales.

You could easily spend a week exploring the park. For example, you could take a boat tour of a fjord named Western Brook Pond which runs for 16 kilometers (10 miles) through 600-meter (2,000-foot) cliffs that have some of North America's highest waterfalls cascading over them. Or, if you're feeling hale and hearty, you could hike the 16-kilometer (10-mile) James Callaghan Trail to the peak of Gros Morne Mountain, a challenging outing that would take a day but offers an unsurpassed view of the entire park. You could laze on one of the many beaches along the coast, or spend hours exploring the picturesque fishing villages inside the park. And you could spend days on the various hiking trails. The visitors center is 3 kilometers south of Rocky Harbour in the heart of the park, and is wheelchair accessible. Several of the trails in the park are wheelchair accessible as well, such as the Berry Hill Pond Trail 10 kilometers (6 miles) north of Rocky Harbour. Admission to the park is $4.25 per day per vehicle, or $20 for a season's pass. Phone: (709) 458-2917 or the province's toll-free tourist information line at (800) 563-6353. (4 hours and up)

✭✭✭ **L'Anse aux Meadows** • This is where the first authentic Viking site in North America was discovered. As far back as 1914, Newfoundlander William A. Munn was suggesting that Norse landings had occurred on this spot, but the remains were not discovered until 1960, when the Norwegian explorer and writer Helge Ingstad and his wife, archaeologist Anne Stine, searched the area. Stine excavated the site through much of the 1960s, after which Parks Canada took over. Three building complexes, each consisting of a large communal dwelling and workshops, were turned up. The site also contained evidence of ironworking and carpentry, which means the Norse here were doing the first known iron-smelting in the New World. Archaeologists believe the Norse were here during a relatively short time between A.D. 990 and 1050; it's further believed that Leif Eriksson established a colony here, which he called Vinland. Declared a UNESCO World Heritage Site in 1978, the site also contained evidence that Groswater, Maritime Archaic, and Dorset people were in the area before the Norse. Visitors can wander through a recreation of the sod houses unearthed at the site, while displays in the park's interpretive center include the floorboard of a Norse boat and iron rivets excavated at the site. The park grounds are open year-round, the visitor center from 9:00 a.m. to 8:00 p.m. daily from mid-June to Labor Day. Admission is free. Phone: (800) 563-6353 toll-free. (3 hours)

✭✭ **Port aux Port Peninsula** • A side trip from the TransCanada west along Route 460 leads to the westernmost point of Newfoundland, Cape St. George, at the tip of the small, triangular Port au Port peninsula. Turn west at Stephenville. The peninsula has 130 kilometers (78 miles) of rocky coastline and the highest proportion of French-speaking residents of any part of Newfoundland (15 percent). Battered by wind and water, the limestone and dolomite cliffs along the peninsula make for some dramatic scenes. Picadilly Head Provincial Park, with camping, hiking trails, picnic tables, lookouts, and a playground, is located on the northeast shore. One of the best times to visit this area is during the annual *Une Longe Veillée* folk festival. Held each August to celebrate French heritage, the festival attracts performers from all over Newfoundland, Atlantic Canada, Quebec, and St. Pierre and Miquelon. (2 hours)

✰✰ **Table Mountain** • Table Mountain is in the Long Range Mountains, part of the ancient Appalachian escarpment, and it's a geological oddity that sends winds whooshing down to the forest below. Sometimes the winds are so strong they disrupt highway traffic. They were even known to topple railway cars, back when Newfoundland had a train system. In fact, a man known as the "human wind gauge" lived in the valley below the mountain and for years was under contract to the railway. He would determine whether the area was safe for the train to traverse on any given day, or whether the wind was so strong it might derail the train. Table Mountain is accessible by a trail that leads to a lookout offering a panoramic view of the surrounding terrain. (1 hour)

✰ **Port au Choix** • An interpretive center at Port au Choix National Historic Park displays skeletons, tools, ornaments, and other artifacts unearthed from a 3,500-year-old burial site here. The site was discovered by accident in 1967 by some construction workers as they dug foundations for a building. The next year, archaeologists found three ancient cemeteries and more than 100 skeletons of the Maritime Archaics, hunters and gatherers who plied the coastal resources between Maine and Labrador more than 4,000 years ago. Also on display are relics from another major archeological site in this area discovered in the 1950s. It turned up the remains of a Dorset Inuit community that lived on nearby Pointe Riche around A.D. 100. There are picnic grounds at Pointe Riche lighthouse if you're toting food. There's a nominal entrance fee to get into the park. (1 hour)

✰ **River of Ponds Provincial Park** • A display at this park includes whale bones that are an estimated 7,000 years old. Found at nearby sites, the bones offer proof that this part of Newfoundland's west coast was once under the ocean. The park, about 60 kilometers (36 miles) north of the edge of Gros Morne, includes a freshwater lake ringed by sand beaches and a forest. Visitors can camp, swim, hike, canoe, or fish. (1 hour)

✵ **Rose Blanche** • The rugged coastal scenery along the 40-kilometer (24-mile) drive between Port aux Basques and Rose Blanche is what makes this short side trip worthwhile. Rose Blanche, a small fishing village, lies to the east of Port aux Basques. Its lighthouse provides a good view of the Cabot Strait, at the bottom of which reportedly lie the wrecks of some 40 ships. (½ hour)

✵ **Wiltondale Pioneer Village** • Just outside the southern entrance to Gros Morne National Park, this recreated nineteenth-century logging village includes a house, a barn, a small school, a general store, and a church. Admission to the pioneer village is $3 for adults, $1 for children and $6 for families. Phone: (709) 453-2464. (1 hour)

## FITNESS AND RECREATION

Western Newfoundland is heaven on Earth for active outdoorsy people. You can scramble over the rocks of the Long Range Mountains, go horseback riding out of the Gros Morne Riding Stables in Rocky Harbour, and windsurf at Cape Ray Sands in the south of the peninsula. If you're there in winter (decidedly the off-season), you can ski at Marble Mountain near Corner Brook. Practically anywhere you happen to find yourself, you can hike until you drop. In Gros Morne National Park, a number of the less strenuous trails are accessible to wheelchairs.

## LODGING

For such a wild landscape, plenty of tourist facilities are available along this route. There are hotels and B&Bs in small communities as well as in larger centers like Corner Brook and Deer Lake. Accommodations are also available in several of the villages inside Gros Morne National Park. Staying inside the park allows you to explore at your leisure. Because it's about halfway up the peninsula, it also makes a good base for day trips up and down the Viking Trail.

Here are some suggestions within the park. **Crocker's Cabins** near the southern boundary of the park offers two-bedroom efficiency units at $60 a night. Weekly rates are also available; phone (709) 451-3236. Efficiency units are also available at **Bay Side**

**Housekeeping Units** in Rocky Harbour. Bay Side has playgrounds and allows pets, so it's a good bet for families. $70 for a double; call (709) 458-2749. **Shallow Bay Motel and Cabins** in Cow Head has both motel rooms and housekeeping units, plus a playground, exercise room, outdoor swimming pool, and mini-golf course. Rates are $56 a night for a double room in the motel, $60 for a one-bedroom efficiency unit, and $65 for a two-bedroom unit; call (709) 243-2471. If bed and breakfasts are more to your taste, there are plentiful options. In Trout River, try **The Feeder Bed and Breakfast**, a nonsmoking establishment that allows pets and charges $49 for a double; call (709) 451-2102. **Terry's Bed and Breakfast** in Norris Point offers a picnic and playground area as well as a view of Bonne Bay. Rates are $45 for a double; call (709) 458-2373. In Rocky Harbour, **Evergreen Bed and Breakfast** doubles are $39; call (709) 458-2692.

Whatever type of accommodation you want, it's vital that you book well ahead if you're traveling in summer. Check the *Newfoundland and Labrador Travel Guide* for complete listings and locations (call 800-563-6353 for a free copy).

## CAMPING

In **Gros Morne National Park** alone there are five attractive campgrounds; note, however, that there are no electrical hookups. Reservations aren't accepted. For details on each of the campgrounds, contact the park at (709) 458-2066.

Most of the numerous provincial parks along the coast also offer camping facilities. Rates begin around $8 a night. The campground at **Barachois Pond Provincial Park** at the base of the Long Range Mountains is one of the largest and most popular in the provincial-park system, and it's also one of the very few to be wheelchair accessible.

## SIDE TRIP: LABRADOR

The most isolated part of Newfoundland, Labrador is for those who want a vacation that's out of the ordinary. Labrador lies north of Quebec, and most of it is a wilderness of towering mountains, wide rivers, and broad lakes. Traditionally, Labrador has attracted hunters and fishermen more than tourists, and if you love the wild, unspoiled outdoors, it's worth a visit.

The native Innu (Indian) and Inuit (Eskimo) have survived in Labrador for thousands of years. The first Europeans to settle the coast were Basque mariners who set up a huge whale oil processing center at Red Bay in the sixteen th century. The Labrador Heritage Museum in Goose Bay depicts the history of the land and the people.

Getting there and getting around takes some planning. In summer, there's a ferry that crosses the Strait of Belle Isle from St. Barbe at the top of the Great Northern Peninsula to Blanc Sablon in Quebec, right next to the Labrador border; from there, the road takes you to Red Bay. There are also car ferries to Happy Valley-Goose Bay in Labrador from Lewisporte in north-central Newfoundland. But the trip takes 35 hours, and from Happy Valley-Goose Bay you must drive through central and western Labrador to Quebec along an unpaved road that's best traveled only in summer. Otherwise, there are sizable airports at Goose Bay, Wabush, and Churchill Falls, while coastal communities are served by smaller airfields. From Baie Comeau, Quebec, you can drive to Labrador City and Wabush in western Labrador. Seasonal coastal boats operate along the north Labrador coast as far as Nain.

The provincial tourism people say you should plan your visit well in advance. Once there, visitors should never venture into unknown territory without an experienced guide. For more information, contact the province's toll-free tourist information line at (800) 563-6353.

# APPENDIX

## METRIC CONVERSION CHART

1 U.S. gallon = approximately 4 liters
1 liter = about 1 quart
1 Canadian gallon = approximately 4.5 liters

1 pound = approximately $1/2$ kilogram
1 kilogram = about 2 pounds

1 foot = approximately $1/3$ meter
1 meter = about 1 yard
1 yard = a little less than a meter
1 mile = approximately 1.6 kilometers
1 kilometer = about $2/3$ mile

90°F = about 30°C
20°C = approximately 70°F

# Planning Map: Eastern Canada

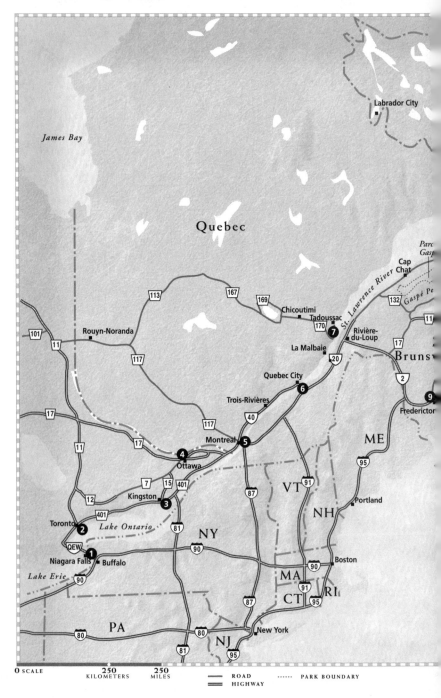

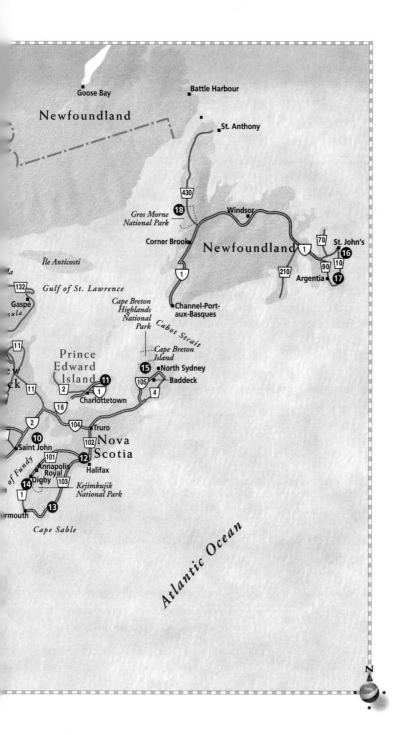

Goose Bay

Battle Harbour

Newfoundland

St. Anthony

430

Gros Morne
National Park

18

Windsor

Corner Brook

Newfoundland

1

70

St. John's

16

210

90

10

Argentia

17

Île Anticosti

132

Gulf of St. Lawrence

Gaspé
ula

Cape Breton
Highlands
National
Park

Cabot Strait

Channel-Port-
aux-Basques

1

11

Prince
Edward
Island

Cape Breton
Island

15

North Sydney

Baddeck

105

11

2

11

1

4

ck

16

Charlottetown

2

104

Truro

10

102

Nova
Scotia

Saint John

101

12

of Fundy

Annapolis
Royal

103

Halifax

14

Digby

Kejimkujik
National Park

1

13

rmouth

Cape Sable

Atlantic Ocean

N

# INDEX

# Other Books from John Muir Publications

## Rick Steves' Books

Asia Through the Back Door, 400 pp., $17.95
Europe 101: History and Art for the Traveler, 352 pp., $17.95
Mona Winks: Self-Guided Tours of Europe's Top Museums, 432 pp., $18.95
Rick Steves' Baltics & Russia, 160 pp., $9.95
Rick Steves' Europe, 560 pp., $18.95
Rick Steves' France, Belgium & the Netherlands, 304 pp., $15.95
Rick Steves' Germany, Austria & Switzerland, 272 pp., $14.95
Rick Steves' Great Britain, 320 pp., $15.95
Rick Steves' Italy, 240 pp., $13.95
Rick Steves' Scandinavia, 208 pp., $13.95
Rick Steves' Spain & Portugal, 240 pp., $13.95
Rick Steves' Europe Through the Back Door, 520 pp., $19.95
Rick Steves' French Phrase Book, 192 pp., $5.95
Rick Steves' German Phrase Book, 192 pp., $5.95
Rick Steves' Italian Phrase Book, 192 pp., $5.95
Rick Steves' Spanish & Portugese Phrase Book, 336 pp., $7.95
Rick Steves' French/ German/Italian Phrase Book, 320 pp., $7.95

## A Natural Destination Series

Belize: A Natural Destination, 344 pp., $16.95
Costa Rica: A Natural Destination, 416 pp., $18.95
Guatemala: A Natural Destination, 360 pp., $16.95

## City•Smart™ Guidebook Series

City•Smart Guidebook: Cleveland, 208 pp., $14.95
City•Smart Guidebook: Denver, 256 pp., $14.95
City•Smart Guidebook: Minneapolis/St. Paul, 240 pp., $14.95
City•Smart Guidebook: Nashville, 256 pp., $14.95
City•Smart Guidebook: Portland, 232 pp., $14.95
City•Smart Guidebook: Tampa/St. Petersburg, 256 pp., $14.95

## Travel✦Smart™ Trip Planners

American Southwest Travel✦Smart Trip Planner, 256 pp., $14.95
Colorado Travel✦Smart Trip Planner, 248 pp., $14.95
Eastern Canada Travel✦Smart Trip Planner, 272 pp., $15.95
Florida Gulf Coast Travel✦Smart Trip Planner, 240 pp., $14.95
Hawaii Travel✦Smart Trip Planner, 256 pp., $14.95
Kentucky/Tennessee Travel✦Smart Trip Planner, 248 pp., $14.95
Minnesota/Wisconsin Travel✦Smart Trip Planner, 240 pp., $14.95
New England Travel✦Smart Trip Planner, 256 pp., $14.95
Northern California Travel✦Smart Trip Planner, 272 pp., $15.95
Pacific Northwest Travel✦Smart Trip Planner, 240 pp., $14.95

## Other Terrific Travel Titles

The 100 Best Small Art Towns in America, 256 pp., $15.95
The Big Book of Adventure Travel, 384 pp., $17.95
Indian America: A Traveler's Companion, 480 pp., $18.95
The People's Guide to Mexico, 608 pp., $19.95
Ranch Vacations: The Complete Guide to Guest and Resort, Fly-Fishing, and Cross-Country Skiing Ranches, 632 pp., $22.95
Understanding Europeans, 272 pp., $14.95
Undiscovered Islands of the Caribbean, 336 pp., $16.95
Watch It Made in the U.S.A.: A Visitor's Guide to the Companies that Make Your Favorite Products, 328 pp., $16.95
The World Awaits, 280 pp., $16.95
The Birder's Guide to Bed and Breakfasts: U.S. and Canada, 416 pp., $17.95

## Automotive Titles

The Greaseless Guide to Car Care, 272 pp., $19.95
How to Keep Your Subaru Alive, 480 pp., $21.95
How to Keep Your Toyota Pickup Alive, 392 pp., $21.95
How to Keep Your VW Alive, 464 pp., $25

## Ordering Information

Please check your local bookstore for our books, or call 1-800-888-7504 to order direct and to receive a complete catalog. A shipping charge will be added to your order total.

Send all inquiries to:
John Muir Publications
P.O. Box 613
Santa Fe, NM 87504